NICHOLSON

ORDNANCE SURVEY GUIDE TO THE RIVER THAMES

River Wey & Basingstoke Canal

Series editor: David Perrott

Robert Nicholson Publications

Also available in this series:

Nicholson/Ordnance Survey Guide to the Waterways 1. South
Nicholson/Ordnance Survey Guide to the Waterways 2. Central
Nicholson/Ordnance Survey Guide to the Waterways 3. North
Nicholson/Ordnance Survey Guide to the Broads & Fens
Nicholson/Ordnance Survey Inland Waterways Map of Great Britain

*The indication of a towpath or footpath in this
book does not necessarily imply a public right
of way. If you are in any doubt, check
before you proceed with the latest published
Ordnance Survey map.*

Pathfinder Series (2½in to 1 mile scale or
1:25 000). These OS walker and rambler maps show
the countryside in great detail, including rights
of way in England and Wales.
Landranger Series (1¼in to 1 mile scale or
1:50 000). This OS series covers the country
in 204 sheets and is ideal for detailed
exploring by car or on foot.

First published 1984 by **Robert Nicholson Publications**
16 Golden Square, London W1R 4BN and
Ordnance Survey, Romsey Road, Maybush,
Southampton SO9 4DH.

2nd edition 1989

© Text, Robert Nicholson Publications 1989

© The maps in this publication are reproduced from
Ordnance Survey maps with the permission of the
Controller of HMSO. Crown Copyright Reserved.

Original research: Paul Atterbury and David Perrott
Natural history section: Alwyne Wheeler
Boat plans: Morag Perrott

Thanks are also extended to the following, who
assisted in the preparation of this book: Thames Water;
Port of London Authority; The National Trust;
the local Tourist Information Offices; the Thames
lock keepers; the boatyards; Surrey and Hampshire
Canal Society; Wey and Arun Canal Trust; David
Bolton, Peter Dobson, Margaret Hughes and
many others who, knowingly or unknowingly,
helped.

Photographs on pages 7, 35, 45, 54, 63, 77, 80, 86,
87, 92, 93, 98, 104, 108, 115, 120, 121, 137, 147, 150,
153, 155 by Derek Pratt.
All other photographs by David Perrott unless
otherwise stated.

Cover photograph: Derek Pratt

Typeset by Rowland Phototypesetting Ltd,
Bury St Edmunds, Suffolk.
Printed in Great Britain by
Scotprint Ltd, Musselburgh

Ordnance Survey ISBN 0 319001 56 3
Nicholson ISBN 0 948576 24 3

INTRODUCTION

Great Britain's most famous river, the Thames, is a natural water highway through the heart of southern England, full of variety and interest and a natural magnet for visitors.

There is something for everyone along its length. For those who enjoy peace and seclusion, the river above Oxford will serve them well. Pleasure seekers who prefer a livelier time will find the middle river, with its plethora of sights, pubs and restaurants, unequalled. And for a special insight into London, the capital's royal river should not be missed.

This book is constructed around the superb Ordnance Survey maps, specially adapted and covering over 140 miles of river from Cricklade to Greenwich at a clear 2½ inches to 1 mile scale. Maps such as these are essential for those who wish to explore the Thames. Alongside the maps is information for boaters, walkers and motorists. Towns, villages and sights are fully described, and riverside pubs and restaurants are there for the thirsty and hungry. Special sections deal with boat hire, navigation, day trips, history, fishing and natural history.

Also covered in great detail is the River Wey, a navigable tributary offering rural calm in the centre of one of the busiest home counties, and the Basingstoke Canal, a triumph of restoration and now a fascinating new area for exploration by water.

So take this book and enjoy a day, a week or longer on these waterways. You will find friendly people and much to occupy your time.

The River Thames map sections

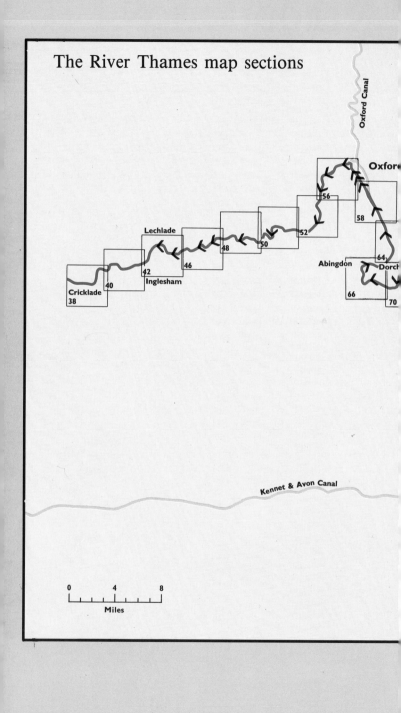

Oxford Canal

Oxford

56

58

Lechlade

48

50

52

64

46

Abingdon

Dorch

42

Inglesham

40

66

70

Cricklade

38

Kennet & Avon Canal

0   4   8

Miles

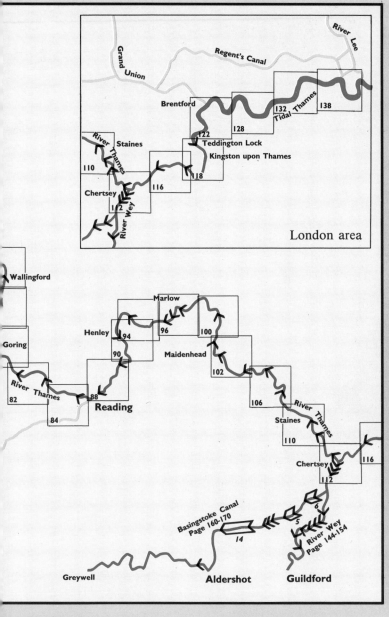

London area

Wallingford

Marlow

Henley 94

Goring 90

Maidenhead

River Thames 82

88 **Reading** 102

84 106 River

Staines 110

Chertsey 116

112

Basingstoke Canal
Page 160-170 5 6

14 River Wey
Page 144-154

Greywell **Aldershot** **Guildford**

Contents

CRUISING ON THE THAMES

Responsibility for the River Thames Navigation between Cricklade and Teddington is vested with:

> General Manager Rivers Division
> Thames Water
> Nugent House
> Vastern Road
> Reading
> Berkshire RG1 8DB

Telephone numbers are:
General enquiries – Reading 593777
Navigation enquiries – Reading 593387
Pleasure boat registration and fishing rod licences – Reading 593300
General fishing enquiries – Reading 593375

The river below Teddington is controlled by the:

> Port of London Authority
> River Division
> Europe House
> World Trade Centre
> London E1 9AA.
> Telephone: 01-481 8484

Navigation rules and hints

Many of these basic rules and hints have been compiled from the *River Thames Handbook* published by Thames Water. Any person wishing to take their own boat on the non-tidal Thames should obtain a free copy of this book, which also contains much of interest to those using hire craft. Those who wish to navigate the tidal river should obtain a free copy of the PLA's *Pleasure Users' Guide to the Tidal Thames*, which is full of useful information.

Registration and licensing

All craft using the non-tidal river must be registered with and licensed by Thames Water, Craft Registration, PO Box 214, Reading RG1 8HQ.

Construction and equipment of launches

All craft must be constructed and equipped in accordance with the specifications published by Thames Water.

Pollution

It is an offence to discharge sewage, oil or any other pollutants into the river, or to throw rubbish into the water or on the river banks. If you suspect or discover a case of pollution, please notify either the relevant Navigation Inspector (listed below), a lock keeper, or ring Freephone 3266.

Hambledon Lock

Navigation Inspectors

Chief Navigation Inspector – Reading 593387
Cricklade to Benson – Oxford 721271
Benson to Hurley Lower Lock Cut – Reading 593284
Hurley Lower Lock Cut to Staines Bridge – Maidenhead 22491
Staines Bridge to Teddington – Sunbury 81946

Fire or explosion on board

In case of a fire or explosion on board, the Chief Navigation Inspector must be notified within 48 hours. Do not move the craft until an inspection has been made.

Course to steer

Keep to the right (starboard) to pass oncoming craft port (left) to port.

Speed

No more than 3mph (a brisk walking pace) and much slower if your wash may cause damage to the river bank or to moored boats, or cause danger to those in small craft such as punts and canoes. Careless or improper navigation on the river is an OFFENCE.

On the tidal river there is a speed limit of 8 knots above Wandsworth Bridge.

Locks

There is a lock keeper on duty at Teddington 24hrs every day of the year. All other locks, except Blake's, are manned as follows:

Nov–Mar	09.15–16.00
Apr	09.00–17.30
May	09.00–18.30
Jun–Aug	09.00–19.00
Sep	09.00–18.00 (18.30 weekends)
Oct	09.00–17.00

Lock keepers usually have their meal breaks 13.00–14.00 and 18.00–18.30, but these times can vary.

Locks may be closed for cleaning on certain weekdays between 07.00–09.00.

When lock keepers are off duty, members of the public may operate the locks at their own risk. Instructions are posted at the locks.

All locks above Godstow are manually operated.

Navigate in single file in the lock cut.

If you have to wait to enter a lock, use the layby.

When passing through a lock, ALWAYS follow the lock keeper's instructions and:

Do not fend off with hands, feet or boat hook.

Never moor upstream of the vertical white line.

Make fast head and stern and then . . .

Switch off your engine (and radio or television).

Keep mooring lines taut and adjust them as the water level changes.

Do not open fuel tanks or strike matches.

You are responsible for ensuring that your boat does not damage/injure other craft/people.

Always be courteous and patient.

Bridges and bends

Pass through the bridge arch indicated as the navigation channel, or the right hand arch if there are two and neither is marked. Those travelling

The church at Bisham

upstream must give way to those travelling downstream, who have less control over their craft. Do not cut corners – it is usually shallow on the inside of a bend.

Mooring

It is good practice to approach a mooring with your boat facing upstream into the current, in order to maintain steerage at very slow speeds. Do not approach the bank or quayside quickly, relying on reverse to stop the boat – if the propeller is fouled or the engine stalls, disaster will ensue. The golden rule is – go dead slow – then if things do not go quite as planned (a not uncommon occurence) the result will be only a gentle bump. Avoid fending off with hands and feet, and take care to keep fingers and feet out of ropes. Most mooring sites are clearly indicated on the river bank, and are also listed in the text accompanying our maps, and are marked on the maps. Do not moor on private ground, or where you will cause an obstruction. Do not allow your ropes to obstruct the towpath. Leave sufficient line, and depth of water under the boat, to allow for a possible rise or fall of 2ft overnight.

Knots

A simple and easy way of securing a rope to a bollard or mooring stake is to use a couple of round turns and a half hitch made with a loop and pulled tight. This can be released quickly by pulling the loose end, which will have been left tidily coiled.

When leaving a mooring, coil all the ropes up again, ready for use when you need them.

Sound signals

It is important to know the basic signals in order to issue or recognise warnings. Remember that starboard is right and port is left when facing towards the bows (front).
One short blast: I am going to starboard
Two short blasts: I am going to port
Three short blasts: I am going astern
Four short blasts: I am unable to manoeuvre
Four short blasts followed by one short blast: I am turning round to starboard.
Four short blasts followed by two short blasts: I am turning round to port.
Continuous sounding of the horn indicates distress.

Lights

If you navigate between sunset and sunrise, you must show the correct navigation lights:
Bright white light on the mast or a staff at the bow, no less than 4ft above the hull, aimed forward.
Green light on the starboard side.
Red light on the port side.
White light at the stern.

Sailing vessels

Power gives way to sail. If a power boat cannot manoeuvre, the correct sound signal is four short blasts. Those sailing must remember that many power craft drivers are inexperienced, and should plan their tacks accordingly.

Bathers

Keep well clear of bathers. If you are tempted to swim, remember there is a current, and that the bottom may shelve steeply in places.

Sub-aqua divers

Keep well clear of divers, who should fly code flag A to indicate their presence.

Code flag A

Marker buoys

These indicate hazards to navigation.
Red can shape: Leave to port (left) when going upstream.
Green triangle: Leave to starboard (right) when going upstream.
Red sphere or two black spheres: Pass either side.
(Don't forget, when coming downstream, leave red cans to starboard, and green triangles to port.)

Weirs

There is a weir at every lock – keep well away from the 'pull' of the weir above the lock, and allow for a possible cross current below.

Strong stream conditions

After prolonged heavy rainfall, the water level will rise, the current will increase and weirs will become very fierce indeed. As this occurs, 'increasing' stream boards will be displayed, and craft should seek sheltered moorings. When it is judged that conditions represent a hazard to navigation yellow or red 'strong' stream boards are displayed at locks. Yellow boards indicate that unpowered craft should moor up; red boards indicate that powered craft should moor up out of the main current. Hire craft are advised to telephone their base for instructions. Lock keepers may not allow hire craft through without an official 'Thames Pilot' on board. To those with no experience of boat handling and navigation these strong stream conditions are DANGEROUS, so be cautious and obey the advice of those better qualified. If you should experience engine failure or a fouled propeller in these conditions, remember that you carry an anchor for just such an eventuality – lower it overboard promptly, taking great care that you do not entangle yourself in the chain or rope. It should hold well in the riverbed. Continuous sounding of your horn will indicate that you are in distress and require assistance. When a 'decreasing' stream is indicated, powered craft may proceed with caution.

Care of boat and engine

Those who own their own craft will have developed a suitable routine. Those with hire craft should follow the company's instructions each day before setting off. These normally are:

>   Check the engine oil.
>   Check the cooling water level in the header tank, or the water inlet filter.
>   Pump the fresh water from the bilges (not the oily black liquid which may follow).

Start the engine *before* casting off, and check that the batteries are charging, by reference to the warning light or ammeter.

Drinking water

Fresh drinking water is available from the privately owned boatyards along the river. A small charge is usually made for this facility. There are also hoses at some locks (usually those with sanitary stations or pump-outs, but there are other sites). The taps at locks are intended only for filling small portable containers, not large built-in tanks. Fill up every day.

Toilets

Many craft now have pump-out toilets, which have to be emptied with a special machine. All boatyards offering this facility are given in the text accompanying the maps. The symbol below indicates this facility. Expect to have to pay.

Chemical 'bucket' type toilets and their more modern counterparts should only be emptied at boatyards offering 'sewage disposal' or at a sanitary station, indicated in the text or on the map. Never throw the contents into the bushes or river. There are male urinals at virtually all locks, so these are not indicated in the text – the few ladies' toilets are mentioned. Many boatyards have toilets for the use of patrons – these are always mentioned in the text.

Fuel

All boatyards offering fuel are indicated in the text. Boaters with diesel engines should take special care not to run out of fuel as the engine may need specialist attention before it will start again. Most hire craft carry fuel sufficient for two weeks normal cruising – your boatyard will advise.

A Thames sailing barge by St Katharine's Yacht Haven

HIRING A BOAT

It can be very disappointing to find the boat you have hired for a week or a fortnight does not live up to your expectations. Minor niggles may cause amusement, but major defects can mar your holiday. So how do you choose? Ideally, if you can see a particular boat before you book it, and talk to the hire company, you will know that all is OK. But for the majority of people this is impractical, as it would likely as not involve an additional long journey to the boatyard. No boatyard worth its salt, however, would turn down a request to view.

Second only to actually viewing the boat is the recommendation of a friend who has personal experience of a particular company, and can give you a first-hand account. All the best hire companies get a good percentage of their bookings either as repeats or by recommendation.

If you are starting from scratch, here is some general advice.

1. A well-produced brochure showing detailed plans, interior photographs and a full specification is a great help. Many of the boat hire companies on the River Thames, and elsewhere, have their bookings handled by two major agencies – Blakes and Hoseasons Holidays – who

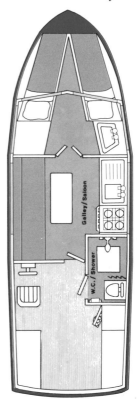

A typical compact four-berth cruiser

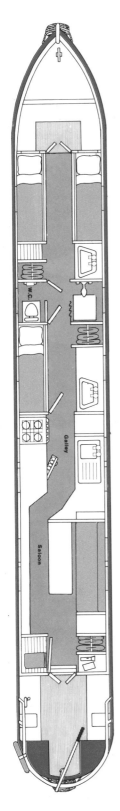

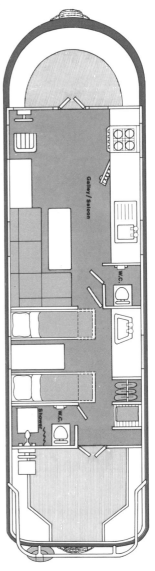

*A typical wide beam holiday boat,
common on rivers and the Norfolk Broads*

*A typical narrowboat, most common
on the canal system*

both produce very comprehensive colour brochures. If you want to know more about a particular craft which they offer, do not be afraid to ask them, or get in touch directly with the boatyard concerned. They are keen to do business with you and will prove extremely helpful.

2. The size of a company is no indication of quality – some of the largest companies have grown because they are good; some of the smaller ones maintain that by remaining small they can offer a better service.

3. Choose a boat suitable for your needs (and see below for special information regarding young children). For example, four large adults could feel very cramped in a small, four-berth, fibreglass cruiser, whereas a four-berth, steel narrowboat would usually offer more space.

4. Make sure you know what you will have to pay. With companies that quote an all-inclusive price you know exactly what your commitments are. However, if your itinerary is not very ambitious, you could be better off with a less expensive boat where the fuel cost is extra. Returnable security deposits are normal practice.

5. Fibreglass cruisers, while admirably suited to river navigations such as the Thames, feel distinctly wrong on narrow canals, where the steel narrowboat, based upon traditional designs, is much more at home.

6. Modern pump-out toilets are preferable to the old chemical type.

7. A water-cooled diesel engine is usually quieter than the air-cooled type.

8. If you are cruising early or late in the year, a boat with central heating and an airing cupboard will be more comfortable than one with just cabin heaters.

9. Generally, a newer boat will be better than an older one.

Choosing a hirecraft with children in mind

With a little forethought, babies who are not yet walking can be coped with easily on a boating holiday. Children between the ages of one and five are probably the most difficult to deal with, and the following points may be helpful:

1. Mum, Dad and two toddlers on a heavily locked length of canal or river will have problems. If you cannot gather a larger crew, then choose a navigation with very few locks, or with locks operated by keepers, such as the Thames.

2. Ensure buoyancy aids are available for the children, and make sure they are *always* worn when on deck.

3. Avoid the traditional style narrowboat which has only a small unprotected rear deck – the children will be forced in fine weather to play in the open front cockpit, where the steerer cannot keep an eye on them.

4. Airing cupboards are useful for drying all the washing produced by small children.

5. Pack favourite toys and games.

6. Allow for plenty of stops where the children can run off their excess energy.

From the age of six, children, properly supervised, become valuable and helpful crew members, requiring few special facilities.

The illustrations show three typical types of craft – a steel narrowboat, most common on the canal network, a narrow fibreglass cruiser, common to both canals and rivers, and a wide berth fibreglass holiday craft, most common on the navigable rivers. All are shown at the same scale.

PLANNING A CRUISE

The enjoyment you derive from a cruise on this attractive and interesting river will depend on many things, but perhaps none more than the schedule you set yourself. The essence of a waterway holiday is that it should be leisurely; taken at a pace that allows time to stop and explore villages and churches, lunch at friendly pubs, and walk the towpath before breakfast. With time in hand, queuing at a lock can be a pleasant break rather than a frustrating delay. Many boating holidays have been spoilt by being too ambitious. On the River Thames, your speed will be about 3mph – remember, excessive 'wash' damages the river bank and inconveniences other river users. When passing moored craft your boat should barely ripple the water, travelling at a speed of 2mph or less.

There are 45 locks on the river, and these will slow down your progress, especially at peak times when you may have to queue before entering. But assuming no untoward delays, it will take about 20 minutes to pass through one lock, or about the same amount of time it takes to travel 1 mile at a speed of 3mph. Here we have the means to calculate an approximate journey time (miles plus locks), although other factors, such as whether you are travelling upstream (slower) or downstream (faster) will affect the result.

Use the mileage chart on p176 to identify your departure and destination points. For example: Kingston to Wallingford, which are 70 miles apart (23–93). Count up the number of locks (printed in bold type) between these two points. You will find there are 24.

70 miles plus 24 locks = 94 'lock miles'

Divide 94 by 3mph – this equals approximately 31 hours cruising.

On a one-week holiday this would mean about five hours cruising each day to complete this one-way trip, with plenty of time for stops and visits. If your planned journey results in more than six hours cruising each day then your stops will have to be limited. More than eight hours cruising each day is probably too ambitious.

During summer peak periods, queues at the locks become inevitable, and a one hour wait is quite common. Expect this, and plan your journey accordingly.

Those who are taking to the inland waterways for the first time may think this all sounds painfully slow, but a few hours of gentle cruising on a fine day is usually enough to convert most people to this pace. For only by proceeding gently can you appreciate the peace and beauty of the countryside, watch the bird life and study the riverside architecture.

DAY TRIPS ON THE THAMES

Britain's most popular river offers the day tripper many opportunities. For those who do not wish to deal with the complications of navigating the tidal section an organised trip is the best way of seeing London's river, from Hampton Court down to the Thames Barrier at Woolwich. In central London your voyage will be enlivened by a well-informed commentary and young people will certainly enjoy a noisy evening on a disco boat.

THE TIDAL RIVER

General information
Recorded information regarding river trip services is available on 01-730 4812.

From Westminster Pier
To the Tower and Greenwich 01-930 4097.
To the Thames Barrier 01-930 3373.
To Kew (and Richmond and Hampton Court in summer) 01-930 4721.

From Charing Cross Pier
To the Tower and Greenwich 01-839 3522.

From Tower Pier
To Westminster and Greenwich 01-488 0344.
A ferry service to HMS *Belfast* also operates from here.

From Greenwich Pier
To the Tower and Charing Cross 01-839 3572.
To Westminster 01-858 3996.
To the Thames Barrier 01-305 0300.

Thames Line
A scheduled river bus service linking Chelsea to Docklands, in craft capable of up to 24 knots. Pick-ups from: Chelsea Harbour – Cadogan Pier – Charing Cross Pier – South Bank Festival Pier – Swan Lane Pier – London Bridge City Pier – Cherry Garden Pier – Greenland Pier – West India Pier. 01-376 3676.

Luncheon and evening disco trips
01-839 3572 and 01-928 9009 (disco only).

The fine traditional steamer 'Belle' (Maidenhead Steam Navigation Co)

THE NON-TIDAL RIVER

On the non-tidal river, many of the companies which operate trip boats are mentioned where appropriate. However, the name which is synonymous with Thames river trips is:

Salter Bros

Folly Bridge, Oxford (243421). Operates a scheduled summer service between the following points – Oxford to Abingdon, Reading to Henley, Henley to Marlow, Marlow to Windsor, Windsor to Staines. It is always advisable to ring and check that space is available on the boats before you turn up – this service is very popular with coach parties, so try to book well in advance.

PRIVATE CHARTER

Most of the trip boat companies listed in this guide also arrange private charter, and some do nothing else. If an 1894 steamboat sounds attractive, the Maidenhead Steam Navigation Co should be contacted (Maidenhead 21770) regarding *Belle*, which carries 100 passengers; and beyond Oxford, at Radcot, the lovely traditional narrowboat *Battersea* is available for hire to parties of up to 48 (Clanfield 313).

HMS Belfast, permanently moored by Tower Bridge

THE HISTORY OF THE RIVER

Geographically the Thames holds the key to the centre of England. 215 miles long, it crosses much of the centre of the country, from west to east. The Romans recognised its importance. Watling Street, the Fosse Way, Ermine Street and the Icknield Way were all built to cross the river. These crossings were usually fords, traces of which remain, but bridges were built at London and Staines. Many of the earliest settlements were close to the river. London grew into a great trading centre and port, and by the 19thC it was the largest port in the world.

Goods were shipped inland from the capital – carried upriver by horse-drawn or sailing barges – and by the end of the 19thC the Thames had been linked to the main canal network, thereby affording access to many other parts of Britain. However, the importance of the river as a transport artery was short-lived and began to diminish with the expansion of the railways.

The economical and geographical importance of the river led to a growth of fortified buildings along its banks. The Romans had a vast military fortification at Dorchester, and another on the site of the Tower of London. The Angles and Saxons, entering the country through the mouth of the Thames, built their fortified settlements on the Kent and Essex banks. The Norman plan to build castles at strategic points throughout England included Windsor and the Tower of London. The Tudors later extended the line of fortresses, under the threat of invasion from France and Spain.

During the Middle Ages the river was a source of livelihood for many people. Great monasteries were established, and mills were built using the river power. From earliest times the Thames held an abundance of fish. Trout and salmon could be caught readily. The latter were once so common that they were eaten by the poor. The river was also thick with eels. The eels would swim up the river in such numbers that they could be caught with sieves and buckets, and were made into a form of cake. In Essex there was a thriving shrimping and cockling industry. From the early 19thC increasing pollution drove all the salmon and eels from the lower river, but a vigorous clean-up campaign has now secured their return, and amateur fishermen are a common sight right through central London.

To catch the fish and power the mills, weirs were built, often in places where they hindered navigation. From earliest times there was constant dispute between the fishermen and millers, and the bargemen. Some weirs, known as flash locks, had movable sections to allow barges to pass through. But even then the bargeman would have to wait for the fierce rush of water to subside before passing the weir. Then he would have to wait on the far side for the depth of water to build up again. Legislation tried unsuccessfully to control the building of weirs, and so allow the river to fulfil its important role as a highway. Navigation did not improve until pound locks were introduced on the Thames, one of the first being built at Swift Ditch, near Abingdon, about 1620. The building of the modern locks accelerated, and by the end of the 18thC navigation had ceased to be a laborious and hazardous business.

In the lower reaches smuggling was a very important source of income. There was a lively trade in contraband along the Kent and Essex coasts until well into the 19thC.

The Thames Barrier at Woolwich (Thames Barrier Visitor Centre)

The Thames has often been the scene of festivity. In the 17th and 18thC Frost Fairs were held in London whenever the river froze. There were stalls, performing bears, fairground amusements and ox roasting on the ice. The last Frost Fair was held in 1814. The removal of the old London Bridge, which had the effect of a dam, and the building of the embankments in the 19thC, narrowed the river, and deepened and speeded the flow of the water, so that it is now no longer possible for the tidal river to freeze over. However in 1963, the non-tidal Thames froze as far as Teddington. Since the early 19thC the river has become the scene of regattas in the summer. The Henley Regatta is now an international event.

Of particular significance to Londoners is the fact that their city is sinking at the rate of about one foot every 100 years. As long ago as 1236 the river flooded the Palace of Westminster; in 1928 central London was flooded with the loss of 14 lives; and the disastrous surge tide of 1953 left 300 dead along the east coast and Thames estuary. To counter this threat the magnificent Thames Flood Barrier has been built at Woolwich. Movable barriers can be raised from the riverbed to hold back the tide – the four main gates having a span of 200ft and the strength to withstand a load of more than 9000 tonnes. The stainless steel shells housing the machinery are built on hardwood ribs, their design reminiscent of the Sydney Opera House.

From the Norman period the City of London exercised control of the river as far as Staines. Above this point it was in the hands of various riparian owners. In 1857 the Thames Conservancy gained control of the river below Staines. In 1866 their jurisdiction was extended as far as Cricklade, giving them control over the navigable part of the river. In 1983 this control was transferred to the Thames Water Authority, now Thames Water. In 1909 the tidal river, from below Teddington, was put under the control of the Port of London Authority. These are the present boundaries.

THE NATURAL HISTORY OF THE THAMES

The Thames is a lowland river throughout most of its course with few of the striking changes in scenery or gradient that one associates with rivers of the north or west of the country. As a result its landscape is gentle and its flood plain contains woodlands, water-meadows and grassland with appropriately modest plant and animal inhabitants. However, the scenery is enriched by the Goring Gap, between Goring and Reading, where the river during the Ice Ages cut a new channel through the south-western end of the Chilterns, isolating the Berkshire Downs on the south bank. The river here passes through chalk hills with rich grassland and beech woods of spectacular appearance. Through most of its length the water meadows overlie river gravels; in many places these have been excavated to win gravel for roads and buildings, leaving water-filled pits in which the richest animal life of all the Thames valley can be found. As a result of these natural and manmade habitats there is a great deal of fascinating natural history interest in the Thames and its surroundings.

Many of the plants associated with the river and its banks are those that can be seen alongside any lowland water, but some are very special, indeed almost unique to the Thames. The snake's-head fritillary is an example. Typical of the meadows and damp pastures of the river, the fritillary became very rare due to drainage of the land and ploughing of ancient meadows in order to reseed them with 'modern' mixtures of grasses. Fortunately, the county naturalists' trusts have been able to preserve several of the meadows in which the fritillary grows and, managing the grassland by traditional methods, have ensured its survival. Thanks to their efforts it is still possible to enjoy the purple drooping heads of these beautiful and rare flowers during May – at Magdalen Meadow in Oxford, and elsewhere in the upper Thames valley.

Another species affected by drainage and management of the meadows is the summer snowflake, sometimes called the Loddon lily from its abundance along this tributary of the river. It grows in the black swampy soil beneath willows and in the wet meadows, but is rare today and efforts are being made to preserve it.

Willows are typical bankside trees, although they are too often grubbed out by river engineers. Nine kinds of willow grow in wetlands but they hybridise and it is often difficult to identify them to species. Osiers were formerly an important and valuable crop beside the river. The shoots were cut in rotation and used for making the fish traps employed at weirs and mills especially to catch eels and salmon. Another typical tree is the alder, which has dark bark, deep green, rather small leaves and produces thousands of minute fruits like miniature pine cones.

In the water, plant life may be sparse because of channel dredging and the disturbance caused by the wash of boats, but in backwaters a rich growth develops. Arrowhead thrusts its arrow-shaped green leaves well above water level, while the pinkish-white flowers grow in clusters. Pond weeds, *Pontamogeton* sp, have most of their long trailing growth below water but their broad oval leaves float on the surface. Close to the banks, but often in quite deep water, grow the familiar sword-like leaves and when ripe, cylindrical brown spears of the reed mace, which is often wrongly called bulrush – a quite different plant.

The varied plants are as important to the bird life of the river, as are the differing habitats. The alders which overhang the water are visited in winter by lesser red polls and siskins – small bright green birds which hang, often upside-down, while feeding on the seeds. Falling seeds may be eaten by mallard, especially when there is a covering of ice on the water. The Thames valley is a great resort for ducks, although the main river usually has limited breeding spaces except for a few mallard, but the gravel pits and reservoirs which line its course contain tufted duck, pochard, teal, and wigeon, as well as mallard. In winter these species are augmented by visitors like golden-eye, goosander and smew. Part of the joy of the river for the bird-watcher is that these ducks, and other rarer ones, are likely to appear on the water at any time.

The mute swan is a constant inhabitant of the Thames, and makes its nest out of a huge mound of reeds or other plants in shallow water or on a quiet bank. When nesting it is particularly aggressive and should be left alone. At other times of the year it may be aggressive in defence of its territory, or simply in soliciting food – but the degree of aggression varies with the personality of the individual swan. Despite popular belief to the contrary it is quite untrue that a swan's wing can break a man's arm or leg, but they are powerful birds and are used to having things their own way. An enraged cob, as the male is known, is quite capable of drowning a swimming child or dog, as they do ducklings, by forcing the head below water by means of pecking and blows with the wings. In recent years they have been found to suffer from lead poisoning, caused by taking lost or discarded angling weights into their gizzard along with small stones (these help crush up the food). The lead dissolves, affecting the muscles and the nervous system and the swan dies slowly. Affected swans had a kink at the base of the neck and were unable to hold their head and neck upright. The mute swan population had declined steadily for 20 years, with only about a dozen breeding pairs left on the river by 1984. Since then public awareness of the problem, plus an outright ban on the use of lead weights by anglers since June 1987 has seen the number of breeding pairs rise to over 40. Incidences of lead poisoning are down from 50 per cent of swan deaths in the early 1980s to around 20 per cent now, indicating that there is still a residue of lead weights on the river bed and, almost unbelievably, the continued (and illegal) use of lead shot by a few anglers.

Almost as large as the mute swan is the Canada goose, an intro-duced bird from North America, and extremely common on the river and adjacent gravel pits. It usually travels in small flocks, and with its greyish-brown plumage, black neck and white cheeks is a familiar sight either on the river or, like the swan, feeding on the soft grass in the meadows. Both swans and geese can damage valuable pastureland if they are present in large numbers.

Moorhens, sooty black birds with white flashes at the tail, and a red and yellow forehead, which swim with a curious nodding motion of the head, are also common all along the river. They build their nest, a heap of dead vegetation, usually in a dense thicket of plants or bushes, but as often in a drainage ditch as in the backwater of the river. Because they lay a large number of eggs, and produce replacement clutches, their small piping chicks can be seen almost all the summer. The adults, but not the chicks, are as often on the bank as in the water, a habit they share with the similar, but larger coot. Coots, however, have a white beak and forehead.

Carrion Crow

Rook

Jackdaw

Magpie

Jay

Starling

Goldfinch

Bullfinch

Chaffinch

Yellowhammer

Reed Bunting

Skylark

Yellow Wagtail

Pied Wagtail

Nuthatch

Treecreeper

Marsh Tit

Great Tit

Coal Tit

Spotted Flycatcher

Long-tailed Tit

Blue Tit

Willow Warbler

Reed Warbler

Blackcap

Whitethroat

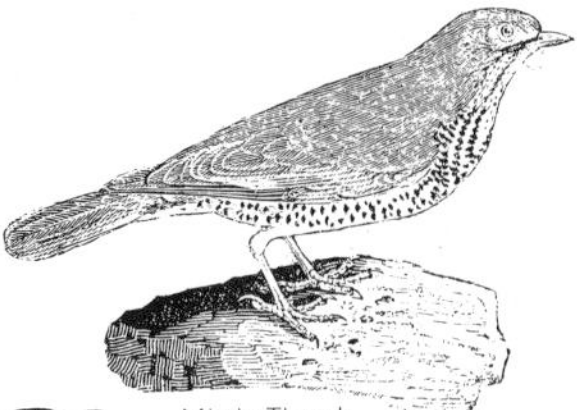

Mistle Thrush

Song Thrush

Blackbird

Nightingale

Robin

Dunnock

Wren

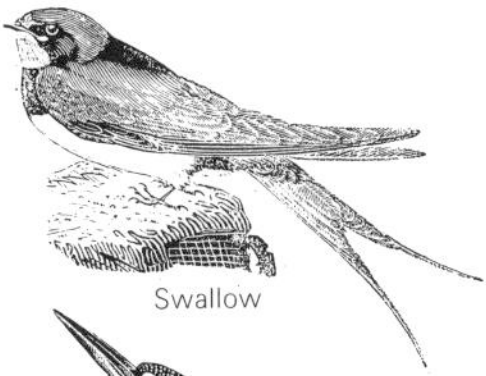

Swallow

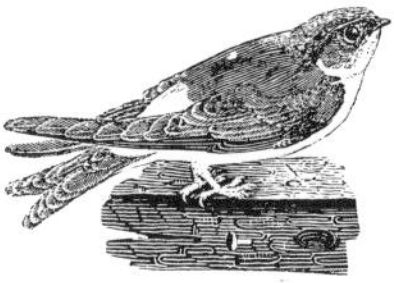

House Martin

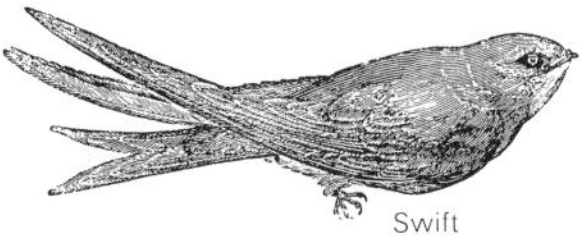

Swift

Kingfisher

Green Woodpecker

Great Spotted
Woodpecker

Cuckoo

Tawny Owl

Turtle Dove

Barn Owl

Kestrel

Common
Buzzard

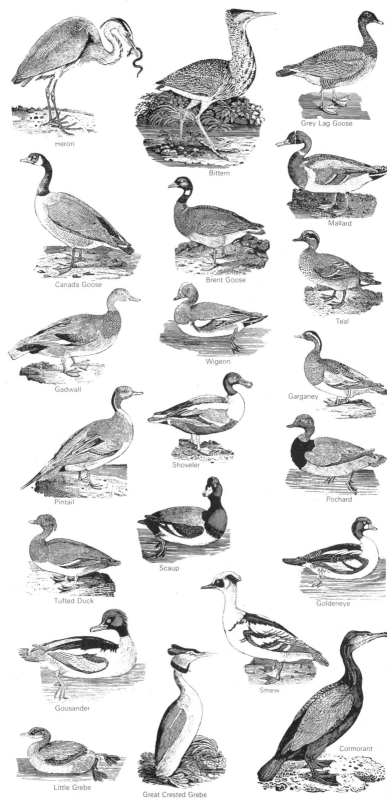

Heron

Bittern

Grey Lag Goose

Canada Goose

Brent Goose

Mallard

Teal

Gadwall

Wigeon

Garganey

Pintail

Shoveler

Pochard

Tufted Duck

Scaup

Goldeneye

Goosander

Smew

Cormorant

Little Grebe

Great Crested Grebe

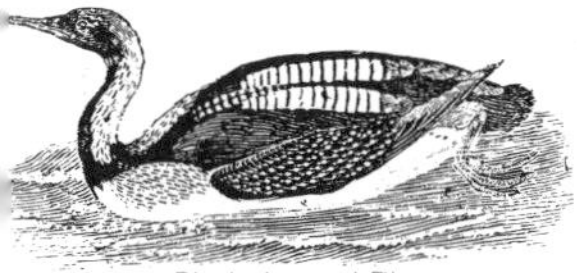

Black-throated Diver

Godwit

Curlew

Snipe

Turnstone

Dunlin

Redshank

Greenshank

Golden Plover

Grey Plover

Lapwing

Oystercatcher

Black Tern

Common Tern

Black-headed Gull

Herring Gull

Great Black-backed Gull

Lesser Black-backed Gull

Coot

Quail

Fish-eating birds are numerous, as one would expect. Virtually anywhere along the Thames the heron will be seen, either in slow and majestic flight overhead, or at dawn and dusk standing silent in the water, fishing. Its favoured food appears to be eels, which are extremely common in the river, and which it holds with little effort. The slime left on the heron's head and neck by an eel will be removed by 'powder down' in its feathers, which acts rather like talcum powder.

The kingfisher is much rarer on the Thames, but is, nevertheless, present in some numbers, although mostly one sees only a flash of blue as it flies low over the water. It lays its eggs in a burrow excavated in the river bank, which eventually becomes carpeted with a smelly mass of fish bones, spat out by the young birds. The most common fish eaten are sticklebacks, minnows, and small bleak.

Relatively few mammals are associated with the Thames, which lacks suitable habitats. Possibly the most often seen is the water vole (usually called water rat) which makes extensive burrows in the river banks and can be glimpsed, briefly, diving into the water when disturbed (they usually swim under water). But the brown rat is also very common, making its home behind bankside piles. Undoubtedly it finds rich pickings from the leavings of bankside picnic parties and anglers, and it swims very capably. The water vole has a blunt rounded snout while the rat's is pointed.

Fish generally manage to pass unnoticed especially in a heavily sedimented river like the Thames, but several kinds may be seen. In the downstream reaches between Teddington and Molesey salmon can be glimpsed leaping in the white water of the weirs while attempting to ascend upstream. Molesey Weir is too high for most to jump so the fisheries staff of Thames Water, who have reintroduced salmon into the river, catch them and transport them to natural spawning beds or to fish hatcheries. In quieter water on a calm sunny day young pike bask near the surface. Their torpedo shape must be very visible to the small fish they habitually feed on, so it seems that they are just enjoying the sun's warmth. In shaded areas, under trees, beneath bridges or landing stages, the quiet-footed may observe the boldly striped shape of a small perch lying quietly in the water waiting for a smaller fish to pass nearby. Larger perch live in the deeper pools of the river, always close to cover, but are shy and rarely seen from a boat or the bank.

Both perch and pike when young feed on the many different kinds of insects and crustaceans that the river holds. May-flies, with their long triple tails, caddis flies, with their big moth-like wings, and alder flies, are all familiar insects for the brief period they fly in May and June, but all spend a year or more underwater as larvae when they are prey for many fish. Dragonflies have a similar life history, but are themselves predators both in the water as larvae and when flying (they eat flies, gnats, and mosquitoes). The largest dragonflies are the several kinds of hawkers, *Aeshna* sp, which are very common on the Thames. Damselflies are much smaller and delicate with a hesitant, hovering flight, frequently alighting on plants or even an angler's float. The males are mostly bright blue, but the females are duller in colour. Because they are not territorial like the large dragonflies they often seem more common at suitable sites along the river. These and a myriad other invertebrates make the river an exceptional habitat and one that is always full of interest.

Northmoor Lock

FISHING THE THAMES

Twenty-five years ago the River Thames was far more peaceful than it is today: there were fewer fishermen and fewer boats. Now, many reaches are often lined with anglers, and boat traffic has grown considerably. As a consequence, during summer and autumn fishing can be very difficult. From June to October the angler who rises early not only has the best chance of success but, equally important, much less disturbance to contend with. During the summer the Thames is usually at its normal height and rate of flow, and is easy to fish. There are, however, exceptions: the abnormally heavy rainfall during the spring of 1983 sent the river soaring over its banks, giving conditions which are generally only expected during winter.

The first essential in fishing is deciding where to fish. Knowledge of where a particular species is most likely to be found is fundamental. The most common fish – with the exception of 'small' species such as bleak, gudgeon and minnows – are roach, which will be found around reed mace, underwater lilies (known as 'cabbages') and where the water flows over a clean gravel bottom. These latter places are easily located should a punt pass by, the sound of the punt pole hitting the gravel being quite audible.

In recent years the bream population has declined although in some reaches big concentrations of this sluggish but popular species are found. Like roach, bream favour gravelly runs, 'cabbages' and reed mace, also weirpools. It is commonly believed that bream dislike fast water: if that is true then vast numbers of bream which have been caught in such water were not aware of it!

Barbel are widespread, and indeed prolific in some reaches – notably above Oxford. They frequent both weirpools and the open river; in the latter, places where the current hits the bank and then runs along it are especially favoured. Only rarely are barbel caught by accident, making it a species primarily for the specialist.

Chub, too, are abundant and in many places they are more common than roach. Chub like cover – overhanging trees, bushes, 'rafts' of rubbish – anything under which they can hide. Nevertheless, chub often venture into open water, but by mid-morning this shy, noise-conscious fish will seek the nearest cover available.

The Thames is full of pike with specimens in excess of 20lbs taken every season. They are usually found close to cover and anyone who likes to feel a good bend in their rod should try fishing for them. Even though those rows of vicious teeth appear frightening there is little to fear, although placing one's hand *in* that unfriendly mouth is definitely not recommended!

Perch – the favourite of dads and boys alike – are, sadly, less in evidence these days although there are signs of a comeback. They are often seen chasing their prey across the surface, their spiky dorsal fin erect, the small, unfortunate fish losing ground all the time in an attempt – usually a forlorn one – to make good its escape.

By far the most prolific species are bleak and gudgeon, popular with the young – and some not so young. A maggot dangling about 18ins below the surface for bleak or in the case of gudgeon close to, or on, the bottom, should almost certainly bring an easy catch.

Where bait is concerned – for better-than-average fish – bread, lobworms, luncheon meat, sausage meat and sweetcorn are the favourites. For the holiday angler, maggots (obtainable from tackle shops) are the most popular. Keep them cool overnight by placing them in the fridge in a tightly closed container. The hook – a number 16 or 18 – is passed through the head (the thick end).

With regard to tackle, the rod should be between 11ft and 12ft long, with 100yds of line, 3–4lb breaking strain (6lb for barbel, 10lb for pike) on a fixed spool reel. Most beginners fail to load the spool properly leaving something like $\frac{3}{16}$in between the line and lip of the spool. This seriously restricts casting. At all times the line should come to within $\frac{1}{16}$in of the lip of the spool.

A near 20lb pike from the upper Thames (Peter Stone)

For floats, choose an Avon or Peacock quill with a loading of about 4 AAA shot. A smaller float carrying one small weight will be necessary for bleak and gudgeon. Hook sizes: for maggot 16s and 18s with a selection of 12, 10, 8 and 6s for meat, worms, bread and sweetcorn.

A question often asked by those embarking on a boating/fishing holiday is not only what fish they are likely to catch but how big they may be. The list below demonstrates the size of fish that can be caught in the Thames – weights are in pounds, ounces, drams. Barbel 13.8.0, J. Ginifer 1968; Bream 11.4.0, S. Martin 1954; Carp 31.0.0, J. Cadd 1974; Chub 7.1.0, S. Mead 1897; Dace 1.0.0, J. Smith 1970; Eel 6.12.0, K. Cummings 1975; Perch 4.5.4, G. Irons 1953; Pike 30.0.0, J. Cadd 1971; Roach 3.9.12, G. Player 1949; Rudd 3.13.0, W. Tucker 1962; Tench 8.8.0, J. Searson 1976. The places where all these were captured is not recorded, although three were taken in Oxford. The barbel came from the reach (Abbey Road) immediately upstream of Botley Road bridge, and both the pike and carp from the Medley reach opposite Port Meadow at Wolvercote.

A few years ago Thames Water introduced salmon fry to the river in an attempt to get them to run the Thames again. This has proved a success and salmon have been seen (and at least one captured) in some weirpools, notably at Teddington in the lower reaches.

Most of the fishing in the Thames is controlled by clubs and associations, with very little free fishing available. The exception to this are the tidal reaches, and around lock structures or where private dwellings adjoin the water. Day/weekly/fortnightly tickets for some reaches are available from tackle shops in towns and villages along the river.

A brace of fine chub from the Thames (Peter Stone)

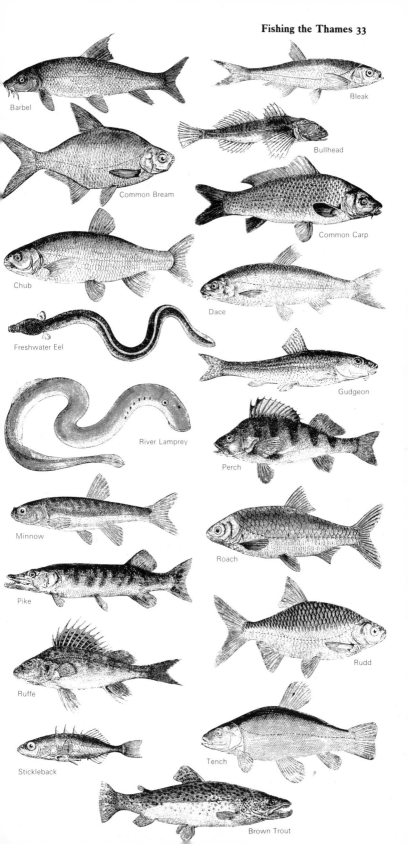

Barbel

Bleak

Common Bream

Bullhead

Common Carp

Chub

Dace

Freshwater Eel

Gudgeon

River Lamprey

Perch

Minnow

Roach

Pike

Ruffe

Rudd

Stickleback

Tench

Brown Trout

Good mixed fishing is available in and around Oxford where much of the river is controlled by the Abingdon and Oxford Anglers Alliance; Secretary M. Pouting (Oxford 67008). The following pubs are a selection of those which have reaches under their control, and tickets can be obtained from them: the Trout Inn at Tadpole, Buckland (234); the Maybush at Newbridge (624); and the Rose Revived, also at Newbridge (221). Local enquiry will reveal others. Fishing in selected weirpools is allowed; special permits can be obtained by writing to Thames Water, Nugent House, Vastern Road, Reading, Berks RG1 8DB. These are valid from 1 January to 31 December. The close season for coarse fishing is from 15 March to 15 June inclusive.

Before fishing the Thames a Thames Water rod licence must be obtained, available either from their Reading office or tackle shops. These cost £7.50 (1989) and are valid from 1 April to 31 March the following year. This licence does not entitle the holder to fish but no-one can fish without one. For those who are tempted to do so, a warning: if caught, the fine can be very high. Confusion often arises regarding fishing from boats. In most reaches this is allowed only if the necessary permit is obtained from the club or association which controls that particular section.

In the late 1970s, the minimum size rule was abolished. The by-laws now state that fish of any size can be retained in a keepnet providing they 'are returned alive to water at the point of capture not later than at the conclusion of fishing'.

Since June 1987 the use of lead shot by anglers has been banned. Lead shot carelessly dropped or discarded into the river was being ingested by swans, which would then subsequently die from lead poisoning. Since the ban the number of swans has increased, although there is evidence to suggest that some irresponsible anglers are still illegally using lead shot. Anglers are also to blame when birds die after becoming entangled in discarded nylon line and while most take the utmost care, a few do not. Discarded line should be taken home, never left on the bank and never tossed into the river. Plastic bags are also dangerous and cattle have died after eating them. Like discarded line, plastic bags should be taken home, along with cigarette packets, cans and bottles.

Many anglers care deeply for the countryside. Many are also conservationists. When a water is polluted, anglers often rescue the fish. They protest when water authorities remove or trim bankside trees prior to dredging, and it is anglers who financially support the Anglers Cooperative Association, a body which fights polluters and which, since its formation in 1954, has never lost a case in the High Court, obtaining thousands of pounds for clubs whose waters have been polluted. They realise that rivers such as the Thames are a vital part of our natural heritage – something for everyone to enjoy.

Near Wargrave

Peter Freebody's Boathouse, Hurley

HOW TO USE THIS GUIDE

SYMBOLS

Used on the map or within the text:

Ⓑ   Boatyard. The text entry describes the facilities in detail.

Ⓡ   Refuse disposal.

Ⓢ   Sewage or 'Elsan' disposal.

Ⓦ   Water, generally charged for at boatyards. Note that hosepipes must not be used at lock water points.

Ⓟ   Petrol.

Ⓓ   Diesel.

M   Overnight mooring. Often this facility must be paid for, and in the high season is in great demand.

🍺   Pub.

23   Mileage.

--   Course to follow.

⟨△⟩   Lock.

....   Footpath (public right of way).

--   Bridlepath (public right of way).

....   Towpath.

....   Path.

L   Recognised launching place or slipway, apart from those at boatyards.

✕   Restaurant.

♠   Licensed to sell alcohol.

L   Open for lunch.

D   Open for dinner.

All the locks on the Thames are accompanied by weirs. An enlarged diagram of each lock has been drawn to clarify your route into the lock.

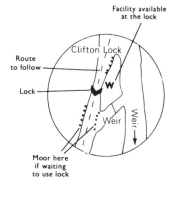

NAVIGATIONAL NOTES

These give telephone numbers and dimensions of locks, facilities available at the locks (note that virtually all locks on the Thames have a gents urinal, sometimes well hidden), the maximum draught and any other relevant navigational instructions.

NOTES FOR WALKERS

Route guidance, plus observations on the type of walking that can be expected. Interesting or useful detours are mentioned where appropriate.

BOATYARDS

Within the descriptions are all the essential services for boaters. Gas is 'Calor' unless indicated otherwise.

MOORING

Indicated on the map and described in this section, but there is also room for initiative, especially on the upper reaches. Don't, however, moor against private property without first seeking permission. Boatyards and pubs may also offer moorings.

BOAT TRIPS

A very good way of seeing the river before you commit yourself to a longer period of hire, or just a nice day out. Mentioned where appropriate and reviewed en masse on page 18.

PUBS AND RESTAURANTS

Virtually all the pubs near the river are included and described. If they offer bar snacks or meals, have a garden or a children's room, this is also mentioned. Where it has been possible we have included information on the brewery, and whether 'real ale' (as defined by CAMRA) is available. Our choice of restaurants is more selective – those included are generally above the usual standard, or have something special to offer. We describe briefly what type of food is offered, and whether L (lunch) or D (dinner) is served. Quite a few pubs have separate restaurants, and this information is also included. If you need to book, the telephone number is there. Finally, riverside pubs and restaurants often have good moorings – M following the entry indicates this facility.

SCALE

The scale of the River Thames and River Wey maps is 2½ inches to 1 mile. The Basingstoke Canal is shown at 2 inches to 1 mile (see page 158).

38 Cricklade

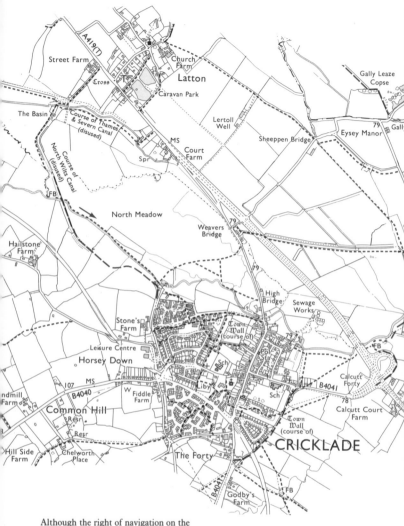

Although the right of navigation on the River Thames begins at Cricklade, the infant river at High Bridge appears little more than a brook. It flows swiftly between steep banks around the northern outskirts of the town before moving into open farmland. To the north lies the abandoned Thames & Severn Canal, which once left the Thames at Inglesham. Above Cricklade, the now derelict Wilts & Berks Canal crossed the Thames on an aqueduct.

NAVIGATIONAL NOTES

There is no navigation for cruisers on this section – those who manage the journey from Lechlade to Cricklade by unpowered craft, and can supply photographic proof of this achievement, can obtain a commemorative scroll by sending an sae to Pam Pugh, 10 Vanner Road, Witney, Oxon. There is an unofficial but well-founded scheme to enable navigation to Cricklade with the proposed construction of three new locks, which is why this book starts here.

NOTES FOR WALKERS

The only footpath to follow the river below Cricklade starts from the eastern outskirts of the town and finishes at Water Eaton House. This involves crossing the A419, a busy M4 motorway feeder road. The scenery is unremarkable.

Cricklade

Wilts. EC Wed. PO, stores, take-away Chinese and fish & chips. The proud Tudor tower of St Sampson's Church dominates this quiet town, relieved of its burden of traffic by a by-pass (A419), which closely follows the original route of Ermine Street, a Roman road, past the town. Apart from the tower, the church exhibits details from 12th–16thC. The heraldic display in the tower vault is fine, showing a curious Spanish influence. The clock outside the Vale Hotel commemorates the Jubilee of

- 77 To Marston Meysey
- Round House
- Marston Meysey Bridge
- N / W / E / S
- 79
- Wd Pp
- Eisey Field Copse
- 78
- Rucks Bridge
- Wd Pp
- North Farm
- 81
- Alex Farm
- Eisey Lock (disused)
- Plague Cottages
- 79
- Course of Thames & Severn Canal (disused)
- 79
- Water Eaton Cottages
- South Farm Cottages
- 81
- South Farm
- River Thames
- 78
- Eysey
- sey Manor
- Lower Part Farm
- 87
- Pp Ho
- FB
- Water Eaton House
- River Ray
- 78
- Manor Farm Cottages
- Calcutt Farm

Queen Victoria. In the churchyard of St
Mary, in the High Street, there is a
complete 14thC cross. Behind the
predominantly 18thC High Street are
several buildings of interest – the remains of
the priory, founded in 1231, can just be
seen, while in Bath Road are the 17thC
buildings of Robert Jenner's School,
founded in 1651. The Museum is in the old
Weigh House. Locally orientated, it
includes silver pennies made at the
Cricklade Mint, which was in operation
from Ethelred to Rufus. The town band,
formed in 1872, still thrives.

St Sampson's Church, Cricklade

Marston Meysey

Wilts. An attractive village with a long
stone-built street. Between the village and
the Thames there is a Round House, a type
of building peculiar to the Thames &
Severn Canal.

PUBS AND RESTAURANTS

Red Lion High Street, Cricklade. An
attractive old coaching inn with a garden,
built on the site of the Mint. Flowers real
ale, snacks and skittle alley.

White Hart Hotel High Street,
Cricklade. (Swindon 750206). Traditional
coaching inn with restaurant (*closed Sun D*),
serving Arkell's real ale.

Vale Inn High Street, Cricklade.
(Swindon 750223). A smart hotel by the
clock, serving Wadworth's real ales, snacks
at *lunchtime* and *evening dinner*. Garden.

Spotted Cow Marston Meysey. A fine
country pub in a stone farmhouse.
Wadworths real ales, bar meals, snacks and
garden.

40 Kempsford

At Castle Eaton the Thames now looks like a river, much wider and deeper than at Cricklade. Its course is secretive, passing Kempsford village almost unnoticed and again flowing through open fields with only livestock for company. There are shallows at Hannington Bridge, the site of an earlier Roman bridge, where the river is hidden from the road between steep sandy banks. South of Sterts Farm there are four enormous earthworks, circles of the Highworth type and thought possibly to be of Roman origin. Being 80 to 100yds in diameter they are far larger than any Bronze Age barrow circles.

NAVIGATIONAL NOTES

This section is not suitable for cruisers, although a 14ft craft, with a draught of 4in and powered by a modified outboard has been known to get as far as Hannington Bridge. The journey was not made without a struggle, and we do not recommend others to try – yet.

NOTES FOR WALKERS

This section has nothing to recommend itself to walkers – no footpaths by the river and little of interest to see outside the villages.

Castle Eaton

Wilts. PO, stores. A small village attractively sited by the river. The sturdy church was restored by Butterfield in 1862, when he

added the quaint bell-turret with a spire. The bridge is disappointing – a plain metal trough.

Kempsford

Glos. PO, store. Kempsford was once the home of the Plantagenet family. Its grandeur has faded and so has its importance after the

closing of the Thames & Severn Canal. The church has a splendid Perpendicular tower built by John of Gaunt in 1390. The tower

worthy of a visit. It is built around the church of St Mary the Virgin, a complete and perfect Perpendicular building. The tower was probably the inspiration for St Sampson's, Cricklade. It contains what is generally considered to be the best 15th–16thC stained glass in England. The glass was buried during the Civil War, and so escaped the attention of Cromwell's vandals. To the south is a large RAF air base, used by giant USAF tanker aircraft.

vaulting has heraldic painting, and there are good examples of Victorian stained glass. It is the only English church that can claim the honour of having an Irish peer buried under the organ.

Fairford

Glos. EC Thur. PO, stores. Over 3 miles north of Kempsford on the River Coln, Fairford is a gracious Cotswold town

PUBS AND RESTAURANTS

Red Lion Castle Eaton. A very handsome red-brick riverside pub with a garden. Courage real ale, bar meals and snacks. Note the picture of the earlier stone Castle Eaton Bridge in the bar.

George Kempsford. An attractive village pub serving Arkell's real ales, bar meals and snacks. Garden.

Axe & Compass Kempsford. Local pub with skittle alley and garden. Courage real ale, snacks and garden.

42 Lechlade

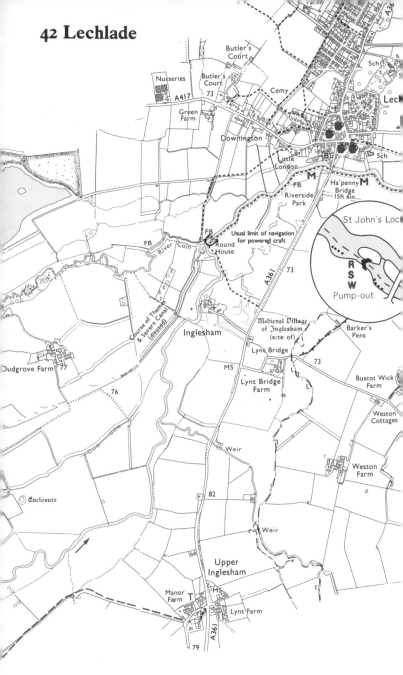

The Thames continues its solitary journey through fields and meadows to Inglesham, an attractive group of buildings by the river's edge. A ¼ mile further down is the usual limit of navigation for powered craft, marked by the Round House at the junction with the Thames & Severn Canal (unnavigable). Now there are moored craft and all the activities of a riverside park as the Thames passes Lechlade, flowing under Ha'penny Bridge, so named because a toll was once taken. The church at Lechlade can be seen from the river – its tall spire always visible as the river meanders to St John's Lock, the highest on the Thames. Note the modern lock house, the quaint miniature buildings in the lock gardens, and the statue of 'Father Thames', which once marked the river's source at Thames Head, north of Kemble, Gloucestershire. Below the bridge the course of the Thames becomes even more extravagant – at one point even doubling back before passing the church and beautiful rectory at Buscot. Beyond Buscot Lock the river is once again in open country, delightfully rural and lonely.

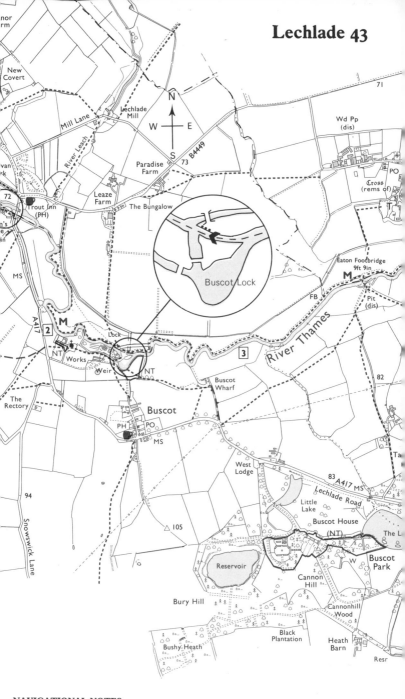

NAVIGATIONAL NOTES

St John's Lock (Faringdon 52309).
110ft 3in × 14ft 10in. Fall 2ft 10in. Manual operation. $\boxed{R}$ $\boxed{S}$ $\boxed{W}$ Pump-out (coin-operated). Ladies toilet.

Buscot Lock (Faringdon 52434).
109ft 10in × 14ft 8in. Fall 5ft 7in. Manual operation.

Max draught: 3ft 10in.

Limit of navigation: for powered craft, this is usually at the old junction with the Thames & Severn Canal, marked by the Round House below Inglesham. Here a full length narrowboat can wind (turn), taking care to avoid the sandbank on the north side. Those not familiar with the river are urged to proceed no further, even though the right of navigation extends to Cricklade and craft drawing 2ft 6in may be able to proceed as far as 3 miles above Lechlade. Canoes and skiffs which complete the journey can obtain a certificate – see Cricklade section.

44 Lechlade

Practical walking along the Thames begins
at Inglesham – however, the path across the
site of the medieval village, although still a
right of way, has become obscured and it is
easier to start from the north bank, at the
confluence of the Rivers Coln and Thames,
or from the Riverside Park above Ha'penny
Bridge. The path is in good shape along this
section, and follows the river continuously,
apart from a detour around the Trout Inn at
St John's Bridge – this has its own reward,
however, as it passes the beautifully
converted Priory Mill (private) on the River
Leach.

Inglesham
Wilts. A marvellous architectural group
around the tiny church. Although of Saxon
origin, the present building is largely 13thC
with later additions: note the bell tower and
the 17thC box pews. William Morris is
responsible for the remarkably original state
of the building – he loved it and saved it
from 19thC 'restoration'. A brass to the
right of the entrance commemorates his
work.

The adjoining farm was once the priory. On
the north bank the Inglesham Round House
is a notable land mark. It once belonged to
the last lock keeper of the Thames & Severn
Canal, which joins the river at this point,
but is unnavigable.

Lechlade
Glos. EC Thur. PO, shops. A golden grey
market town dominating the river in all
directions and best seen from St John's
Bridge, with the tall spire of the
Perpendicular 'wool' church rising above
the surrounding cluster of buildings. By
Ha'penny Bridge is the highest boatyard on
the river, a friendly and helpful concern
occupying the old wharves. Shelley's Walk
leads from the river to the church, where his
Stanzas in a Summer Evening Churchyard is
quoted on a plaque in the churchyard wall.
Shelley, Peacock, Mary Godwin and Charles
Clairmont stayed in Lechlade in 1815 after
rowing from Windsor.

Little Faringdon Mill 1 mile outside
Lechlade on the A361 to Burford. A perfect
18thC mill in its original state, with farm

and outbuildings. Private.

Buscot
Oxon. A small village off the A417, notable

for the very beautiful Queen Anne rectory
(private) which stands on the riverside by
the church, itself unremarkable apart from
its Burne-Jones windows. The National
Trust own a picnic site by the weir pool.

Buscot Old Parsonage A Cotswold stone
building of 1703 on the riverbank. *Open
Wed afternoons by written appointment with
the tenant.* National Trust.

Buscot Park Built about 1780 in the Adam
style, with a park and gardens laid out by
Harold Peto. Fine furniture and paintings by
Rembrandt and Murillo. Burne-Jones room.
*Open Wed to Fri, 2nd and 4th weekends,
afternoons only, Apr–Sep. Charge.* National
Trust.

Buscot Wharf Little trace remains of the
wharf from which brandy was shipped to
France. The short arm was known as
'Buscot Pill'.

BOATYARDS

Ⓑ **Riverside Lechlade** Lechlade.
(Faringdon 52229). Ⓦ Ⓟ Ⓓ Gas, hire craft,
day hire boats, chandlery, maps, boat sales,
pub. *Closed Sun in winter.*

MOORING

Possible below Ha'penny Bridge on the
towpath side, and above Buscot Lock on the
towpath side. Many isolated rural moorings.

PUBS AND RESTAURANTS

🍺 **Swan** Lechlade. Courage real ale,
morning coffee, snacks and meals in a
friendly town centre pub. Garden.

🍺✕ **Crown Inn** Lechlade. (Faringdon
52218). Excellent choice of real ales, and
good food such as home-made soups and
hamburgers make this a very popular pub.
There is also a French restaurant (*open D
Wed–Sun*) and a garden.

🍺 **Appletree** Lechlade. Arkell's real ales,
snacks and meals in this town centre hotel.

🍺✕ **New Inn** Lechlade. (Faringdon 52296).
Right by the church. Courage real ale,
snacks and cordon bleu restaurant meals
every evening except Sun.

There are several small restaurants/tea rooms
in Lechlade, such as Katies, all easily
found.

🍺✕ **Trout Inn** St John's Bridge, nr
Lechlade. (Faringdon 52313). A justly
famous 13thC Cotswold stone pub, with
plenty of wood panelling, low beams and
stuffed pike. There are tasty bar meals and
Courage real ale, with a separate dining room
for more elaborate meals *in the evening.* The
riverside garden borders the weir stream.
Children are welcome. Fishing rights on 2
miles of the Thames. Ⓜ(limited).

🍺 **Red Lion** Buscot. Main road pub,
serving Hall's beers.

St John's Lock, with Lechlade in the distance

46 Kelmscot

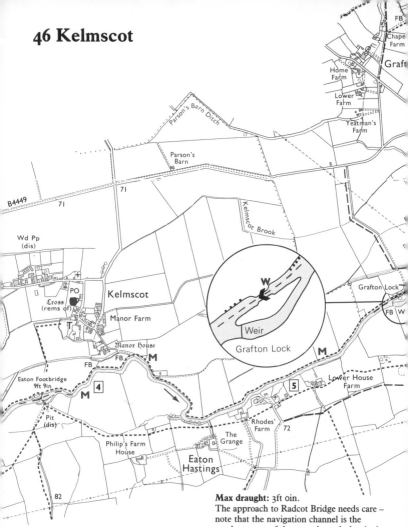

Max draught: 3ft 0in.

The approach to Radcot Bridge needs care – note that the navigation channel is the northernmost of the two, through the single arched bridge, and that the approach is blind and the current sometimes difficult.

NOTES FOR WALKERS

The towpath, apart from a short stretch below Grafton Lock, is in good condition and follows without detour the wholly rural course of the river. Kelmscot is fortunately on the towpath side, and the walk up the lane past the manor provides relief from the endless water-meadows. The pub at Radcot Bridge is a welcome sight – it's a long lonely walk to the next.

Kelmscot

Oxon. A pristine village of elegant grey stone houses, firmly entrenched against development. Kelmscot Manor, a beautiful

A very isolated, rural stretch of river, meandering through meadowland and having little contact with civilisation. Boats moored in a backwater at Eaton Footbridge indicate the presence of a boatclub, below which is Kelmscot Manor, standing close to the river in an area very popular with anglers. The church at Eaton Hastings is also by the river and provides interest before reaching Grafton Lock, a lonely outpost. At Radcot the river divides and two fine bridges, the ever popular Swan Inn and the large picnic area opposite are busy with pleasure seekers on sunny summer afternoons. In summer there are river trips aboard a colourful traditional narrowboat, moored opposite the pub. Caravans line the north bank as once more the Thames enters open meadowland around Radcot Lock.

NAVIGATIONAL NOTES

Grafton Lock (Clanfield 251).
113ft 6in × 15ft 1in. Fall 3ft 8in. Manual operation. W

Radcot Lock (Faringdon 20676).
113ft 6in × 15ft 0in. Manual operation. W
Ladies toilet.

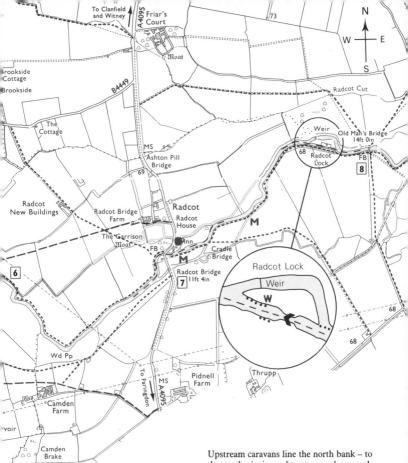

16thC house behind high walls, was the home of William Morris from 1871 until his death in 1896, and he shared it with Dante Gabriel Rossetti until 1874. William Morris was buried in the churchyard here after his death in Hammersmith; his tomb is the work of Philip Webb. The quiet 15thC church has a strong medieval atmosphere. *Manor open first Wed of month, Apr–Sep or by written application (sae required). Charge.*

Eaton Hastings

Oxon. An inaccessible village. The 13thC church is well situated by the river – the rest of the village is a mile away.

Radcot

Oxon. A small hamlet centred around the popular Swan Hotel. The triple arched 13thC bridge is the oldest surviving on the

Thames. The single arched bridge spanning the navigation channel, an artificial cut, was built later, in 1787. The old bridge, made of Taynton stone, was the scene of a Civil War skirmish when Prince Rupert's Royalist cavalry pounced on Cromwell's men, marching to an attack on Faringdon.

Upstream caravans line the north bank – to the south picnics and tents sprawl across the meadow.

Faringdon House *Oxon.* 2½ miles south of Radcot Bridge. An 18thC house built by George III's 'dogged and dull' poet laureate Henry James Pye. The surrounding parkland is reputedly haunted by a headless Hampden Pye, an earlier member of the family decapitated at sea. His story is recalled in *The Ingoldsby Legends*, 1840. The folly on Faringdon Hill, an octagonal Gothic lantern, was built by the artist and author Lord Berners in 1935.

BOAT TRIPS

Thames Cruises 5 Bourton Close, Clanfield, Oxon. (Clanfield 313). Scheduled trips *Apr–Sep*, and private charter in the beautiful narrowboat *Battersea*, moored opposite the Swan Inn at Radcot.

PUBS AND RESTAURANTS

Plough Inn Kelmscot. A fine 16thC pub with flagstone floors, serving Arkell's, Hook Norton and Morland's real ales, snacks and meals (*not Sun evening*). Garden, fishing rights. M

Swan Radcot Bridge. A very comfortable and friendly old inn of great character. The interior is decorated with stuffed fish, plenty of brass and features a William Morris oak chair. Morland's real ales and bar food. There is a pleasant garden. M and fishing rights.

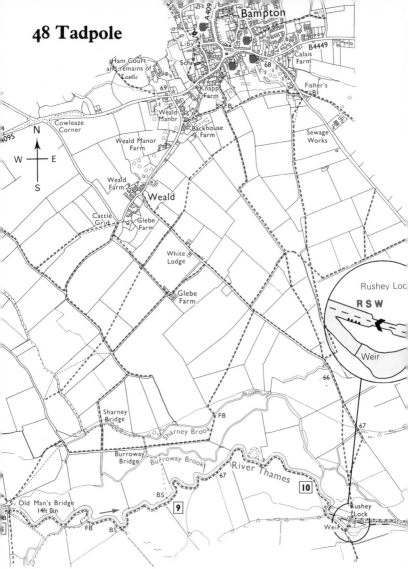

48 Tadpole

A section of flat and featureless water-meadows. The only things of interest are the splendid Rushey Lock, with its charming house and fine garden, and the handsome 18thC Tadpole Bridge. About as 'far away from it all' as you can get on the Thames, if you like that sort of thing.

NAVIGATIONAL NOTES

Rushey Lock (Buckland 218).
113ft 6in × 15ft 1in. Fall 6ft 0in. Manual operation. R S W Pump-out (coin-operated).
Max draught: 3ft 0in.

NOTES FOR WALKERS

The path from Radcot Lock stays on the south side, and is in reasonable shape. At Rushey Lock it crosses the weir and the lock to continue along a good vehicle track to Tadpole Bridge – here the road can be followed to the handsome town of Bampton or to Buckland. From Tadpole to well beyond Shifford, large parts of the towpath resemble something between a jungle and an assault course, recommended only to those who are fit and determined to follow the river at all costs. The right of way half a mile south of Tadpole could provide a sensible detour to Duxford; alternatively the towpath can be followed as far as Tenfoot Bridge, and a crossing made here to join the Duxford path, or a visit to Bampton could be followed by a walk via Aston and Standlake to Newbridge. The villages provide more interest than the river at this point.

Bampton

Oxon. PO, tel, shops. A very attractive grey stone town 1½ miles from the river, easily approached by a variety of footpaths or by road from Tadpole. It has a timeless appearance in that much of the new development is built from the same materials as, and often in a style similar to, the old. The result is both unusual and pleasing

without being consciously archaic. The
church, largely 13th and 14thC, is
dominated by a slightly uneasy octagonal
spire. Inside, the 14thC reredos is cut from a
single piece of stone, while the Horde Chapel
contains excellent Baroque monuments.
Beside the church is the old Grammar
School, founded in 1653. There are an
unusually large number of pubs in Bampton,
many featuring well painted signs in the
traditional style. Perhaps the many fairs
associated with the town explain this
profusion. You may notice on some of the
pub signs the town is called 'Bampton in the
Bush' – this dates from before the 18thC
when no roads served the community.
Morris dancing is reputed to have originated
here, a tradition celebrated each year at the
Bampton Horse Fair (*Aug*) and the Spring
Bank Holiday Fair.

Buckland
Oxon. 1 mile south of Tadpole Bridge. A
village intimately connected with Buckland
House, and best approached from the river
as there is a fine view over the Thames
Valley. The church has an unusually wide
12thC nave. The south transept is
splendidly decorated in rich late Victorian
mosaic, dating from about 1890.

Buckland House Built in 1757 by Wood of
Bath, it is one of the most imposing 18thC
homes in Oxfordshire. The wings were
added in 1910, but are nonetheless quite
convincing. There is a Gothic stable in the
park (private).

MOORING

There may be overnight moorings available
at the Trout Inn, and plenty of isolated
rural moorings elsewhere.

PUBS AND RESTAURANTS

Trout Inn Tadpole Bridge. (Buckland
234). A fine traditional riverside pub
recently refurbished. Real ale, bar meals
and snacks. Garden, camping and fishing
rights. M

It is not difficult to find a pub in Bampton –
this is a small selection of those available:

Morris Clown High Street, Bampton.
12thC pub with a wonderful sign and
superb garden full of mangles. Courage real
ale and bar meals.

Romany Inn Bridge Street, Bampton.
(Bampton Castle 850237). There are Saxon
arches in the cellar of this fine old pub.
Usher's real ale and extensive bar meals.

Jubilee Market Square, Bampton. The
sign celebrates Queen Victoria's Jubilee on
21 June 1887. One bar, where Wadworth's
real ales are dispensed.

Eagle Church View, Bampton. The
famous Morris Dancers have their
headquarters here. Naturally there is a
garden to dance in, and Morrell's real ale to
drink.

50 Newbridge

The river winds its way through remote countryside to Shifford, where the navigation channel passes through the tree-lined cut to Shifford Lock, the last to be built on the Thames (in 1898). Shifford church stands near the river below its junction with the Great Brook – again the countryside is flat farmland glimpsed here and there over the steep river banks which are in places heavily overgrown. Electricity pylons do little to improve the scene. Welcome relief appears at Newbridge, with a fine pub on each side of the handsome old bridge. The nearest village is Standlake, a mile to the north.

NAVIGATIONAL NOTES

Shifford Lock (Buckland 247).
113ft 8in × 15ft 1in. Fall 7ft 4in. Manual operation. Ladies toilet.
Max draught: 3ft 0in.
The original course of the river is navigable for small craft from below Shifford Lock to Duxford Ford, but the turning area is restricted to the width of the river.

NOTES FOR WALKERS

Those who have fought their way along the towpath to Shifford should cross the lock cut by the footbridge and proceed to Duxford Ford, which is passable in boots when the river is not in spate. It is not possible to cross the river at the lock. The path from Duxford to the junction with the Great Brook is heavily overgrown and difficult, involving a scramble across a drainage ditch. The next 1½ miles is acceptable until the point below Harrowdown Hill where woods come down to the river's edge and a way has to be forced through, to make a field edge detour, before reaching Newbridge. Those who have made the detour via Bampton, Aston and Standlake will have had an altogether easier time, and seen a lot more. Below Newbridge the path, now on the north side, improves.

Shifford

Oxon. A church and a few houses surrounded by lush pastureland are all that remain of a once important town. Alfred held a meeting of the English Parliament here in AD890. The church is situated in the middle of a field less than ¼ mile from the river.

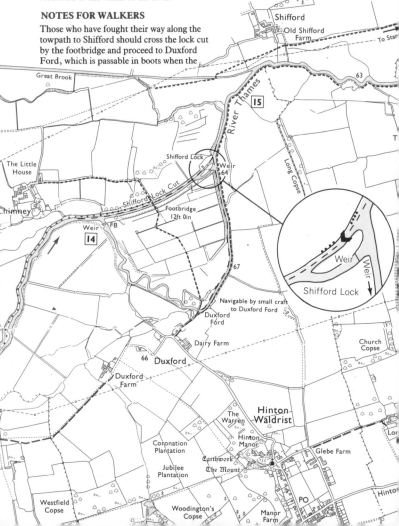

Hinton Waldrist and Longworth
Oxon. PO, stores. Two pleasant straggling
villages up on a ridge overlooking the

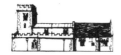

valley. Longworth church contains a good
example of Arts and Crafts stained glass by
Heywood Sumner, 1906. The Old Rectory,
Longworth, was the birthplace of Dr John
Fell, 1625–86, who participated in the early
development of the Oxford University
Press, especially with regard to printing
types; and also Richard Doddridge
Blackmore 1825–1900, author of *Lorna
Doone* (1869), who spent only the first four
months of his life here – sadly his mother
died shortly after his birth.
Harrowdown Hill A very dominant breast-
shaped hill, approached by footpath from
the river.

Standlake
Oxon. PO, stores, launderette. On the River
Windrush, 1 mile north of Newbridge.
There are some very fine houses here,
hidden amongst untidy modern
development.
Newbridge
Oxon. A fine 13thC stone bridge with
pointed arches, one of the oldest on the
river and the site of a Civil War battle when
the Parliamentarians tried, and failed, to
approach Faringdon. The River Windrush
joins the Thames here.

MOORING

Plenty of isolated rural moorings
throughout – especially above Shifford
Lock; better moorings at Newbridge.

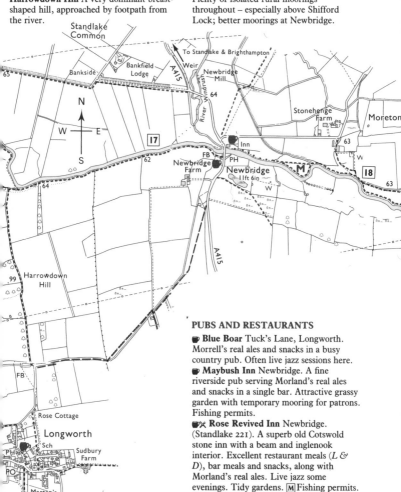

PUBS AND RESTAURANTS

🍺 **Blue Boar** Tuck's Lane, Longworth.
Morrell's real ales and snacks in a busy
country pub. Often live jazz sessions here.
🍺 **Maybush Inn** Newbridge. A fine
riverside pub serving Morland's real ales
and snacks in a single bar. Attractive grassy
garden with temporary mooring for patrons.
Fishing permits.
🍺✕ **Rose Revived Inn** Newbridge.
(Standlake 221). A superb old Cotswold
stone inn with a beam and inglenook
interior. Excellent restaurant meals (*L &
D*), bar meals and snacks, along with
Morland's real ales. Live jazz some
evenings. Tidy gardens. M Fishing permits.
🍺 **Bell** High Street, Standlake. A pleasant
pub with a small front garden and vast car
park. Morland's real ales and *lunchtime* bar
meals.

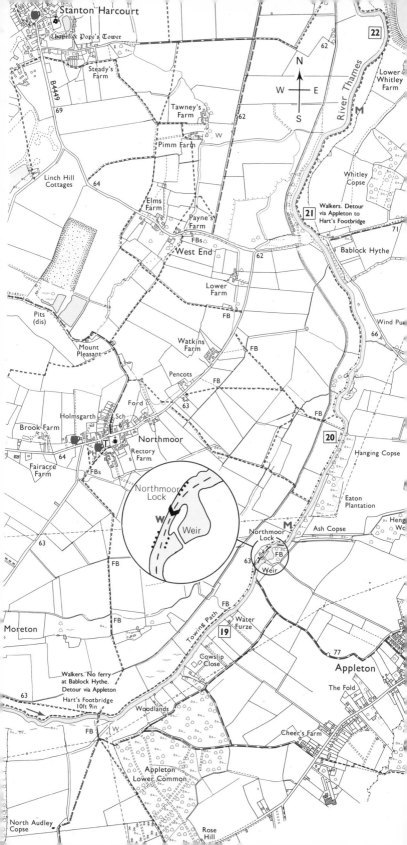

Stanton Harcourt

Chapel & Pope's Tower

Steady's Farm

B4449

69

Tawney's Farm

Pimm Farm

W

62

N

W ← → E

S

River Thames

22

Lower Whitley Farm

M

Linch Hill Cottages

64

Elms Farm

Payne's Farm

FBs

West End

62

Whitley Copse

21

Walkers. Detour via Appleton to Hart's Footbridge

71

Bablock Hythe

Lower Farm

FB

Pits (dis)

Mount Pleasant

Watkins Farm

FB

Wind Pu

66

Pencots

FB

Ford

Sch

63

Holmsgarth

Brook Farm

Northmoor

64

PH

Rectory Farm

Fairacre Farm

FBs

FB

FB

20

Hanging Copse

Eaton Plantation

Northmoor Lock

W

Weir

Northmoor Lock

M

Ash Copse

Heng Wo

63

FB

63

FB

Weir

FB

Towing Path

Water Furze

19

Moreton

FB

Cowslip Close

77

Appleton

The Fold

Walkers. No ferry at Bablock Hythe. Detour via Appleton

63

Hart's Footbridge 10ft 9in

Woodlands

Cheer's Farm

FB

W

Appleton Lower Common

North Audley Copse

Rose Hill

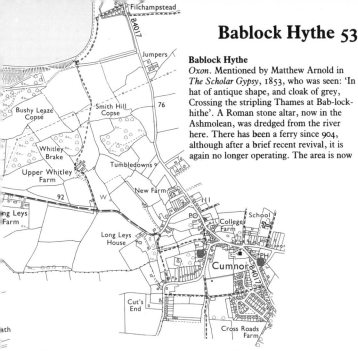

Bablock Hythe

Oxon. Mentioned by Matthew Arnold in
The Scholar Gypsy, 1853, who was seen: 'In
hat of antique shape, and cloak of grey,
Crossing the stripling Thames at Bab-lock-
hithe'. A Roman stone altar, now in the
Ashmolean, was dredged from the river
here. There has been a ferry since 904,
although after a brief recent revival, it is
again no longer operating. The area is now

As the hills close in from the east the
countryside loses much of the bleakness of
the upper reaches and the villages come a
little closer. There are attractive woods
below Northmoor Lock, and Bablock
Hythe is soon reached. To the north, the
grassy banks of the vast Farmoor Reservoir,
much loved by anglers, come down to the
river's edge.

NAVIGATIONAL NOTES

Northmoor Lock (Oxford 862923).
113ft 6in × 15ft 1in. Fall 4ft 1in. Manual
operation. Ⓦ

NOTES FOR WALKERS

The path on the north bank to Northmoor
Lock and on to Bablock Hythe is in good
shape, and the hills opposite make the walk
quite enticing but there is, alas, no longer a
ferry at Bablock Hythe, so a detour over
Hart's Footbridge and through the woods to
Appleton, then on by road to Bablock
Hythe is required.

Northmoor

Oxon. A remote village. The 13thC
cruciform church contains a restored bell-
loft, dated 1701 – note the dedication poem.
Behind the church is a Tudor rectory. The
tiny Dun Cow pub is a delight.

Appleton

Oxon. PO, store. A meandering thatch and
stone village, with new development to the
west. Appleton Manor, situated beside a
splendid weatherboarded barn and gateway,
was built at the end of the 12thC. An
astonishing amount remains: note especially
the doorway.

surrounded by an unwelcoming estate of
temporary homes. The Ferry Inn has been
closed down.

Stanton Harcourt

Oxon. PO, stores. A superb grey village
between the Thames and the Windrush, the
waters reflecting the quiet glory of the
buildings. The grand cruciform church, still
predominantly Early English and
Perpendicular, has fine monuments in the
Harcourt Chapel. The Harcourts built the
15thC manor (Oxford 881928). Only Pope's
Tower, the scene of his translation of the
Iliad, and the unique Great Kitchen, survive
(*open B. Hols, and various Sun & Thur, Apr–
Sep, afternoons only; charge*). Well worth the
walk from the river.

Cumnor

Oxon. PO, store. A pleasant 1½-mile walk
from Bablock Hythe. It was the scene of the
tragedy of Amy Dudley, wife of Elizabeth I's
courtier Robert Dudley, Earl of Leicester.
She was discovered dead at the foot of a
'paire of staires' in the medieval Cumnor
Place, which stood to the west of the church.
Now, apart from a few stones from the house
in the churchyard wall, only the memory
remains. The church, begun in the 12thC,
contains much Jacobean and Georgian
woodwork; note the splendid spiral staircase
in the tower, dated 1685, the choir stalls and
the two-decker pulpit. Hidden away in the
vestry is a life-like statue of Queen Elizabeth
I, reputedly erected by the Earl of Leicester.

54 Bablock Hythe

MOORING

There are plenty of opportunities for isolated rural moorings.

PUBS AND RESTAURANTS

Dun Cow Northmoor. A lovely old cottage pub with no bar. Morland's real ales served straight from the cask. Garden. A genuine unspoilt gem.

Red Lion Northmoor. (Standlake 301). A good village pub, by the church. Courage real ale, food and garden.

Thatched Tavern Appleton. An attractive tiled pub, the sign showing its earlier roof. Hall's beers, food and garden.

Plough Inn Eaton Road, Appleton. A comfortable 17thC inn serving Morland's real ales. No electronic machines or juke box. Snacks and garden.

Three Horseshoes Oaksmere, Appleton. (Oxford 862130). A good country pub and restaurant (*open D, closed Sun & Mon*) with a large garden and pub games such as skittles and Aunt Sally. Interesting tool collection. Bar meals and snacks.

Harcourt Arms Stanton Harcourt. (Oxford 881931). A large and handsome 16thC inn with a beamy interior. Morrell's real ales, bar food, snacks and garden. Meals in the restaurant (*L & D*).

Vine Cumnor. A pretty pub with the aforementioned vine growing along the front wall. Hall's beers, food and garden.

Bear & Ragged Staff Cumnor. (Oxford 862329). A large 16thC edifice close to the village pond. Morrell's real ale, good restaurant with a varied and imaginative menu (*closed Sat L, Sun D & Mon*), snacks and garden.

The Ferry Inn, Bablock Hythe

The Thames meanders extravagantly past Farmoor Reservoir and the very pretty Pinkhill Lock, with its picnic site, towards Swinford. Below Eynsham Lock the entrance to the Wharf Stream can be seen on the east side, followed by the Cassington Cut, which by-passed the lower reaches of the Evenlode, when that river was navigable. Opposite are the dense woodlands of Wytham Great Wood, falling steeply down Wytham Hill to the river's edge. The Seacourt Stream leaves the Thames at Hagley Pool, and a short distance below is King's Lock, the lowest manually operated lock on the river. The lock sells mature cheddar cheese, honey and fresh produce when available. Access to the Oxford Canal can be gained via a backwater and the Duke's Cut, which join the weir stream. Pixey Mead lies to the west, its peace shattered by the incessant traffic of the Oxford by-pass, which crosses the river above Godstow. On the weir stream is the old Trout Inn; overlooking the lock cut are the ruins of Godstow Abbey. By Port Meadow the river is now significantly wider,

flowing between sandy banks to Binsey, where a small jetty indicates the presence of the village and its handsome thatched pub.

NAVIGATIONAL NOTES

Pinkhill Lock (Oxford 881452).
113ft 6in × 16ft 1in. Fall 3ft 6in. Manual operation. W

Eynsham Lock (Oxford 881324).
113ft 3in × 16ft 4in. Fall 2ft 9in. Manual operation. R S W

King's Lock (Oxford 53403).
113ft 1in × 16ft 4in. Fall 2ft 6in. Manual operation. W

Godstow Lock (Oxford 54784).
110ft 0in × 16ft 3in. Fall 5ft 2in.

Max draught: 3ft 0in.

Access to the Oxford Canal can be gained via the weir stream above King's Lock and through Duke's Cut. Maximum dimensions on this charming rural canal are: length 70ft 0in, beam 7ft 0in, headroom 7ft 0in. The canal is described in detail in *Nicholson/OS Guide to the Waterways 1. South*.

Take great care at Godstow Bridge, where the arches are narrow and low.

Cruising by Wytham Great Wood

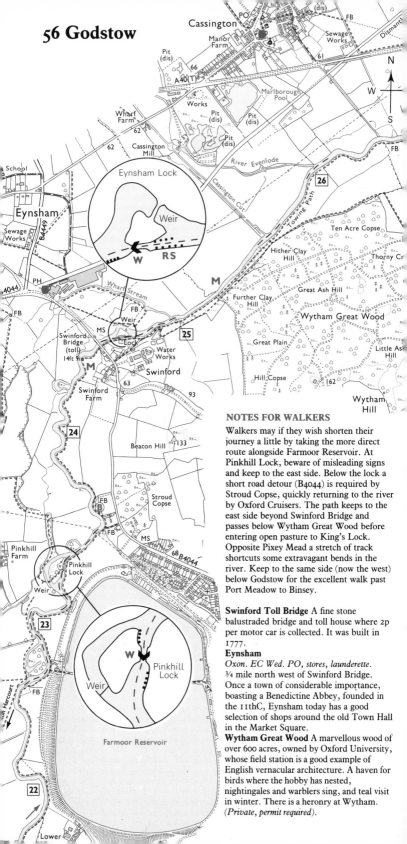

56 Godstow

NOTES FOR WALKERS

Walkers may if they wish shorten their journey a little by taking the more direct route alongside Farmoor Reservoir. At Pinkhill Lock, beware of misleading signs and keep to the east side. Below the lock a short road detour (B4044) is required by Stroud Copse, quickly returning to the river by Oxford Cruisers. The path keeps to the east side beyond Swinford Bridge and passes below Wytham Great Wood before entering open pasture to King's Lock. Opposite Pixey Mead a stretch of track shortcuts some extravagant bends in the river. Keep to the same side (now the west) below Godstow for the excellent walk past Port Meadow to Binsey.

Swinford Toll Bridge A fine stone balustraded bridge and toll house where 2p per motor car is collected. It was built in 1777.

Eynsham
Oxon. EC Wed. PO, stores, launderette.
¾ mile north west of Swinford Bridge. Once a town of considerable importance, boasting a Benedictine Abbey, founded in the 11thC, Eynsham today has a good selection of shops around the old Town Hall in the Market Square.

Wytham Great Wood A marvellous wood of over 600 acres, owned by Oxford University, whose field station is a good example of English vernacular architecture. A haven for birds where the hobby has nested, nightingales and warblers sing, and teal visit in winter. There is a heronry at Wytham. *(Private, permit required).*

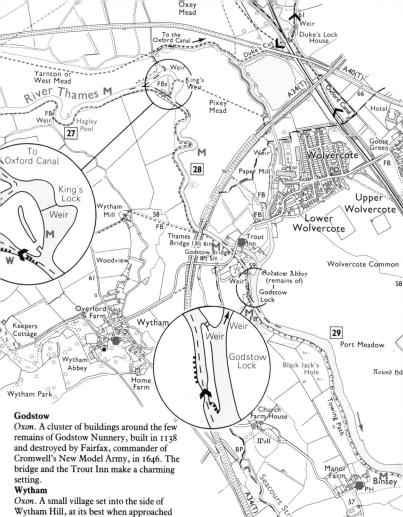

Godstow

Oxon. A cluster of buildings around the few
remains of Godstow Nunnery, built in 1138
and destroyed by Fairfax, commander of
Cromwell's New Model Army, in 1646. The
bridge and the Trout Inn make a charming
setting.

Wytham

Oxon. A small village set into the side of
Wytham Hill, at its best when approached
from the river. Wytham Abbey, originally
16thC, has many later additions: the whole is
pleasingly irregular.

BOATYARDS

Ⓑ **Oxford Cruisers** Eynsham, Oxford
(881698). R S W P D Pump-out, gas, hire
craft, day hire boats, long-term mooring,
winter storage, slipway, dry dock, books and
maps, boatbuilding, boat and engine repairs,
toilets, showers. M

MOORING

There are many opportunities for isolated
moorings, but more convenient spots
include: above Swinford Bridge (small fee to
Swinford Farm Shop), above Godstow
Bridge, and below Binsey (but watch the
shallows).

PUBS AND RESTAURANTS

Talbot Oxford Road, Eynsham. North
west of Swinford Bridge. An attractive small
pub on the now unnavigable Wharf Stream,
serving Hall's real ale, bar meals and snacks.
Tables at the roadside, swings and a little
wooden house to amuse the children.
Chequers Cassington. Morrell's real ales,
bar food and snacks in a village local.
Children's room and garden.
Trout Inn Godstow Bridge, Oxford
(54485). A lovely ivy-covered stone building,
with a riverside terrace, built in 1138 as a
hospice for Godstow Nunnery. Peacocks
roam the gardens, and the weir stream – not
fished for the last 20 years – is full of shoals
of large chub, swimming tamely near the
surface among the ducks. One is left
wondering how many fish would be seen in
the rest of the Thames if the anglers found
some other pastime. Good restaurant (*L &
D, Reserve*), bar meals and snacks.
White Hart Wytham. An old village pub
with flagstone floors and 16thC dovecote.
Hall's real ale and excellent food. Garden.
Perch Binsey. (Oxford 240386). Moor at
the jetty and walk 50yds along a path to this
large and handsome 17thC thatched pub,
standing in a superb garden with willow
trees. Hall's and Ind Coope real ales in the
low-ceilinged bar, where the ghost of a sailor
is said to appear. Bar meals and snacks. M
nearby.

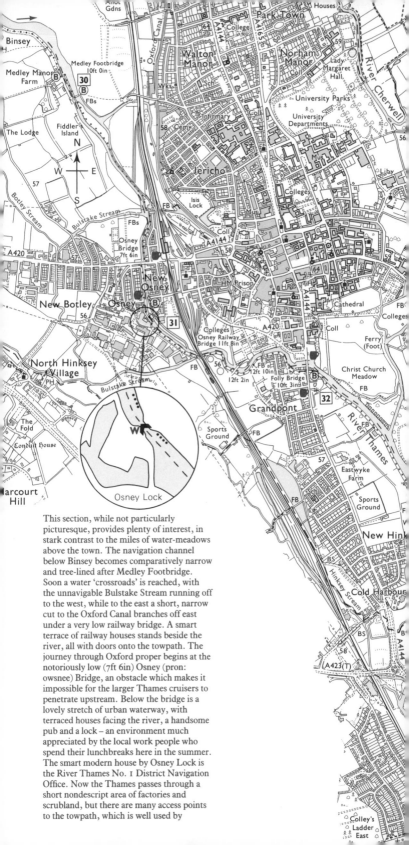

This section, while not particularly
picturesque, provides plenty of interest, in
stark contrast to the miles of water-meadows
above the town. The navigation channel
below Binsey becomes comparatively narrow
and tree-lined after Medley Footbridge.
Soon a water 'crossroads' is reached, with
the unnavigable Bulstake Stream running off
to the west, while to the east a short, narrow
cut to the Oxford Canal branches off east
under a very low railway bridge. A smart
terrace of railway houses stands beside the
river, all with doors onto the towpath. The
journey through Oxford proper begins at the
notoriously low (7ft 6in) Osney (pron:
owsnee) Bridge, an obstacle which makes it
impossible for the larger Thames cruisers to
penetrate upstream. Below the bridge is a
lovely stretch of urban waterway, with
terraced houses facing the river, a handsome
pub and a lock – an environment much
appreciated by the local work people who
spend their lunchbreaks here in the summer.
The smart modern house by Osney Lock is
the River Thames No. 1 District Navigation
Office. Now the Thames passes through a
short nondescript area of factories and
scrubland, but there are many access points
to the towpath, which is well used by

cyclists, joggers and walkers. Just above Osney Railway Bridge stands a touching memorial to Edgar Wilson who on 15 June 1889 saved the lives of two boys here, at the cost of his own. A little cheer is brought to the river by a gaudily painted iron road bridge as the river curves past more terraced houses which look across to new

development on the north side. Folly Bridge is always a hive of activity during the summer; Salter's Boatyard is here, along with a large riverside pub. Punts are available for hire and small motor and rowing boats proceed up and down. Christ Church Meadow lies to the east, and is thronged with tourists and sunbathers during the summer. Below is a long row of boat houses, facing the mock Tudor of the

University Rowing Club building. Downstream of Donnington Road Bridge, suburbia keeps its distance and the river proceeds along a green passage, past George Harris' boat house, where he builds racing boats, and on to Iffley Lock, with its pretty balustraded footbridges and fine lock house, all surrounded by trees, with a white painted pub nearby. There is an area of parkland to the west, on an isthmus created by the Weirs Mill Stream, followed by the functional steel of Kennington Railway Bridge. As the river dog-legs past Rose Isle pylons run parallel, but still the houses and factories, for the most part, keep away. A fascinating stretch of river.

NAVIGATIONAL NOTES

Osney Lock (Oxford 247050). 113ft 8in × 17ft 3in. Fall 6ft 3in. W Ladies toilet.
Iffley Lock (Oxford 777277). 154ft 11in × 21ft 3in. Fall 2ft 9in. R
Max draught: above Oxford 3ft 0in; below Oxford 4ft 0in.
Proceeding downstream below Binsey, note that the navigation channel is under the iron footbridge on the west side, by the boatyard. Access to the Oxford Canal can be made along the channel above Osney Bridge. Full details of the Oxford Canal are in the *Nicholson/OS Guide to the Waterways 1. South*. The headroom at Osney Bridge is 7ft 6in at normal levels, less when the river is in spate. Those proceeding upstream who are in any doubt regarding the headroom should consult the lock keeper. And remember, the water levels can change very quickly, so you could get stuck *upstream*. The approach downstream to Osney is made difficult by the strong weir stream. There are two channels at Folly Bridge; go slowly through either.

NOTES FOR WALKERS

Below Binsey walkers should cross the iron footbridge (dated 1865) by the boatyard and walk along the narrow Fiddler's Island, ignoring the next footbridge unless they wish to visit the second boatyard or walk into Oxford through the backstreets. The path is now shaded by trees, with water on both sides – the river and a backwater covered with lilies. A footbridge crosses the entrance to the Oxford Canal, and a little below here walkers should cross Osney Bridge to stay on the west side through the remainder of Oxford. It is a fascinating walk – rarely pretty, but always interesting. Access to the centre of Oxford is via St Aldates, north of Folly Bridge. There are enchanting walks along the Cherwell from Christ Church Meadows.

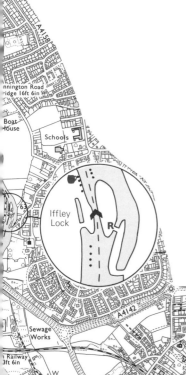

60 Oxford

City of Oxford

Oxon. All shops and services. The town was founded in the 10thC and has been a university city since the 13thC. Today it is a lively cosmopolitan centre of learning, tourism and industry. Visitors from the river intending to explore should proceed up St Aldates from Folly Bridge to the:

Tourist Information Centre St Aldates Chambers, Oxford (726871) where they will find a good selection of city guides and maps, and helpful and informative staff.

COLLEGES

It is, of course, the 39 colleges which give Oxford its unique character – they can all be visited, but opening times vary, so consult with the Tourist Centre. Those noted here have been selected as being particularly representative of their periods.

Merton College

One of the earliest collegiate foundations, dating from 1264, the buildings are especially typical of the Perpendicular and Decorative periods. The chapel was begun in 1294 and Mob Quad was the first of the Oxford quadrangles. The library, mainly 14thC, has a famous collection of rare books and manuscripts. During the Victorian era, the college was enlarged and the Grove Buildings are by William Butterfield with alterations in 1929 by T. Harold Hughes.

New College

The college was founded by William of Wykeham, Bishop of Winchester, in 1379. The chapel, a noble example of early Perpendicular, has been greatly restored by Sir George Gilbert Scott in the 19thC. The great west window, after a cartoon by Reynolds, and Epstein's *Lazarus* are noteworthy. The 14thC cloister and the workmanship of the wrought-iron screen, 1684, between the Garden Quad and the Garden, are outstanding memorials of their times.

Keble College

Built by William Butterfield in 1870, Keble is the only Oxford college entirely in the Victorian Gothic style. The frontage of red and grey patterned brickwork and the tracery windows wears a god-like self-confidence. The chapel, with its glass and mosaics, bricks, tiles and brass, contains Holman Hunt's *The Light of the World*.

St Catherine's College

An important and interesting example of the new university by the Danish architect, Arne Jacobsen, 1964. The entrance to the college is reached through an unprepossessing car park area, but in the main quadrangle the effect is one of stark impact. The mass of glass windows with their bands of ribbed concrete stretch like concertinas on either side of the quadrangle. All is bleak but full of atmosphere. The furniture and college plate were also designed by Jacobsen.

St Anne's College

This college reflects some of the most exciting modern building in Oxford. The Wolfson block in the main quadrangle was designed by Howell, Killick and Partridge, 1964. With its two curving wings and square jutting windows, all of pre-cast concrete, this building is impressive and original. Facing the block is the Dining Hall by Gerald Banks, 1964, and to one side is Hartland House, mainly 1930s but with 1951 additions by Sir Giles Gilbert Scott.

INTERESTING BUILDINGS

Radcliffe Camera

Radcliffe Square. Dr Radcliffe left £40,000 for the building of this library by James Gibbs, 1739, to house his 'Physic' library. It is a vast domed Italianate rotunda, now a Bodleian reading room, and not open to the public. The staircase and skylight can be admired through the doorway.

Sheldonian Theatre

Broad Street. Built by Christopher Wren in the mid 17thC under the auspices of Gilbert Sheldon, Archbishop of Canterbury, who disapproved of the annual irreverent performances of plays taking place in St Mary's. The theatre was also designed to be used for university ceremonies. Degrees are awarded here. For many years it also housed the workshops of the University Press. The interior with its ceiling by Robert Streeter is delightful.

The Old Bodleian

Schools Quadrangle, Oxford (277165). Named after Thomas Bodley, who died in 1613 leaving a fine collection of rare manuscripts. The old Bodleian buildings, mainly 16thC and early 17thC, also incorporate Duke Humphrey's library, 15thC. Bodley extended Duke Humphrey's

Oxford County Hall

Old Tom Tower

St Peter's College

Worcester College

Clarendon Building

Carfax Tower

St John's

Magdalen Bridge

St Michael's Church

Trinity

Botanic Gardens Gateway

Martyrs' Memorial

Christ Church, Oxford

library and also financed the entire rebuilding of the Schools Quadrangle. Under the Copyright Act the Bodleian is entitled to claim a copy of every book published in the British Isles. It currently holds some 5½ million volumes and 136,000 manuscripts.

St Cross Building
St Cross Road. The new Bodleian English and Law Library by Sir Leslie Martin, 1965, is a striking composite structure of some originality. A long flight of steps, a central feature of the building, leads between graded massive blocks. The structural frame is of reinforced concrete clad externally with brickwork. The building won a Civic Trust award in 1966.

Christ Church Cathedral
Christ Church. The cathedral, with its inconspicuous entrance in Tom Quad, was originally part of the Priory of St Frideswide. It is mainly 12thC with later additions and is typically Romanesque. The most splendid feature is the 16thC stone-vaulted fan roof of the choir. There is medieval glass and also 19thC glass by Burne-Jones. The Chapter House is a 13thC masterpiece.

St Mary the Virgin
High Street. The fine 14thC spire is a landmark. The church is typical of the Perpendicular style apart from the magnificent Baroque porch with its twisted columns by Nicholas Stone, 1637. The iron-work gates are 18thC. Before the building of the Sheldonian Theatre the church was also used as a theatre.

St Philip & St James
Woodstock Road. This church by G. E. Street, 1860–6, with its bands of pink sandstone in the brickwork, has an originality of its own, particularly noticeable on the west front.

MUSEUMS AND GALLERIES

Ashmolean Museum
Beaumont Street, Oxford (278000). The oldest public museum in Britain (opened in 1683) and one of the most rewarding museums outside London. It has an outstanding collection of Near Eastern and European archaeology, as well as the Farrer collection of 17th and 18thC silver. The Heberden Coin Room has a vast display of early coins, while in the Department of Fine Art, the Michelangelo and Raphael drawings are to be admired. The museum also has the bulk of the archaeological material from the Upper Thames. Much of this is exhibited and there is a permanent display of aerial photographs of sites in the Thames Valley. *Open 10.00–16.00 Tue–Sat, 14.00–16.00 Sun. Free.*

Christ Church Picture Gallery
Christ Church Oxford (276150). Built by Powell and Moya, 1967, the gallery displays Christ Church's private collection. Exceptional Renaissance drawings by Michelangelo, Veronese and Tintoretto, as well as 14th–18thC paintings, mainly Italian.

Museum of Modern Art
30 Pembroke Street, Oxford (728608). Although there is a small standing exhibition of painters of the 1960s including Paolozzi, Hilton, Hitchens and Frost, this gallery specialises in unusual exhibitions. *Open 10.00–18.00 Tue–Sat, 14.00–18.00 Sun. Charge.*

Museum of Dolls
Grove House, Iffley Turn Oxford (777935). The museum is intended for collectors and no children under 16 are allowed. There is an exceptional collection of early dolls' houses, 1700–1885, displayed with their furniture and silver – a marvellous

illustration of social history. 10 mins by bus from the centre of Oxford. *Open Sun May–Sep 14.15–17.15 only. Charge.*

The Oxford Story
Broad Street, Oxford (728822). Eight centuries of Oxford University's history told through sights, sounds and smells. *Open daily 09.00–19.00 Apr–Oct, to 17.30 Nov–Mar. Charge.*

University Museum
Parks Road, Oxford (272950). The building by Deane and Woodward, 1855–60, in high Victorian Gothic was much admired by Ruskin. Built to house a collection of the Natural Sciences, the interior is a forest of columns and skeletons covered by a glass roof. One great rarity is the head and claw of a dodo. *Open 12.00–17.00 Mon–Sat. Free.*

Christ Church Meadows
The meadows lie behind Christ Church and Merton and have fine views and a path leading down to the river. The path is lined with college barges, not many remaining, and boat houses. In the afternoon one can watch the rowing Eights. Enter the Meadows from St Aldates.

Magdalen Water Walks
Access to the Water Walks is through Magdalen College. Close to the Walks lies the Deer Park. The 50 fallow deer can sometimes be seen over the railings. The Walks pass beside the streams from the Cherwell and sturdy shoes are advised.

University Botanic Garden
High Street. Oldest botanic garden in Britain founded by Henry Lord Danvers. In the 17thC the garden was intended for the culture of medical plants, but today it fosters an extensive collection of rare plants for research and teaching. The gateway is by Inigo Jones.

UNIVERSITY CELEBRATIONS

Commemoration Balls
The Balls are held in the college quadrangles at the end of the summer term. They are lavish, all-night affairs with marquees and champagne. Tickets are expensive and limited.

Eights Week
Late in May the college boat races take place on the Isis close to Folly Bridge. Saturday, the finals day, is a social occasion with tea-parties and champagne in the boat houses and barges. The races are followed by the Eights Week Dances.

May Day
At *06.00* on May Morning (*May 1st*) a Latin hymn is sung from Magdalen Tower in the medieval tradition. Then Morris dancers dance through the streets.

Feast of St Giles
On the *Monday after the first Sunday in September*, there is a fair in the middle of St Giles. Roundabouts and side-shows block the road.

THEATRE AND MUSIC

Oxford has three main venues:
Apollo
George Street. Built in 1933, it is visited by major ballet and opera companies, and also stages plays and concerts.

Oxford Playhouse
Beaumont Street. Built in 1938, it has student and professional productions.

Holywell Music Room
Holywell Street. The oldest music room in Europe.

The Tourist Information Centre has details of current productions, and there is a booking kiosk at the centre, telephone Oxford 727855.

WALKING TOURS

Conducted walking tours leave the TIC *daily for most of the year*. Tours last 2 hours.

BOATYARDS

Ⓑ **Bossoms Boatyard** Medley, Oxford (247780). Ⓦ Long-term mooring, winter storage, slipway, dry dock, chandlery, boat building (esp steam launches), boat and engine sales, repairs (esp wooden craft), toilets, showers. *Closed Sat afternoon & Sun.* Ⓜ

Ⓑ **Medley Boat Station** Port Meadow, Walton Well Road, Oxford (511660). Ⓡ Ⓦ Ⓓ Pump-out, gas (Calor and Super), hire craft, day hire boats, long-term mooring, winter storage, dry dock, crane, chandlery, books and maps, boat building, boat and engine sales and repairs, toilets. *Closed weekends in Dec.* Ⓜ

Ⓑ **Osney Marine Engineering** Osney Mill, Mill Street, Oxford (241348). Ⓦ Ⓓ Gas, long-term mooring, winter storage, slipway, boat and engine repairs, club room. Ⓜ

Ⓑ **Salter Bros** Folly Bridge, Oxford (243421). Ⓢ Ⓦ Ⓟ Ⓓ Pump-out, gas, hire craft, day hire boats, winter storage, dry dock, provisions, books and maps, boat building and sales, boat and engine repairs. *Closed winter weekends.*

BOAT TRIPS

Salter Bros Folly Bridge, Oxford (243421). Scheduled services *daily from mid-May to mid-Sep*, from Oxford, Abingdon, Reading, Henley, Marlow, Windsor and Staines, with some intermediate stops. These trips are heavily booked in the main holiday season – so telephone first, don't just turn up. Boats also available for party hire. Bar on board.

PUBS AND RESTAURANTS

There are many fine pubs and restaurants in Oxford. Listed first are those nearest the river, followed by a few further afield that you should enjoy visiting.

🍺 **Old Gatehouse** 2 Botley Road, Oxford. Hall's real ale in what was once a toll house. *Lunchtime* bar food and snacks. Between Osney Bridge and Oxford Station.

🍺 **Watermans Arms** 7 South Street, Osney. A very fine riverside local near Osney Lock, once used by the bargees. Morland's real ales and snacks. Some grass to sit on near the river. Ⓜ

🍺✕ **Head of the River** Folly Bridge, Oxford (721600). Pub and restaurant complex built

Iffley Lock

in a converted grain warehouse, with an upstairs bar, which contains the winning 1908 Olympic twin scull and opens onto a balcony. Hall's and Ind Coope real ale, *lunchtime* carvery, restaurant, and bar snacks. Punts for hire close by.

🍺✗ **Folly Bridge Inn** 38 Abingdon Road, Oxford (790106). South of Folly Bridge. A pleasant pub backing onto Oxford Football Club. Choice of real ales, extensive range of bar food and snacks. Cocktails upstairs.

🍺 **Isis** Iffley Lock. A large white isolated pub, once a farmhouse, in a pleasant garden with mature trees. With no direct road access, the beer was once delivered from the river. The bars contain memorabilia of university boat races. Morrell's real ale and *lunchtime* bar meals.

🍺 **Bear Inn** Alfred Street, Oxford. Near the junction of Cornmarket Street and High Street. The original inn on this site dated from the 13thC, but the present building is 17thC. Huge tie collection and fine old handpumps, dispensing Hall's and Ind Coope real ale. Bar meals and snacks.

🍺✗ **Chequers** 131a High Street, Oxford (243733). A 15thC inn, with the original panelling and fireplace in the 'Monks Bar' at the front. Hall's and Ind Coope real ale, food and snacks.

🍺✗ **Golden Cross** 5 Cornmarket, Oxford (242391). A famous 800-year-old inn where martyr bishops Latimer and Ridley spent their last night before being burnt at the stake in 1555. The building is an intriguing mixture of Tudor and Georgian. Usher's and Wadworth's real ales, snacks and garden. Three restaurants with a wide range of dishes (*L & D*).

🍺✗ **Mitre** 17 High Street, Oxford (244563). Parts of this building date from the 13thC, but the main part of this well-known hotel is 17thC. Past patrons include Peel, Gladstone and Elizabeth Taylor. The cellar bar has

medieval vaulting. Wethered real ale straight from the cask, steak house restaurant (*L & D*), garden, snacks, and afternoon teas *during the summer.*

🍺 **King's Arms** 40 Holywell Street, Oxford. A 17thC 'university' pub with a choice from seven real ale breweries. The back bar was 'men only' until as recently as 1975. Bar meals and snacks.

🍺 **Turf Tavern** 10 St Helen's Passage, off Holywell Street, Oxford. Well hidden away, this low-beamed 13thC tavern, mentioned by Hardy in *Jude the Obscure*, is worth searching for. It used to be a Victorian gambling place, hence the name. Large choice of real ales, including Hook Norton. Punch in winter, bar meals, snacks (fine Stilton cheese) and garden. Children welcome.

✗🍷 **Restaurant Elizabeth** 84 St Aldates, Oxford (242230). Some excellent dishes and delicious sweets, and a good, but not cheap, wine list. Just a short walk up from Folly Bridge. *L & D. Closed Mon. Reserve.*

✗🍷 **Liaison** 29 Castle Street, Oxford (242944). A gourmet restaurant, with generous helpings and a reasonably priced table d'hôte. Good cheese and sweets, sensible wine list. *Open D Mon–Sat. Reserve Fri & Sat.*

✗ **Munchy Munchy** 6 Park End Street, Oxford (245710). East of Osney Bridge. Exciting Indonesian cooking washed down with tea, or bring your own wine. *L & D. Closed Sun & Mon. Reserve D* if your party exceeds four.

✗🍷 **Opium Den** 79 George Street, Oxford (248680). Original Cantonese food, plenty of tea and sake. *L & D. Reserve D.*

✗ **Heroes** 8 Ship Street, Oxford (723459). Home-made soup, filling sandwiches and home baking. *Open daily, closed Sun & B. Hols.*

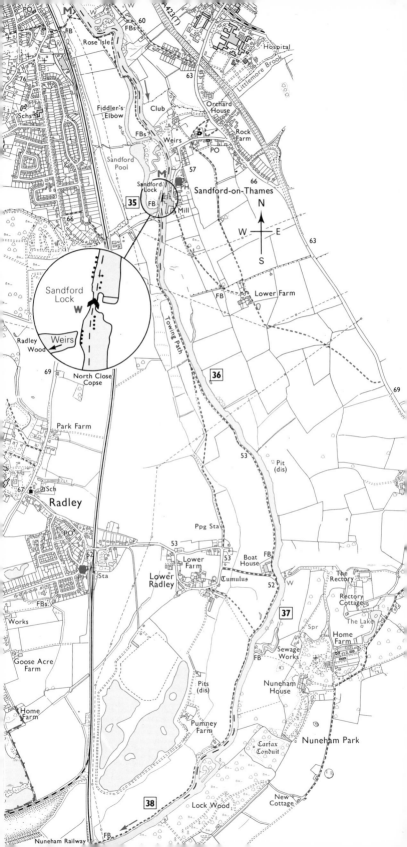

Sandford 65

Gradually the Oxford conurbation is left behind as the river passes through a mixture of woodland, suburbia and light industry, then curves through a maze of backwaters, used as boat club moorings, to Sandford Lock, the deepest on the river above Teddington and distinguished by the presence of large mill buildings. Below here the river passes through open country criss-crossed by electricity pylons. Hills close in from the east as Radley College Boat House is passed and the landscaped grounds of Nuneham House come into view, followed by the steeply wooded slope of Lock Wood. Flooded gravel pits lie to the west.

NAVIGATIONAL NOTES

Sandford Lock (Oxford 775889).
174ft 0in × 21ft 9in. Fall 8ft 10in. W
Max draught: 4ft 0in.

NOTES FOR WALKERS

The path stays to the west of the river, crossing the backwaters at Sandford by a series of footbridges. Those who wish to visit the pub may cross at the lock. The towpath continues on the west bank to Abingdon.
Sandford-on-Thames
Oxon. PO, stores. A small village with a useful shop and a pub.

Radley
Oxon. PO, shop. A straggling commuter suburb on the main London–Oxford railway, with much indiscriminate new development. The church is predominantly Perpendicular, with unusual wooden pillars in the aisle. Note the 15thC pulpit canopy, reputedly from the House of Commons, and the 17thC choir stalls.

Radley College Founded in 1847. The college is based on Radley Hall, 1721–7, with many later additions. It is famed as a rowing school.
Nuneham Park Nuneham Courtenay, Oxon. An 18thC Palladian mansion by Leadbetter, splendidly situated in landscaped grounds (see Nuneham Courtenay, below) by Mason and Brown. Rousseau stayed here in 1767, and planted foreign wild flowers in the gardens. The Temple is by 'Athenian' Stuart. Particularly noticeable from the river, standing on a wooded slope, is the Carfax Conduit, an ornamental fountain built in 1615 and once part of Oxford's water supply system. Originally situated in Carfax, it was moved here in 1786. In times of celebration wine and beer were run through it. The house and grounds are owned by the University of Oxford and are *opened for a few days in Aug & Sep.*
Nuneham Courtenay
Oxon. An 18thC model village of startling regularity along the A423, the result of a mass upheaval around 1760 when the 1st Earl of Harcourt required the original village site as part of his landscape garden. Oliver Goldsmith (1730–74) wrote bitterly of this practice in *The Deserted Village* (1770):
'The man of wealth and pride
Takes up a space that many poor supplied'.
However, whether the early villagers, moving from ancient clay-built cottages into far more modern houses would have seen it that way is open to question. The site of the original village is by the estate road.

MOORING

On the towpath side by Rose Isle. Isolated rural moorings elsewhere.

PUBS AND RESTAURANTS

🍺 **King's Arms** Sandford Lock. A fine lockside pub, with ceiling beams of old barge timbers. Courage real ales, bar meals and snacks.
🍺 **Bowyer Arms** near Radley Station. A large pub with a garden containing peacocks and swings for the children. Morland's real ales, *lunchtime* bar meals and snacks.
🍺✕ **Harcourt Arms** Nuneham Courtenay (209). Originally the 'New Inn'. Pub and restaurant (*L & D*) in a listed Georgian building. Bar meals, snacks, garden and Wethered real ales.

66 Abingdon

Below Nuneham Railway Bridge the river passes the entrance to the Swift Ditch – once the main navigation channel – where one of the earliest pound locks on the Thames was built in about 1620. Its remains were incorporated into one of the overspill weirs in 1967.

Above Abingdon Lock the handsome river frontage faces the open fields and sports grounds of Andersey Island, where there are pleasant moorings, in an area noted for mute swans.

The River Ock, once the entrance to the disused Wilts & Berks Canal, enters the Thames under a bridge by the Old Anchor Inn, a mellow and welcoming building. Now the river heads for open country and enters Culham Reach, passing the wooden bridge across the Swift Ditch, standing beside the old road bridge and its more modern replacement. A sharp turn east marks the entrance to Culham Cut, overlooked by the 17thC grey stone manor. There is a footpath to the pub and village from the footbridge, but, of course, no moorings in the cut. Sutton Courtenay lies to the south beyond the weir stream and Sutton Pools. After Culham Lock the river resumes a more direct course, passing under a steel girder railway bridge before starting its eccentric sweep to Dorchester.

NAVIGATIONAL NOTES

Abingdon Lock (Abingdon 23044).
120ft 0in × 18ft 9in. Fall 6ft 2in. R S W
Pump-out (coin-operated).
Culham Lock (Abingdon 22061).
130ft 10in × 17ft 6in. W Ladies toilet.
Max draught: 4ft 0in.
Go slowly at west entrance to Culham Cut – blind corner.
Go slowly through Culham Lock bridge – narrow.

NOTES FOR WALKERS

The path changes sides at Abingdon Bridge. Below here, the towpath continues to Clifton Hampden. The high spot of this section is the superb Abingdon waterfront, seen across the river from the east side.

Abingdon

Oxon. EC Thur. All shops and services, and extensive shopping precinct with launderette. A busy and attractive 18thC market town which grew up around the abbey, founded in AD675. Little of the original building now remains, except the Gateway and Long Gallery. Abbey Meadow, by the river, is a public park with a swimming pool, toilets, café and putting green. The best views of the town are from the river or the bridge, which is of medieval origin but was rebuilt in 1927. The river is dominated by the gaol, an impressive stone bastille built 1805–11 (now a leisure and sports centre) and St Helen's Church. Set among 17th and 18thC almshouses, the church has five aisles, making it broader than it is long. Perpendicular in style with a 17thC painted roof, it has a notable pulpit (1636), and the reredos is by Bodley (1897).

What is recognised as one of the finest town halls in England stands in the Market Place. Built 1678–82 by Christopher Kempster, one of Wren's city masons, it is high and monumental with an open ground floor, once used as a market. The upper floor, which was a court room, now houses a local museum. *Open 14.00–17.00 daily, closed B. Hols.* (Abingdon 23703). St Michael's Church, Park Road is a quiet and dignified design by Gilbert-Scott 1864–7.
Each year in Abingdon, *on the Saturday closest to 19 June*, the people of Ock Street

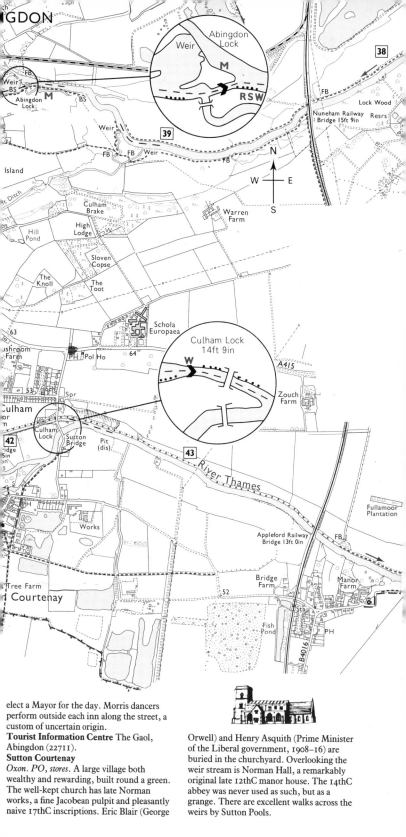

Abingdon
Lock

Weir

M

RSW

38

Lock Wood

39

Nuneham Railway
Bridge 15ft 9in

Resrs

FB

Weir
BS

Abingdon
Lock

M

BS

FB

Weir

N

W ← → E

S

Island

t Ditch

FB   FB   Weir

FB

Culham
Brake

Warren
Farm

Hill
Pond

High
Lodge

Sloven
Copse

The
Knoll

The
Toot

63

Schola
Europaea

Culham Lock
14ft 9in

A415

ushroom
Farm

PH Pol Ho

64

W

Zouch
Farm

53

Spr

Culham

or

42
idge
sin

Culham
Lock

Sutton
Bridge

Pit
(dis.)

43

River Thames

Fullamoor
Plantation

H

Works

Appleford Railway
Bridge 13ft 0in

FB

Tree Farm

Courtenay

52

Bridge
Farm

Manor
Farm

Fish
Pond

PH

B4016

elect a Mayor for the day. Morris dancers
perform outside each inn along the street, a
custom of uncertain origin.
Tourist Information Centre The Gaol,
Abingdon (22711).
Sutton Courtenay
Oxon. PO, stores. A large village both
wealthy and rewarding, built round a green.
The well-kept church has late Norman
works, a fine Jacobean pulpit and pleasantly
naïve 17thC inscriptions. Eric Blair (George

Orwell) and Henry Asquith (Prime Minister
of the Liberal government, 1908–16) are
buried in the churchyard. Overlooking the
weir stream is Norman Hall, a remarkably
original late 12thC manor house. The 14thC
abbey was never used as such, but as a
grange. There are excellent walks across the
weirs by Sutton Pools.

68 Abingdon

BOATYARDS

Ⓑ **Abingdon Boat Centre** The Bridge, Abingdon (21125). W P D Pump-out, gas, hire craft, day hire, long-term mooring, winter storage, 20ft slipway, chandlery, milk and eggs, books and maps, boat and engine repairs, dinghy spares, toilets.

Ⓑ **Red Line Cruisers** Wilsham Road, Abingdon (21562). R S W P D Pump-out, gas, hire craft, long-term mooring, chandlery, books and maps, boat building and sales, boat and engine repairs, outboard sales. *Closed Sun in winter.* M

MOORING

Abingdon – 24hr mooring above and below bridge on payment. Free moorings above Abingdon Lock and in Culham Reach (rather isolated).

PUBS AND RESTAURANTS

There are many pubs and eating places to be found in Abingdon. Fish & chips and hamburgers in The Precinct and in Ock Street (continuation of the High Street).

🍺 **Nags Head** By the bridge, Abingdon. Riverside terrace, *lunchtime* food. Usher's real ale.

🍺✗ **Crown & Thistle** Bridge Street, Abingdon. Large Berni Steak House pub and restaurant.

🍺 **Broad Face** Bridge Street, Abingdon. Has a lovely sign. Morland's real ale, bar food, garden.

🍺 **Old Anchor** St Helens Wharf, Abingdon. A very handsome pub by the confluence of the Rivers Ock and Thames, but alas, no mooring outside. Morland's real ale. Launching site for small craft opposite.

✗🍷 **Upper Reaches** Thames Street, Abingdon (22311). Smart restaurant/hotel in a converted mill on the Abbey Stream. Children's menu. M

✗🍷 **Abingdon Bridge Restaurant** Abingdon (25066). Grills and light snacks. *Open Mon-Sat.* Garden. M

🍺✗ **Ox Inn** 15 Oxford Road, Abingdon (20962). About 1 mile north of Abingdon Bridge, but worth the walk for excellent home-made food including three course meals (*L & D, not Sun*) and Morland's real ale. Garden.

Peking House Bridge Street (opp Crown & Thistle), Abingdon (21570). Chinese takeaway.

🍺 **New Inn** High Street, Sutton Courtenay. A snug village local near the church. Morland's real ale.

🍺 **Fish Inn** Appleford Road, Sutton Courtenay. A large pub serving Morland's real ale. Bar meals, garden.

🍺 **Lion Inn** Culham. A short walk from Culham Cut. Morrell's real ale, bar snacks and garden.

🍺 **Waggon & Horses** Culham, on the main A415. Morrell's real ale, food, and separate restaurant. Children's play area.

Abingdon waterfront

The main navigation passes through Clifton Cut and the lock, below which is the entrance to the weir stream, navigable as far as the Plough at Long Wittenham. Beyond a caravan park to the east is Clifton Hampden Bridge, with the church and thatched cottages clustered on rising ground beyond – a superb setting.

Burcot stands above the river to the north, which now begins to head south past Dorchester. The cooling towers of Didcot Power Station dominate the area and appear in front, behind, to the left and to the right as the Thames makes an extravagant winding journey, passing the massive 114 acres of earthworks known as the Dyke Hills before making a sharp turn to the east below Day's Lock at the base of Wittenham Clumps. This is a particularly attractive stretch of river. The River Thame joins opposite Little Wittenham Wood – very small craft can pass under the footbridge to moor below Dorchester Bridge. Above the confluence, the Thames is sometimes romantically known as 'Isis'.

NAVIGATIONAL NOTES

Clifton Lock (Clifton Hampden 7821). 129ft 10in × 19ft 0in. Fall 3ft 5in. W
Day's Lock (Clifton Hampden 7768). 154ft 0in × 21ft 2in. Fall 5ft 2in. R S
Max draught: 4ft 0in.
Take care at the blind corner below Little Wittenham Bridge.

NOTES FOR WALKERS

There is no towpath connection between Clifton Hampden and Little Wittenham – detour via Long Wittenham or Burcot and Dorchester. The excellent views over the valley from the top of Castle Hill are just reward for the walk up from Day's Lock. Dorchester can also be reached from the lock – the path crosses the Dyke Hills – or by walking alongside the River Thame.

Long Wittenham
Oxon. EC Wed & Sat. PO, stores. Access by boat along the weir stream from Clifton Lock. A fine straggling village along the original course of the river. The 13thC church contains choir stalls from Exeter College, Oxford, and a late Norman font.
Pendon Museum At the far end of Long Wittenham village (Clifton Hampden 7365). A museum of miniature landscapes and transport. *Open afternoons at weekends & B. Hols. Modest charge.*
Clifton Hampden
Oxon. EC Tue. PO, store. A cluster of thatched cottages away from the brick bridge (a Norman folly built in 1864). The small church on a mound was delicately remade by Gilbert Scott. Very picturesque.
Little Wittenham
Oxon. The church is well situated among woods. There are good walks through Little Wittenham Woods to the summit of Castle Hill, topped with an Iron Age hill fort.

Clifton Hampden

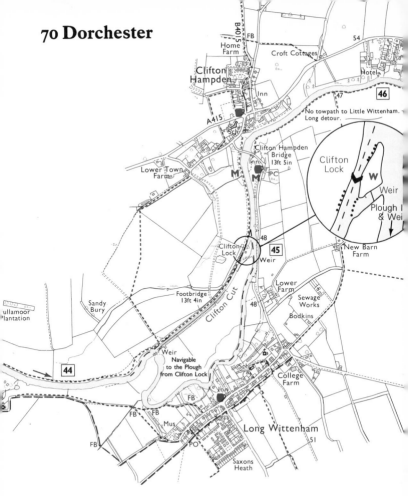

Dorchester

Oxon. PO, stores. This large main road
village of antique shops and hotels was once
a small Roman town sited on the River
Thames. It is accessible from the Thames by
footpath over Dyke Hills from Day's Lock.
Today only the Abbey Church of SS Peter

and Paul, founded in the 7thC, shows that it
was once the cathedral city of Wessex, then
Mercia. Approached through a Butterfield
lych gate the mostly Decorated abbey gives
little clue to the splendid size and proportion
of its interior. The most important feature is
the Jesse window, with stonework imitating
trees. The figures seem to grow organically
from the body of Jesse. Note also the tomb
of Sir John Holcombe: the realism and
fluidity of the effigy has inspired many
modern sculptors. The Old Monastery Guest
House, used in the 17thC as a grammar
school, now houses a museum, although
most Roman finds are in the Ashmolean,
Oxford. Small craft may navigate up the
River Thame to Dorchester Bridge.

MOORING

There are moorings on the towpath side
above Clifton Hampden Bridge and on the
opposite side (fee); there is a large expanse of
isolated moorings below Burcot, also on the
towpath side. The moorings below Day's
Lock and Little Wittenham Bridge are
convenient for the walk to Dorchester or
Castle Hill.

PUBS AND RESTAURANTS

Plough Long Wittenham. The weir
stream is navigable from Clifton Lock to this
attractive pub. Usher's real ale, food,
restaurant, garden. Handy for the Pendon
Museum. M

Barley Mow East of Clifton Hampden
Bridge (Clifton Hampden 7847). A
deservedly famous and superbly old-
fashioned thatched pub built in 1350. It was
described by Jerome K. Jerome as having
'quite a story book appearance'. Usher's real
ale, restaurant, garden, children's room.

Plough North of Clifton Hampden
Bridge. Another fine thatched pub,
deserving a visit. The 1948 Olympic torch is
displayed here. Ask who carried it. Usher's
real ale, food, garden. *PO and store* opposite.

Chequers Burcot. Worth the walk from
Clifton Hampden to visit this handsome

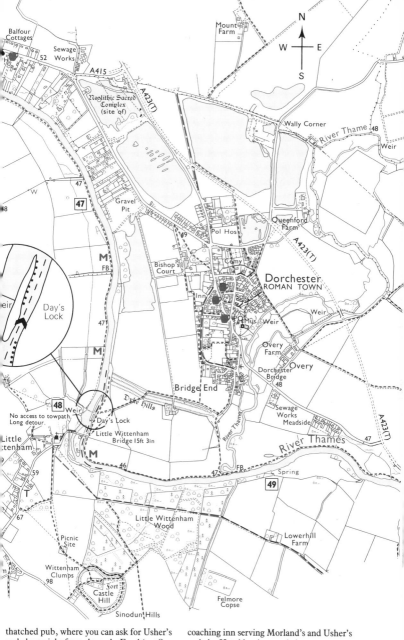

Map labels:

Balfour Cottages
Mount Farm
52 Sewage Works
A415
A423(T)
Neolithic Sacred Complex (site of)
Wally Corner
River Thame 48
Weir
47
Gravel Pit
47
Queenford Farm
W
Pol Hos
A423(T)
47
FB
Bishop's Court
Comy
Dorchester ROMAN TOWN
M
Day's Lock
eir
Inn
47
M
Mus Weir
Overy Farm
Overy
Day's Lock
48 Weir
Dyke Hills
Bridge End
Dorchester Bridge
48
No access to towpath. Long detour.
Day's Lock
Little Wittenham Bridge 15ft 3in
Sewage Works
Meadside
47
Little ttenham
M
46
River Thame
River Thames
59
47
FB
Spring
49
T
67
Little Wittenham Wood
Lowerhill Farm
Picnic Site
Wittenham Clumps 98
Fort Castle Hill
Felmore Copse
Sinodun Hills

---

thatched pub, where you can ask for Usher's real ale straight from the cask. Food (*not Sun L*), garden.

Several pubs in Dorchester, including:
🍴 **George Hotel** High Street, Dorchester. (Oxford 340404). Built in 1449 as the brewhouse of the nearby abbey, this comfortable galleried inn was once a coaching stop. Brakspear's and Morland's real ale, food, restaurant serving English à la carte (*L & D*).
🍺 **Fleur de Lys** High Street, Dorchester. Friendly and comfortable pub opposite the abbey. Good food. Usher's real ale, garden.
🍴 **White Hart Hotel** High Street, Dorchester. (Oxford 340074). 17thC

coaching inn serving Morland's and Usher's real ale. Hotel has its own bakery. Restaurant and snack bar.
🍴 **Dorchester Abbey Tea Room** High Street, Dorchester next to the abbey. Delicious biscuits, cakes and scones, all home baked. *Open from 15.00 'until the food runs out' every day except Mon during the summer.* All in aid of charity, so call in.

Wallingford

Open flat farmland flanks the river on its approach to Shillingford, marked by the smart hotel and stone bridge, which replaced an earlier wooden structure built in 1784. A caravan park and many moored boats announce the presence of Benson and the lock. Aircraft can usually be seen taking off and landing from the RAF Transport Command base near here.

Below the lock the river makes a bee-line for Wallingford, passing Howbery Park Institute of Hydrology, once the home of Jethro Tull (1674–1741), a pioneer of mechanised farming, to flow through only a few of Wallingford Bridge's 17 arches. After passing some attractive Georgian buildings and the busy Wallingford Marina the river continues south.

Court Farm

Warborough

48

49

The Green

PO

N
W   E
S

Sch

MP
Leave towpath.
Detour via road.

A423(T)

Shillingford
Farm

50

No crossing

Shillingford

48

48

47

FB

48

Spr

Shillingford
Bridge
7ft 8in

49

MS

Elm
Bridge

47

A423(T)

Littleworth

Sch

Hotel
Shillingford
Hill

Reservoir

MS

51

W

47

Caravan
Park

Benson

River Thames

Sotwellhill
Barn

61

Moat

W

No crossing.
Detour via road.

B

R

Severalls
Cottages

Rush
Court

A329

52

Benson Lock

Weir

Severalls
Farm

Severalls
Farm

Copse
Cottages

Mill

Sotwell Hill

Benson
Lock

Preston
Crowmarsh

44

A4130

51

Nursery

Weir

Moat

R

Slade End
Farm

56

PH

Res
Sta

Fir Tree
Cottage

Hospital

Cemy

Towpath gone.
Detour via road.

44

53

Sch

School

51

WALLINGFOR

Slade End
Barn

Hospl

Sch

Sch

Howbery Pa
Inst of Hydrol

FB

T

Sch

Park

Castle
(rems of)

M

B

Wallingford
Bridge
16ft 5in

Works

Allot
Gdns

A329

Sch

Coll

DY

FB

Newn
Mur

Bradford's Brook

WALLINGFORD CP

Hospl

B

Bradford's Brook

Bradford
Bridge

No crossing

Old Hithercroft

Winterbrook

54

48

NAVIGATIONAL NOTES

Benson Lock (Wallingford 35255).
133ft 1in × 17ft 11in. Fall 6ft 2in. W
Wallingford Bridge – use the central arch.
Max draught: 4ft 0in.

NOTES FOR WALKERS

Leave the towpath about a mile above
Shillingford Bridge for a detour through the
village to rejoin the path at Shillingford
Bridge and proceed as far as Benson, then
detour through Crowmarsh or cut straight
across to Wallingford. The towpath above
Wallingford has eroded away and there is no
crossing above Benson Lock. Below
Wallingford, walkers should rejoin the
towpath by Wallingford Marina. Not really a
lot of river to see on this section, but the
Shillingford to Wallingford road is
pleasantly tree-lined.

Shillingford
Oxon. Tel. The extremely handsome triple-
arched bridge and the hotel stand away from
the village, a discreet residential area to the
north.

Warborough
Oxon. A traditional English village built
round a green. Buildings of all periods.

Benson
Oxon. EC Wed. PO, shops, launderette. A
friendly airforce town with a pleasant river
frontage, but the old coaching inns are
surrounded by married quarters and
supermarkets, and it is hard to believe this
was once a seat of the kings of Mercia. The
13thC church has Saxon foundations.

Wallingford
Oxon. EC Wed. All services. One of the
oldest Royal Boroughs, the town received its
charter in 1155. Well preserved banks and
ditches of Saxon defences still remain. From
the river the town is dominated by the
unusual openwork spire of St Peter's
Church, built by Sir Robert Taylor in 1777.

Behind the boatyard by the bridge,
footpaths lead to the remains of the Norman
castle built on a mound by Robert D'Oilly in
1071, and destroyed by Fairfax in 1646. The
Town Hall, built in 1670, has a typical open
ground floor. Wallingford Museum is

housed in Flint House, in the traffic-choked
High Street – it is *open afternoons Tue–Fri &
all day Sat. Closed Dec–Feb.* The 17-arched
bridge is of medieval origins (possibly as
early as 1141). It was rebuilt in 1809 when

the balustrade was added. The town is now
the HQ of the Habitat empire.
Tourist Information Centre Stone Hall,
High Street, Wallingford (35351, ext 249).

BOATYARDS

Ⓑ**Benson Cruiser Station** Benson.
(Wallingford 38304). R S W P D Pump-
out, gas, hire craft, long-term mooring,
winter storage, slipway, provisions, books
and maps, toilets, showers, restaurant.
Closed winter weekends. M

Ⓑ**Wallingford Bridge Boat House**
Wallingford (38005). Gas, chandlery, hire
craft, day hire boats, boat and engine sales
and repairs, long-term mooring. Nautical
Wheel Restaurant above.

Ⓑ**Maidboats** The Marina, Wallingford
(36163). R S W D Pump-out, gas, hire
craft, slipway, winter storage, books and
maps, boat building, boat and engine
repairs, toilets. *Closed winter Suns.* M

MOORING

On the towpath side above Shillingford
Bridge (fee), above Benson and above
Wallingford. Also below Wallingford Bridge
(fee).

PUBS AND RESTAURANTS

🍺✕ **Shillingford Bridge Hotel** (Warborough
8567). A very smart riverside hotel with
excellent moorings (modest fee). Patrons
may use the squash courts, and the outdoor
heated swimming and paddling pools (*closed
after 19.00*). Courage real ale, *lunchtime* bar
food, terrace, garden, function rooms,
fishing. M

🍺 **Kingfisher** North of Shillingford on the
A423. Usher's real ale, buffet.

🍺 **Six Bells** By the cricket green,
Warborough. Over a mile's walk north of
Shillingford Bridge to this thatched pub
serving Brakspear's real ale.

✕🍷 **Rivers** Benson. (Wallingford 38331).
Night club and restaurant. Bar snacks, live
music, cabaret and disco nights.

🍺✕ **Castle** Benson. (Wallingford 35349).
Georgian coaching inn in the centre of the
village. Restaurant (*closed Sun & Mon D*)
and bar meals. Brakspear's, Hook Norton
and Wadworth's real ale.

🍺✕ **Farmer's Man** Brook Street, Benson.
Various real ales, garden. Music on *Thur.*

🍺✕ **Sun** Watlington Road, Benson. Usher's
real ale, bar meals.

✕🍷 **Nautical Wheel** By Wallingford Bridge,
Wallingford (36507). Restaurant in a
converted boat builder's loft. *Closed Sun D
& Mon.*

🍺 **Town Arms** by Wallingford Bridge.
Congenial local with knowledgeable licensee.
Usher's real ales. Lunches (*not Sun*).

✕🍷 **Stoneys** High Street, Wallingford
(36249). Varied menu based around steak,
veal, chicken and scampi. Home-made ice
cream. *Closed Sun L & Mon.*

74 Wallingford

Wine Bar High Street, Wallingford (33426). Soup, bread, pizzas, burgers. *Closed Sun D & Tue.*

George High Street, Wallingford (36665). Smart Tudor hotel serving Usher's real ale to young patrons. The 'Teardrop Room' recalls a Civil War story of the landlord's daughter's grief at the loss of her love, a Royalist sergeant.

Trapps Table Castle Street, Wallingford (39606). Good home-made food in basement bar under an antiques arcade. *Open lunchtime only. Closed Sun & B. Hols.*

Mamtaj Tandoori High Street, Wallingford (35394). The aroma here says it all. *L & D.*

Lamb Coffee Shop High Street, Crowmarsh. (Wallingford 33581). Excellent self-service food above a shopping arcade. *Open daily until 17.00.*

Bell Crowmarsh. Morland's real ale and food (*not Sun L*) in large comfortable pub. Garden.

Queen's Head Crowmarsh. Low beams and open fires. Usher's real ale. Food, garden.

Above Wallingford

Rowing at Pangbourne

76 Moulsford

Winterbrook

54 48
Carmel College Farm

School

Winterbrook — White Cross

Mon

The Lodge

Monge

Bucklands

Carmel College

Mongewell Park

River Thames

MS

Mead Furlong

The Ridgeway Path

46

Mill Court

Blackall's Farm

Cholsey Stables

55

N

Bow Barn

Bow Bridge

49

Neolithic Axe found

5

B4009

W E

S

Cholsey

FB

North Stoke

P

FB

49

MS

Fair Mile Hospital

Chy

Hospl

Tumulus

Hospl

Papist Way

Tumulus (site of)

Hospl

FB

No crossing here. Detour via road.

43

Tumuli

Reading Road A319

56

49

.77

59

Hotel

46

The Gables

Littlestoke Manor Farm

Ash Cottages

MS

58

Offlands Farm

Moulsford Rly Bridge 21ft 8in

The Oak

The Ridgeway Path

Sch

Sch

Freedom Cottages

B

57

Lower Farm

52

Moulsford

Sch

P

South Stoke

South Stoke

Hotel

No crossing here. Detour via road.

PH

P

Glebe Cottages

Sowberry Court

South Bank

MP

River Thames

The Ri

A broad stretch of river, pleasant but unremarkable. The buildings of Carmel College stand in wooded grounds in Mongewell Park, which fronts the Thames for a mile. North Stoke lies back from the river to the east, while the Fair Mile Hospital for the Disabled is passed to the west. The islands above Brunel's lovely skewed brick arched railway bridge are supposedly haunted. Gradually the hills close in as the valley narrows towards Goring. The Beetle & Wedge Hotel marks the site of the old ferry which once linked Moulsford and South Stoke, facing each other across the river, but now totally separate.

NAVIGATIONAL NOTES

Max draught: 4ft 0in.
Pass to the east of the islands above Moulsford Railway Bridge.

NOTES FOR WALKERS

There is no river crossing below North Stoke, so a detour via Papist Way and the Reading Road to rejoin the river by the Beetle & Wedge is necessary. On the east bank, the Ridgeway Path shares the tow-path. This easy 85-mile walk stretches from Marlborough to Ivinghoe, and crosses the Thames at Goring.

North Stoke
Oxon. An attractive red-brick village among trees. The church is pleasingly original and unrestored, with notable wall paintings and a canopied pulpit.
Moulsford
Oxon. A roadside village with large houses by the river. The small, secluded church was rebuilt by Gilbert Scott in 1846: his fee was reputedly £64.
South Stoke
Oxon. EC Tue. Shop. A pretty residential

Beetle & Wedge

village among trees. St Andrew's Church is 13thC. Access can be gained from the river opposite the Beetle & Wedge.

BOATYARDS

Ⓑ **Sheridan Line** Moulsford. (Cholsey 652085). Ⓢ Ⓦ Ⓓ Pump-out, gas, day hire boats, winter storage, slipway, boat lift, provisions, books and maps, boat and engine repairs, boat sales. This used to be Hobb's Boatyard.

MOORING

There are moorings on the towpath side above and below North Stoke.

PUBS AND RESTAURANTS

🍺 **Waterloo Hotel** Reading Road, Cholsey. Up Papist Way and left at the crossroads. Interesting choice of real ales. Food and garden.
🍺 **Morning Star** Papist Way, Cholsey. Morland's real ale in an unspoilt village pub. Food, garden.
🍺✕ **Beetle & Wedge Hotel** Moulsford. (Cholsey 651381). A *beetle* is a mallet used to hit the *wedge* which split trees into planks for floating downriver to London; a practice last recorded in 1777 but recalled in the name of this justly famous pub, where H. G. Wells stayed while writing *Mr Polly* – it features in the book as the Potwell Inn. The building is a former manor house, standing in a superb riverside situation, with a lovely garden and a jetty. A choice of real ales, good bar meals and a restaurant. Children welcome, fishing day tickets, accommodation. Ⓜ
🍺 **Pike & Perch** South Stoke. Stuffed fish on the walls and painted fish on the plates. Fresh sandwiches to eat with Brakspear's real ale (the Special is served straight from the cask). Nice garden with swings for the children. Fishing day tickets.

78 Goring

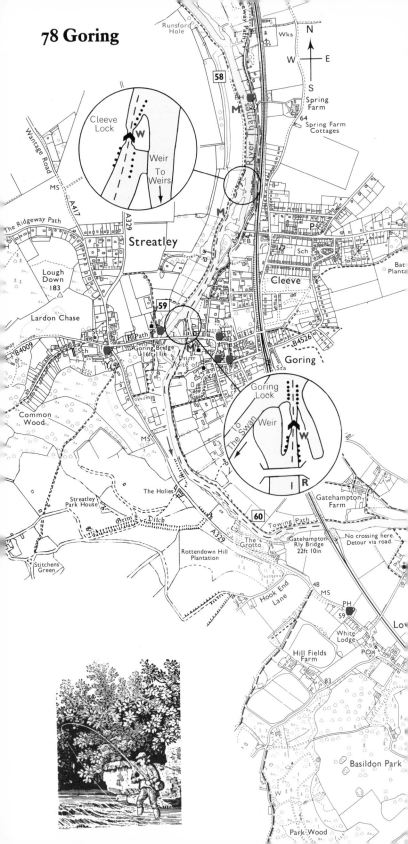

Runsford Hole

58

N
W   E
S

Wks

River Thames

Spring Farm

64   Spring Farm Cottages

Cleeve Lock

Weir
To Weirs

MS

The Ridgeway Path

Wanage Road

A417

A329

Streatley

Lough Down 183

Lardon Chase

Cleeve

Sch

P

Bat Planta

B4009

Sch

59

Path

Goring Bridge 16ft 11in

Priory Site of

B4526

Goring

Sta

Goring Lock

To The Swan

Weir

W

R

Common Wood

MS

The Holies

Streatley Park House

Grim's Ditch

Stitchens Green

Rottendown Hill Plantation

The Grotto

60

A329

Towing Path

Gatehampton Farm

Gatehampton Rly Bridge 22ft 10in

No crossing here. Detour via road.

Hook End Lane

48   MS

PH

59

White Lodge

PO

Hill Fields Farm

83

Lo

Basildon Park

Park Wood

Goring 79

Approaching Cleeve Lock the valley narrows, with Lardon Chase rising steeply to the west behind Streatley. Little of Goring can be seen from the river – boat houses, the mill and a glimpse of the church as the river enters one of its most attractive parts. In the meadows to the east of Basildon there is a picturesque group of buildings around a church, while on the east bank beech woods rise steeply from the river's edge. Basildon House stands in wooded grounds beyond the Child Beale Wildlife Park. The brick Gatehampton Railway Bridge was built by Brunel.

NAVIGATIONAL NOTES

Cleeve Lock (Goring 872608).
133ft 7in × 18ft 2in. Fall 2ft 3in. W Ladies toilet.
Goring Lock (Goring 872687).
179ft 5in × 21ft 0in. Fall 5ft 10in. R W
Max draught: 4ft 0in.

NOTES FOR WALKERS

As there is no longer a ferry below Gatehampton Bridge, walkers should follow the A329 and rejoin the towpath by the church at Lower Basildon. The river passes through an area of outstanding beauty, and the walk here is particularly rewarding. A detour up Lardon Chase will give fine views over the valley. The Ridgeway Path crosses at Goring.

Goring

Oxon. EC Wed. PO, general store by bridge and shops and supermarket in High Street; launderette. One of the most important prehistoric fords across the river, linking the Icknield Way and the Ridgeway. The village is set in a splendid deep wooded valley by one of the most spectacular reaches on the river. A holiday paradise of indeterminate age, it retains many pretty brick and flint

cottages. The church, of handsome proportions, is well situated by the river. Its

bell, dating from 1290, is one of the oldest in England. Goring Mill, now a showroom full of crafts and pottery, stands below the bridge, an approximate replica (built 1923) of the earlier timber structure. Between Goring and Henley, the Thames passes through the Chilterns Area of Outstanding Natural Beauty, covering 309 square miles.

Streatley

Berks. Shops. A continuation of Goring on the west bank, its 18thC charm is diminished by the traffic roaring through. Of note are the old malthouses converted into a village hall by W. Ravenscroft in 1898, and Wells Stores at the crossroads, opposite the Bull, renowned for its choice of 150 properly kept cheeses from Great Britain and Europe. Lardon Chase (NT) rises to the north.

Lower Basildon

Berks. An attractive group of buildings surrounds the church in a superb riverside

situation. The 13thC church is over restored, but note the Flaxman monument to Sir Francis Sykes, and the portrait group of two boys drowned in 1886. Jethro Tull (1674–1741), pioneer of agricultural mechanisation, lies buried in the churchyard.

Basildon Park (Pangbourne 3040). Built by John Carr of York for Sir Francis Sykes in 1776, this is the most splendid Georgian

mansion in Berkshire. Rescued from virtual dereliction in 1952 by Lord and Lady Iliffe, the building has been carefully restored. Octagon Room, Shell Room, Anglo-Indian objects in Nabob's Room, and many fine pictures and pieces of furniture. Superbly landscaped grounds. Teas. *Open afternoons Apr–Oct. Closed Mon, Tues & Good Fri. Charge.*

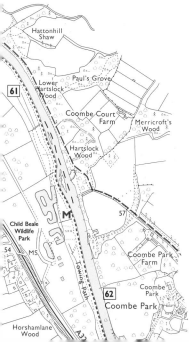

Child Beale Wildlife Park (Pangbourne 5172). Lying in the meadowland south east of Basildon, and fronting the river, it specialises in birds, including peacocks. Also collection of statuary. *Open 10.00–18.00 daily Mar–Sep. Phone for winter hours. Charge.* M

MOORING

There are casual isolated moorings on the towpath side above and below Cleeve Lock, and good moorings below Goring Bridge. Visitors to the Child Beale Wildlife Park may moor there.

PUBS AND RESTAURANTS

Old Leatherne Bottel Riverside, above Cleeve Lock. An original riverside pub serving Brakspear's real ales straight from the cask. There was a well here in Roman times which produced medicinal water. Food, bar billiards, garden. M

Swan Streatley. (Goring 873737). A beautifully situated and very smart hotel/ restaurant dating from around 1700. Plush interiors, fine riverside gardens and ornate 'College Barge' for private functions. The food is excellent, with fine cheeses from Wells Stores. Morland's real ale and bar meals. M for patrons.

Bull Streatley. (Goring 872507). 16thC restaurant/pub at busy crossroads. Usher's real ale, bar snacks, garden.

Miller of Mansfield High Street, Goring (872829). Up the road from the bridge, this is a very comfortable brick and flint pub. Parts of the building are 13thC. Courage real ales, separate restaurant (*L & D*) and excellent bar meals. Children welcome. Accommodation.

John Barleycorn Manor Road, Goring (872509). Brakspear's real ale, bar food and restaurant.

Catherine Wheel Station Road, Goring. Brakspear's real ale in an attractive 16thC building. Food, garden.

Crown Lower Basildon. Courage real ales and food in a comfy road house. Garden.

Goring Lock

The wide reach above Whitchurch Lock is often busy with sailing and rowing boats from Pangbourne College. The lock and its attractive lock house are well sited on an island, with the fine white Victorian toll bridge completing the scene. Open farmland flanks the river below here. Hardwick House can be glimpsed through trees on the north bank while to the south, the vineyards of Westbury Farm can be seen as Mapledurham is approached. The weir probably dates from the 13thC and the pound lock from 1777 – it was the first lock on the Thames to be mechanised, in 1956. The mill, church and house are in a superbly romantic setting. Now the residential outskirts of Reading begin, and the main railway line joins the river on an embankment – the Inter City trains rush by, a vivid contrast with the pace of the river.

NAVIGATIONAL NOTES

Whitchurch Lock (Pangbourne 2448). 135ft 3in × 18ft 0in. Fall 3ft 4in. [S][R]

Mapledurham Lock (Reading 417736). 202ft 5in × 21ft 1in. Fall 6ft 9in. [R]
Max draught: 4ft 0in.

NOTES FOR WALKERS

The towpath is not continuous below Mapledurham – detour from the lock along roads to rejoin near the Roebuck Hotel. Those who wish to visit Mapledurham (and this route is recommended) should take the minor road east out of Whitchurch and rejoin the towpath at Caversham Bridge. There are excellent walks on the downs north of Whitchurch.

Pangbourne

Berks. EC Thur. All services. A large, well-equipped commuter town, still preserving traces of Edwardian elegance, built at the confluence of the Thames and the Pang, a famous trout stream. The Nautical College, an imposing William and Mary style mansion, is by Sir John Belcher, built 1897–8. Pangbourne Meadow is now a National

Pangbourne

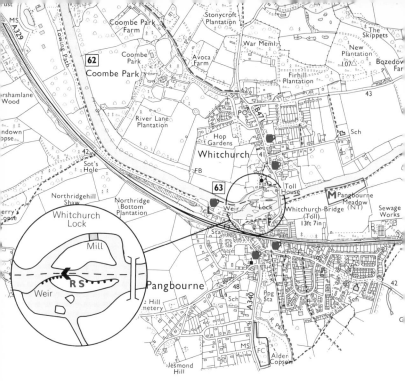

Trust property of 7 acres. The Scottish author of *The Wind in the Willows*, Kenneth Grahame (1859–1932), who was also Secretary to the Bank of England, lived in Church Cottage, Pangbourne, and told this story to his four-year-old son Alastair in 1904.

Whitchurch

Oxon. EC Sat. PO, store. Quiet and attractive with a good group of mill buildings, overlooked by the mainly Victorian church. A 4p toll for cars is collected at the Victorian iron bridge.

Westbury Farm The Thames Valley Vineyards may be visited by largish groups who book in advance (Pangbourne 3123) for a tour, lecture and tastings. No casual visits. Also trout ponds.

Hardwick House *Oxon*. The gardens almost reach down to the river, with the house nestling among trees. Mainly Tudor, it was restored after the Civil War, and has two 'real' tennis courts. Queen Elizabeth I slept in one of the bedrooms. There is a stud farm in the grounds. Private.

Mapledurham

Oxon. A cluster of period houses and cottages stand in the water-meadows close to the restored and working water mill, one of

the oldest corn and grist mills on the Thames. The scene is typical of an early 19thC landscape painting and should be visited (but see below).

Mapledurham House (Reading 723350). A huge Elizabethan mansion built in 1588 by the Blount family. The park runs down to the Thames. Beside the house, which was frequented by Alexander Pope, and was also the setting of the closing chapters of Galsworthy's *The Forsyte Saga*, stands the church of St Margaret. There are many fine

memorials, in particular the 17thC tomb to Sir Richard Blount and his wife. *House and mill open weekends & B. Hol afternoons Easter Sun–Sep. Charge*. There is no direct access from the river at Mapledurham – you cannot cross the river or moor on the north bank. The moorings above Hardwick House are about 2 miles walk away, and Caversham Bridge is 3 miles walk away. A trip boat, the *Caversham Lady*, carries visitors from Reading (details: Reading 481088). Plenty of taxis at Reading Railway Station.

Purley

Berks. EC Thur & Sat. PO, stores. A straggling village approached from Mapledurham Lock and marking the western extremity of the Reading conurbation. St Mary's Church is well sited among old trees by the river, close to the private marina. The building is mostly by Street, 1870, apart from the 17thC brick tower. Purley Park, beyond the railway and overlooking the river, is a fine white house of Portland stone by James Wyatt, 1800 – notice the free use of bays and columns. Purley Hall, a private 17thC house, stands in

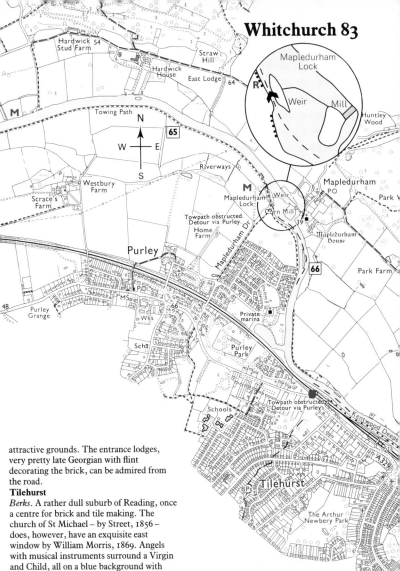

attractive grounds. The entrance lodges,
very pretty late Georgian with flint
decorating the brick, can be admired from
the road.

Tilehurst

Berks. A rather dull suburb of Reading, once
a centre for brick and tile making. The
church of St Michael – by Street, 1856 –
does, however, have an exquisite east
window by William Morris, 1869. Angels
with musical instruments surround a Virgin
and Child, all on a blue background with
yellow flowers. Other fine windows by
Wailes.

MOORING

There are moorings for patrons of the Swan
Hotel at Pangbourne, and further moorings
below the lock at Pangbourne Meadow.
Half-a-mile downstream there are isolated
moorings on the non-towpath side (*small
fee*).

PUBS AND RESTAURANTS

Swan Hotel Above Whitchurch Lock.
(Pangbourne 3199). A well known,
rambling, and beautifully situated riverside
venue, with a restaurant. It was here that
Jerome K. Jerome, his two colleagues and a
'shamed looking dog' abandoned their *Three
Men in a Boat* journey (on the way back) and
took the train to London. (*L, & D until
21.15*). M

Copper Inn Reading Road, Pangbourne
(2244). A good choice of local real ales in an

old coaching inn with restaurant. Food,
garden.

Ye Olde George South of the bridge
and under the railway (Pangbourne 2237).
Usher's real ale straight from the cask. Food,
garden. Restaurant *L & D Mon–Sun*.

Greyhound North of Whitchurch Bridge.
Hall's and Ind Coope real ales, *lunchtime*
food (*Mon–Fri*), garden and collection of
brasses.

Ferryboat North of Whitchurch Bridge.
Courage real ales in a cottagy country pub.

Roebuck Tilehurst. (Reading 27517).
Access from the towpath across the railway.
Courage beers, bar meals (*Mon–Fri*).

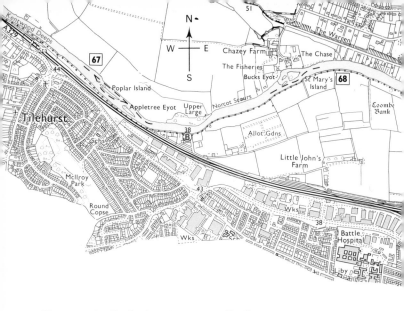

The entrance into Reading from the west is not unpleasant. The railway parts company below Appletree Eyot as the river curves round to Norcot Scours and on past St Mary's Island, becoming quite wide and often busy with rowing and sculling boats. Well-kept chalets and tidy gardens line the north bank, followed by landscaped public gardens above Caversham Bridge, which was built in 1926. The original bridge on this site was erected in the 13thC, and at one time had a chapel on it. Fry's Island is situated between the bridges; on it are two boatyards. By Reading Bridge are the tall office block and moored maintenance craft of Thames Water, the authority in charge of the non-tidal Thames. Just below the bridge is Caversham Lock, on the edge of King's Meadow. To the east, under the railway bridge, is the entrance to the Kennet & Avon Canal (River Kennet).

NAVIGATIONAL NOTES

Caversham Lock (Reading 575764). 131ft 4in × 17ft 11in. Fall 4ft 9in.
Blake's Lock (on River Kennet) (Reading 572251). 122ft 8in × 18ft 11in. Fall 3ft 6in.
Max draught: 4ft 0in.

The Kennet & Avon Canal is navigable on a TW licence through Blake's Lock (the only TW lock *not* on the Thames) to about 70yds below High Bridge.

NOTES FOR WALKERS

From the Roebuck Hotel the towpath can be followed throughout this section, crossing Caversham Bridge to the north bank, under Reading Bridge and back across the weir to Caversham Lock, where it skirts King's Meadow and crosses Kennet Mouth on the railway bridge. As urban waterways go, this is quite attractive, although at the western and eastern extremities any peace is shattered by the railway. Walkers heading west who wish to visit Mapledurham should cross to the north at Caversham Bridge and walk out past 'The Warren' to Mapledurham.

Reading

Berks. All services. A very busy town lacking a cohesive centre – it is an amalgam of university and industry – but historically and architecturally has interest. The university buildings are disappointing, but there are numerous Victorian buildings and the museum houses one of the most fascinating archaeological collections in the country.
Abbey Ruins Fragmentary remains of the 12thC abbey, built by Henry I, lie on the edge of Forbury Park. The Abbey was one of the largest in England and at one time comparable with Bury St Edmunds. The 13thC Gatehouse still stands. It was once the Abbey School where Jane Austen studied in 1785–7, although the structure was greatly altered by Gilbert Scott in 1869. The Church of St Lawrence near the Market Place was originally attached to the outer gate.
Gaol Forbury Road. Designed by Scott & Moffat, 1842–4 in Scottish Baronial style. Oscar Wilde (1854–1900) wrote *De Profundis* in 1897 while imprisoned here for 'homosexual practices'. (The *Ballad of Reading Goal* was actually written in Paris in 1898.)
Royal Berkshire Hospital London Road. This magnificent façade of Bath stone with

its grand classical portico would be worthy of a Royal residence. Henry Briant, 1837–9.
Reading Museum and Art Gallery Blagrave Street, Reading (575911). The museum has an exceptional natural history and local archaeological collection. The Silchester collection is displayed so that the visitor can obtain a vivid picture of everyday life in the Romano-British town of Calleva Atrebatum (Silchester). The Thames Conservancy Collection includes prehistoric metal work, palaeolithic hand axes, Iron Age and Roman pottery and Saxon grave goods. There is also a changing art exhibition. *Closed Sun.*

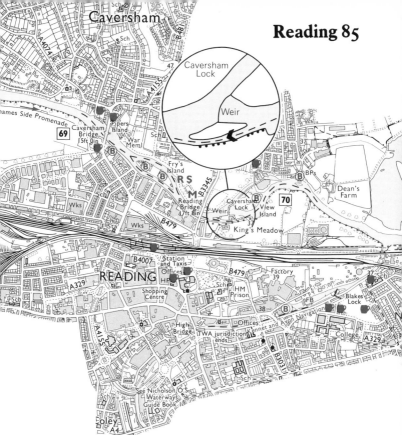

Museum of English Rural Life
Whiteknights, University of Reading
(318660). All aspects of rural life in England,
before the invention of the tractor. *Closed
Sun, Mon & B. Hols. Small charge.*
Ure Museum Whiteknights, University of
Reading (318420). Greek antiquities. *Closed
weekends & University holidays. Free.*
Tourist Information Centre Civic Offices,
off Castle Street, Reading (390375).

Caversham
*Berks. EC Wed. PO, stores, launderette, fish
& chips.* A residential continuation of
Reading, at its best by the river, where parks
and gardens stretch alongside. The library in
Church Street is worth a look – an amusing
Edwardian building, 1907, with a central
green copper clock supported by an angel.

Kennet & Avon Canal
One of the most splendid lengths of artificial
waterway in Britain, cutting across southern
England from Reading to Bath and opened
in full in 1810. It is 57 miles long with a
summit level 474ft above sea level, and was
built to a broad gauge with many handsome
architectural features. Currently navigable
from the Thames as far as Aldermaston, and
expected to open throughout by 1990.
Navigation above High Bridge, Reading,
requires a British Waterways Board licence
(enquiries Watford 26422; or purchase from
Reading Marine Co on the Kennet & Avon
Canal). Below here, the river is administered
by Thames Water. The Kennet & Avon
Canal Trust are to be found at The Wharf,
Couch Lane, Devizes (Devizes
71279). This waterway is described in detail
in the *Nicholson/OS Guide to the Waterways
1. South.*
Blake's Lock Museum Kenavon Drive,
Forbury Industrial Park, Reading (575911).
Waterways Exhibits and The Industrial
History of Reading. *Open 10.00–17.00
Mon–Fri, from 14.00 Sat & Sun. Free.*

BOATYARDS
Ⓑ**Reading Marine Company** Kenavon
Drive, Forbury Industrial Park, Reading
(573917). Pump-out, gas, hire craft, books
and maps, boat and engine repairs and sales.
Licences for Kennet & Avon.
Ⓑ**Reading Marine Services** Scours Lane,
Oxford Road, Reading (27155). Ⓦ Ⓟ Ⓓ Gas,
mooring, winter storage, slipway, crane,
chandlery, books and maps, boat building,
boat and engine sales and repairs, toilets,
showers.
Ⓑ**Salter Bros** Caversham Bridge, Reading
(572388). Ⓦ Ⓓ Pump-out, hire craft, engine
repairs.
Ⓑ**Bridge Boats** Fry's Island, Reading
(590346). Ⓡ Ⓢ Ⓦ Ⓓ Pump-out, gas, hire
craft, winter storage, mooring, slipway,
chandlery, books and maps, boat building,
boat and engine repairs and sales, toilets,
showers. *Closed winter weekends.*

Ⓑ**Caversham Boat Services** Fry's Island, Reading (574323). Ⓡ Ⓢ Ⓦ Ⓓ Pump-out, gas, hire craft, day hire boats, moorings, slipway, boat and engine repairs (24 hr breakdown service).

Ⓑ**Better Boating** Mill Green, Caversham, Reading (479536). Ⓦ Ⓓ Pump-out, gas, engine repairs, provisions, crane.

Ⓑ**Caversham Marina** View Island, Reading (472792). Long-term mooring, winter storage, books and maps, boat building, boat and engine sales and repairs, crane, DIY facilities.

MOORING

There are very good (if a little expensive) moorings by Christchurch Playing Fields, above Reading Bridge (swings, playground, paddling pool, ½ mile to shopping streets).

BOAT TRIPS

Thames River Cruises Mapledurham House, Mapledurham. (Reading 481088). *Caversham Lady* available for private charter. Also regular *summer* trips to Mapledurham, when the house is open.
Salter Bros 204 Caversham Bridge Road, Reading (572388). Scheduled *summer* service up and down river.

PUBS AND RESTAURANTS

Caversham Hotel (Reading 391818). A smart riverside hotel with a real ale tavern. Lovely gardens and lawns edged with chestnut trees.
🍺 **Griffin** Church Road, Caversham. North of Caversham Bridge. Courage real ale, food, garden.
🍺 **Crown** Bridge Street, Caversham. North of Caversham Bridge. Courage real ale, food.
🍺 **Golden Key** Queens Road, Caversham.

North of View Island. Large pub with Brakspear's real ale, not far from Reading Bridge moorings. Food, garden.

There are many pubs in Reading, especially around the shopping centre, and many of them serve real ale.
🍺 **Rising Sun** Forbury Road, Reading. South of Reading Bridge and under the railway. Brakspear's real ales and food. Handy for the museum.
🍺 **Riverside Bar** Not riverside, but on platform 4 of Reading Station (buy platform ticket). Arkell's real ale.
🍺 **Blagrave Arms** Blagrave Street, Reading. Courage real ale and food. Handy for the museum.

The following four pubs are close to the Kennet:
🍺 **Jolly Anglers** Kennet Side, Reading. Decorated with fish. Courage real ale, garden.
🍺 **Plasterers Arms** Rupert Street, Reading. Morland's real ale.
🍺 **Dove** Orts Road, Reading. Brakspear's real ale, garden.
🍺 **Fishermans Cottage** Kennet Side, Reading. A good choice of real ales, right by the river. Garden.

Fish & chip shops, take-away Chinese, and burger bars can be found in plenty around the main shopping area of Reading. Try:
✕♟ **Mama Mia** 11 St Mary's Butts, Reading (581257). Typically informal Italian restaurant. *Open L & D. Closed Sun & B. Hols.*
✕♟ **Sirdar Tandoori** Queen Victoria Street (up from the station), Reading (573122). For those who must have curry. *Open L & D.*

Sonning Lock

Moorings near Caversham

88 Sonning

Downstream of Reading the scenery is uninspiring. This all changes, however, when Sonning Lock and Mill (now a theatre) appear among the willows. The 18thC bridge and the large white hotel by it mark the western extremity of Sonning village, which lies back from the river. About a mile below Sonning, St Patrick's Stream (unnavigable, with the River Loddon flowing in), makes its detour around Borough Marsh. The main course of the river passes numerous islands and skirts Warren Hill, a chalk ridge, before reaching Shiplake Lock. Beyond the railway bridge, Wargrave village stands on a hill overlooking the Thames.

NAVIGATIONAL NOTES

Sonning Lock (Reading 693992).
156ft 1in × 17ft 11in. Fall 5ft 4in. R Ladies toilet.
Shiplake Lock (Wargrave 3350).
133ft 4in × 18ft 3in. Fall 5ft 1in. R S W Ladies toilet.
Max draught: 4ft 6in.
Sonning Bridge – use the large central arch and go slowly. St Patrick's Stream is unnavigable by powered craft. Hallsmead Ait and The Lynch should be passed to the east.

NOTES FOR WALKERS

Cross from the east side to the west at Sonning Bridge to follow the towpath to Shiplake. Those who wish to visit Wargrave should take the road out of Sonning via Charvil and Twyford. Once the factories and pylons of Reading are left behind, the walk is extremely pleasant. A detour into Sonning, to see the church and the pubs, is really a must.

Sonning

Berks. EC Tue. PO, stores. As you walk into Sonning from the 11-arched 18thC bridge, you could be forgiven for thinking you had stumbled upon a film set, for surely this is every American director's idea of what a Thames-side village should look like. The

red brick houses are pretty, but the preservation is too desperate and the village has, as a result, become sterile. The largely 19thC church by Woodyer and Bodley has remarkable monuments, and some 15thC brasses. The most interesting house in the town is Lutyens' Deanery Gardens, built for Edward Hudson in 1901. To the west of Sonning is Holme Park – the Reading Blue Coat School – its wooded grounds drop steeply to the river. The railway passes in a spectacular cutting to the south, built by Brunel.

Wargrave

Berks. EC Wed. PO, stores. A well-situated town on rising ground among trees, overlooking the Thames. The church was burnt down in 1914 by the Suffragettes – some say it was because the vicar refused to take the word 'obey' out of the marriage service. As rebuilt, the church has a pleasing architectural unity – note particularly the woodwork. In the churchyard the Hannen Mausoleum was designed by Lutyens. The striking Woodclyffe Hall, in the High Street, was built in 1901. Henry Kingsley (1830–76), the novelist, often stayed here. East of the town is Wargrave Manor, an early 19thC building. The River Loddon joins St Patrick's Stream to the south west – here, in black swampy soil, the Loddon Lily (*Leucojum aestivum*), or summer snowflake, is native. Loddon Pondweed (*Potamogeton nodosus*), its leaves beautifully veined, may also be found.

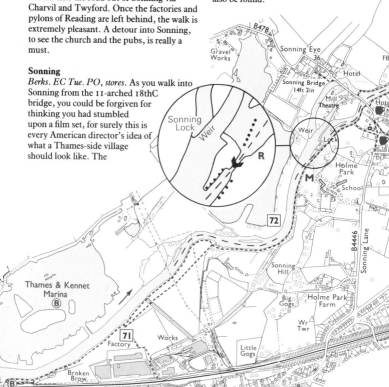

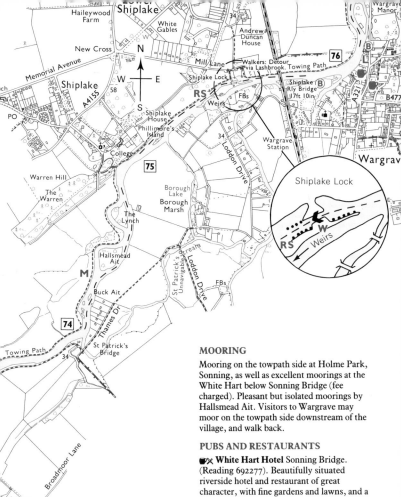

MOORING

Mooring on the towpath side at Holme Park, Sonning, as well as excellent moorings at the White Hart below Sonning Bridge (fee charged). Pleasant but isolated moorings by Hallsmead Ait. Visitors to Wargrave may moor on the towpath side downstream of the village, and walk back.

PUBS AND RESTAURANTS

White Hart Hotel Sonning Bridge. (Reading 692277). Beautifully situated riverside hotel and restaurant of great character, with fine gardens and lawns, and a terrace lined with lime trees. One dining room is 700 years old; the main bar is a beamy room with a stone fireplace and talking parrot. Wethered and Young's real ales and good bar food complete the treat. M

Bull By Sonning church. A lovely old half-timbered pub, used by locals and visitors alike. Comfy cushioned settles, massive beams and inglenook fireplaces inside. Wooden tables in a flower decorated courtyard facing the church outside. Wethered's real ale, *lunchtime* bar meals, separate dining room for the *evening*.

St George & Dragon Henley Road, Wargrave (2815). Courage real ale. Visited by Jerome K. Jerome. There are views over the Thames from the bar, which has the old hotel sign displayed inside. Garden. M

Bull High Street, Wargrave. A comfortable brick built pub serving Brakspear's real ales and excellent buffet meals. Patio, children's room.

White Hart High Street, Wargrave (2590). Old inn serving Wethered's real ale and bar lunches.

Greyhound High Street, Wargrave. Courage real ale, *lunchtime* snacks and *evening* meals in a half-timbered corner pub. Garden.

BOATYARDS

Thames & Kennet Marina Caversham Lakes, Henley Road, Reading (482911). The following facilities are available to privately owned craft only – *not* to hire craft. R W D Pump-out, gas, winter storage, chandlery, boat sales, toilets, showers, groceries, gifts.

John Bushnell Wargrave (2161). R S W D Moorings, winter storage, crane, boat building, boat and engine repairs, boat sales, toilets. *Closed Sat afternoon & Sun.*

Swancraft Wargrave (2577). R W Pump-out, gas, electric day boat hire, engine repairs.

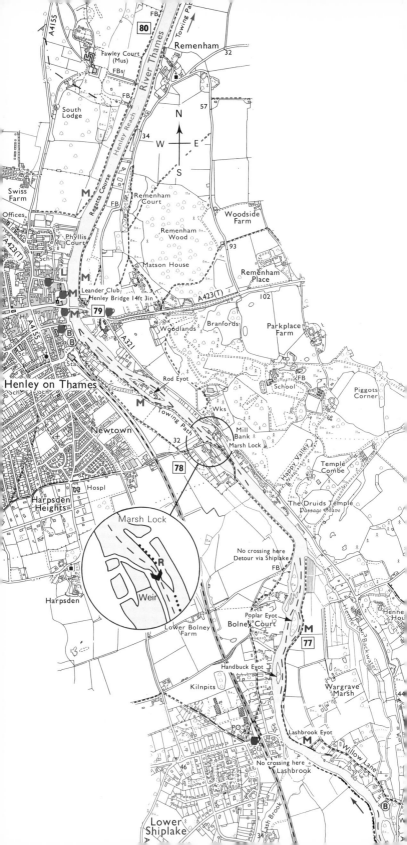

The river passes Shiplake and weaves
through a group of islands to the west of
Wargrave Marsh, a low lying area enclosed
by the Hennerton Backwater (navigable only
by small boats). To the north east, Temple
Combe Woods rise steeply. This part of the
river is noted for Brent Geese and some
handsome wooden boat houses. To the north
of Marsh Lock is Park Place; in the grounds
is part of Wren's original spire for St Bride's
Church, Fleet Street. The house was once
occupied by General Conway whose
daughter, Mrs Damer, sculpted the masks of
Thames and Isis on Henley Bridge. Henley
lies to the west of the river, with an attractive
waterfront, many moored boats and resident
swans, facing the rise of Remenham Wood to
the east.
Between May and July piles and booms mark
the famous regatta course, 1 mile 450yds
long, and overlooked by the buildings of
Fawley Court.

NAVIGATIONAL NOTES

Marsh Lock (Henley 572992).
135ft 2in × 21ft 1in. Fall 4ft 4in. R

Max draught: 4ft 6in.

NOTES FOR WALKERS

Those on the Oxfordshire (west) side should
leave the river at Shiplake Lock to make a
detour alongside the Lash Brook through
Shiplake, to rejoin the towpath below Bolney
Court. Cross Henley Bridge to the Berkshire
(east) side where the towpath is continuous
to Hambleden, or take the road out of
Remenham through Aston to visit Hurley.
The walk by Marsh Lock, with the steep hill
on the east bank, is particularly attractive.
The river front at Henley, with its fine old
inns, handsome bridge and many moored
craft looks good from across the river.

Shiplake

Oxon. PO, stores. A village of desirable
commuter houses climbing up into the hills
that border the river. The splendidly
situated Church of SS Peter and Paul
contains some medieval Belgian glass of
great beauty. Tennyson married Emily
Sellwood here in 1850. In the village note
The White House, built by George Walton
in 1908. Further north, near the station,
George Orwell lived as a boy at 'Roselawn',
Station Road.

Henley on Thames

*Oxon. All shops and services, launderette,
swimming baths, theatre.* A fine market town
and one of the most popular resorts on the
river, described by Dickens as 'the Mecca of
the rowing man'. The main street, running
down to the Thames from the Victorian
Town Hall, has a feeling of timelessness and
Edwardian elegance almost out of place
today. From the river the most obvious
features are the 18thC stone bridge (note the
masks of Thames and Isis) and the
Decorated and Perpendicular church, a large
and gloomy building. The Red Lion Hotel,
near the church, has received some notable
visitors, including King Charles I (1632 and
1642), the Duke of Marlborough (early
18thC), the poet William Shenstone (1750)
and Johnson and Boswell (1776). The
Kenton Theatre in New Street is the fourth
oldest in the country, being built in 1805.
The first Oxford and Cambridge boat race
was rowed between Hambleden and Henley
on 10 June 1829 – it is now rowed between
Putney and Mortlake. The first Henley
Regatta was held in 1839, becoming Royal in
1851 with Prince Albert as patron. This is
now held *annually in the first week of July*; the
town becomes very busy indeed, and
everyone seems to be on a picnic. The
epitome of an English summer (when the
sun shines).
Tourist Information Centre 4 West Street,
Henley (571626).

Remenham

Berks. An untidy village scattered along the
south bank, backed by the woods of
Remenham Hill.
Fawley Court *Bucks.* (Henley 574917). A
fine riverside situation. The court was
designed by Wren and built in 1684, later to
be decorated by Grinling Gibbons and
classicised by James Wyatt. The grounds
were laid out by Capability Brown in 1770. It
now houses the Divine Mercy College and a
museum consisting of a library, various
documents of the Polish monarchy and
Polish militaria, and paintings and sculpture
illustrating ancient history and the Middle
Ages. *Open Wed & Sun afternoons (also Thur
in Jul & Aug). Closed Christmas, Easter,
Whitsun, Jun. Charge.* Teas in *Jul & Aug.*
You may moor your boat and walk up from
the river.

92 Henley on Thames

BOATYARDS

ⓑ Val Wyatt Marine Wargrave (3211/3836).
W P D Gas, long-term mooring, winter
storage, slipways, hoist, chandlery,
provisions, books and maps, boat building,
boat and engine sales and repairs, toilets.
Specialists in the repair and renovation of old
wooden craft.

ⓑ Hobbs & Sons Station Road, Henley
(572035). W P D Hire craft, day hire boats,
long-term mooring, winter storage, slipway,
hoist, chandlery, books and maps, boat
building, boat and engine repairs and sales,
toilets. *Closed Sat afternoon & Sun in winter.*

ⓑ Alf Parrott 14 Thameside, Henley
(572380). Gas, hire craft, day hire boats,
long-term mooring, chandlery, books and
maps, boat sales, fishing tackle and bait.
Closed Sun in winter.

MOORING

Downstream of Wargrave there are
moorings a short walk from the village.
Henley has good moorings on the waterfront
above and below the bridge, and in Fawley
Meadows – at most a fee is payable. This is,
of course, a busy and popular area.

PUBS AND RESTAURANTS

⚑✕ Baskerville Arms Station Road,
Shiplake. (Wargrave 3332). Wethered's real
ale. Restaurant serving scampi, steaks and
seafood. *Closed Mon, & Sun D.* Garden.

Henley has a wonderful selection of pubs,
the majority serving real ale brewed by
Brakspear in their 18thC brewhouse in New
Street, by the river. In warm calm weather
the aroma of malt and hops wafts over the
water tempting all devotees of good beer to
search hastily for a mooring. None of the
pubs in Henley is far from the river – those
below are simply the closest, and the rest are
easily found.

⚑ Anchor Friday Street, Henley.
Brakspear's real ales, children's room, food,
garden.

⚑✕ Angel on the Bridge Henley Bridge,
Henley (574977). Beautiful and historic
14thC inn adjoining the bridge. Bistro
restaurant serves prawns, lasagne, fish, curry
and home-made fudge cake. Brakspear's real
ales, riverside garden, bar food. M

⚑✕ Little White Hart Hotel Riverside,
Henley (574145). Half-timbered riverside
inn with jetty moorings across the street.
Restaurant specialises in fine fish, steaks,
and international dishes. *Open for D & Sun
L.* Brakspear's real ales. M

⚑ Rose & Crown New Street, Henley.
Close to Brakspear's brewery and the
Kenton Theatre. No prizes for guessing
which beer.

There are many places to eat in Henley,
including:

✕⚑ Jasmine 25 Duke Street, Henley
(575854). A very dark Chinese restaurant
doing all the usual things very well. *Closed
afternoons Mon–Thur.* Take-away service.

✕ Henley Tea Shop 26 Hart Street, Henley
(576536). Lovely cakes and teas, with an
antique shop combined. *Closed evenings, Sun
morning & Wed.*

✕ Copper Kettle 18 Thameside, Henley
(575262). Home-made lunches and teas in
quaint cottagey surroundings. Patio. *Open
10.00–18.00 Mon–Sun.*

✕⚑ Barnaby's 2 New Street, Henley
(572421). Charcoal grilled steaks and
burgers, among a range of international
dishes. *Closed Sun L.*

⚑✕ Little Angel East of Henley Bridge,
Henley (572160/574165). Brakspear's real
ale in the bar and seafood specialities in the
expensive cordon bleu restaurant. Garden.

Henley

Hambleden Mill

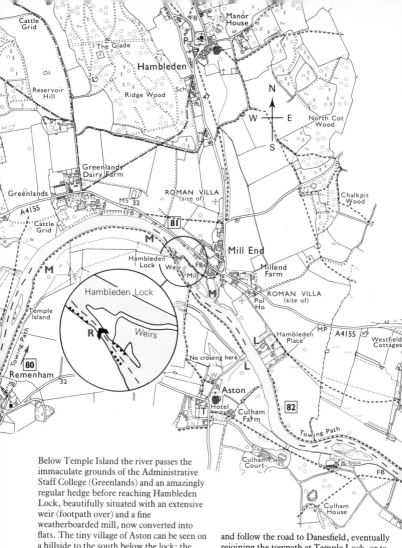

Below Temple Island the river passes the immaculate grounds of the Administrative Staff College (Greenlands) and an amazingly regular hedge before reaching Hambleden Lock, beautifully situated with an extensive weir (footpath over) and a fine weatherboarded mill, now converted into flats. The tiny village of Aston can be seen on a hillside to the south below the lock; the Thames then divides around thickly wooded islands and meanders past Medmenham and St Mary's Abbey. Beyond the next group of islands a large caravan site heralds the approach of Hurley, where the weir streams rush among more islands by the lock. To the north, on top of the chalk cliffs, is a Ministry of Defence police training base, behind Danesfield, a home built at the turn of the century by a Manchester millionaire.

NAVIGATIONAL NOTES

Hambleden Lock (Henley 571269). 135ft 2in × 17ft 9in. Fall 4ft 9in. R
Hurley Lock (Littlewick Green 4334). 130ft 8in × 19ft 11in. Fall 3ft 5in. R S W
Ladies toilet.
Max draught: 4ft 6in.
Keep to the west side of Temple Island to avoid rowers.

NOTES FOR WALKERS

There is no river crossing at Aston, so walkers are advised either to take the exciting footbridge across Hambleden Weir and follow the road to Danesfield, eventually rejoining the towpath at Temple Lock, or to stay on the south bank and walk through Aston and rejoin the river near Culham, where the path is continuous to Hurley. The two locks on this section provide the highlights – Hambleden with its weir and mill; Hurley with a maze of islands.

Temple Island The temple was built by James Wyatt in 1771 as a vista for Fawley Court and has a set of hand-painted wall decorations by him. It is thought to be the earliest example in England of the 'Etruscan' style. Owned by the Mackenzie family for over 130 years, the island was sold in 1988. Visited by King Edward VII and Queen Alexandra, it is a pretty ornament, with views down the river to Henley.
Greenlands A sumptuous 19thC Italianate mansion in impeccable grounds, once owned by the first Viscount Hambleden, better known as W. H. Smith. Now an Administrative Staff College.
Hambleden
Bucks. PO, store. Set back from the river and surrounded by heavily wooded hills, this is

one of the most attractive villages in Bucks, and worth the walk up from the river. All mellow flint and brick with a marvellous original unity. The 14thC church and the houses round the green make it a perfect village setting with the 17thC Manor House in the background. The church tower was built in 1721.

Hambleden Mill On the river the white weatherboarded mill, converted into flats, and mill house form a fine group by the lock and weir.

Medmenham

Bucks. A village straggling up from the now defunct ferry into the woods behind. Medmenham Abbey (St Mary's Abbey) is a charming agglomeration of building styles: 1595, 18thC Gothic and mostly 1898. It was the house of the orgiastic Hell Fire Club, under the auspices of Sir Francis Dashwood. It was decorated in a suitably pornographic and sacrilegious style, but understandably

BOATYARDS

Ⓑ **Peter Freebody's Boatyard** Mill Lane, Hurley. (Littlewick Green 4382). Primarily a boat builder, also boat and engine repairs, long-term mooring, winter storage, slipway, some chandlery.

MOORING

Between Temple Island and Hambleden Lock, on the towpath side above Hambleden Lock, above Medmenham on the towpath side, and above Hurley Lock by the caravan site (fee charged).

PUBS AND RESTAURANTS

🍺 **Flowerpot** Aston. An out of the way pub serving Brakspear's real ales. Snacks, garden.

🍺 **Stag & Huntsman** Hambleden. Wethered's real ales in a fine Victorian pub. Bar food, garden.

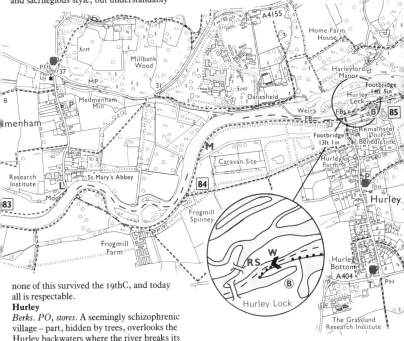

none of this survived the 19thC, and today all is respectable.

Hurley

Berks. PO, stores. A seemingly schizophrenic village – part, hidden by trees, overlooks the Hurley backwaters where the river breaks its course around a number of islands – the rest is given over to indiscriminate surburban development, and to a huge riverside caravan sprawl in the east. In the old part of the village the long, dark and narrow nave of the church is all that remains of Hurley Priory (St Mary's), founded before 1087 for the Benedictine Order. Opposite the church are a 14thC tithe barn (now a dwelling) and a dovecote.

Harleyford Manor On the north bank opposite Hurley. The manor was built in 1755 by Sir Robert Taylor for Sir William Clayton. The splendid grounds, reputedly by Capability Brown, sweep down to the river, and now enclose a caravan park and marina. The manor is used as a club house – how times change!

🍺 **Dog & Badger** Medmenham. Dates from 1390. Historical associations with the Hell Fire Club (see Medmenham description). Wethered's real ales. Bar food (*not Sun*).

🍺 **Black Boy** Hurley. South of Frogmill Farm. Brakspear's real ales, food, garden.

🍺✕ **East Arms** Henley Road, Hurley. (Littlewick Green 3227). Brakspear's, Wethered and Wadworth's real ales, cocktail bar, dinner dances, bar food and restaurant meals – steak, fish and duck.

🍺✕ **Olde Bell Hotel** Hurley. (Littlewick Green 4244). Built in 1135 as the guest house for the monastery: there is still a connecting underground passage. Fine Norman porch. Expensive French, Italian and English food in the restaurant. *Open L & D.*

96 Marlow

Hurley Lock is swiftly followed by Temple Lock. Below here you may well see canoeists and dinghy sailors from the National Sports Centre at Bisham Abbey. At the end of this long wide reach is the elegant white Marlow suspension bridge, with the lock just beyond and day hire boats close by. The Marlow–Bisham by-pass crosses; below here is the Scouts Boating Centre, so the river is again usually full of small craft. Now the river turns to skirt the steep hills of Quarry Wood. Below the beech woods, at the water's edge, are many smart chalets, a strange, grey, castellated building housing holiday flats, and Woottens Boatyard with splendid decaying boat houses nearby, dated 1885. To the north the Marlow branch line hides flooded gravel workings and a sewage works.

NAVIGATIONAL NOTES

Temple Lock (Littlewick Green 4333). 134ft 7in × 17ft 11in. Fall 4ft 1in. Ladies toilet.
Marlow Lock (Marlow 2867). 151ft 3in × 19ft 11in. Fall 7ft 1in. $\boxed{R}$ $\boxed{W}$ Ladies toilet.
Max draught: 4ft 6in.

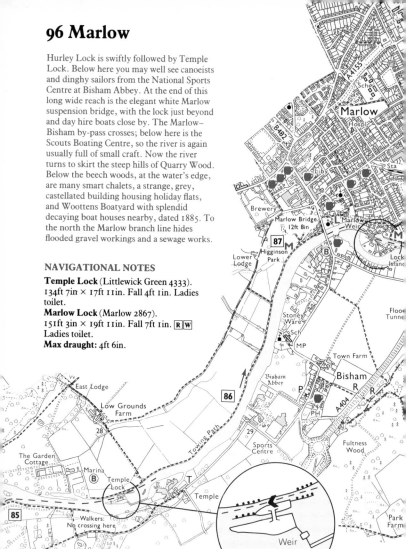

Temple Lock
Weir

NOTES FOR WALKERS

Whether you arrive at Marlow on the north or south bank, a detour into this fine town should be made. Below Marlow Bridge walkers should keep to the south side where there are excellent walks through Quarry Wood and past Winter Hill, to rejoin the riverside before Cock Marsh, where the towpath continues to Cookham. The walks around Cookham Dean are very pretty.

Bisham
Berks. EC Thur. Shop. A largely Georgian village set back from the river, behind the abbey. The church is set apart from both, being superbly sited almost at the river's edge. Although rebuilt, it still has a Norman tower. Inside are the fine 17thC Hoby monuments, especially that to Margaret, one of the most unusual of the period.
Bisham Abbey The abbey, built mainly in the 14th and 16thC, was a private house from 1540. It is now a sports centre of the Central Council of Physical Recreation, a hive of activity where young players and coaches come together under the aegis of their respective governing bodies of sport. They train in the sport of their choice, ranging from archery to weight lifting. River activities feature strongly in the training programme. The facilities include five 'tennis quick' courts and a large sports field. The centre is not open to casual visitors.

Marlow
Bucks. EC Wed. All shops and services, launderette. A very handsome and lively Georgian town, with a wide tree-lined High Street connecting the bridge with the Market Place. A marvellous view of the weir can be had from the white suspension bridge, built by Tierny Clarke in 1831–6 and

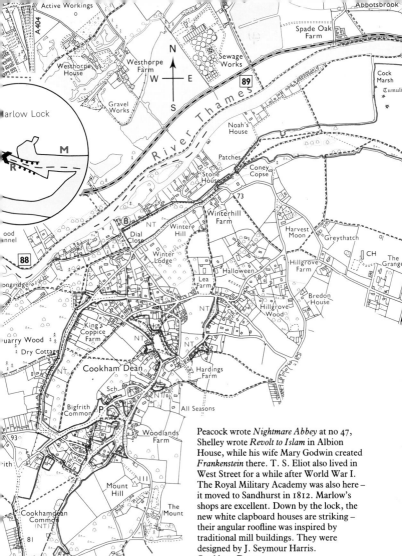

Active Workings

Spade Oak
Farm

Westhorpe
House

Westhorpe
Farm

Sewage
Works

Gravel
Works

89

RIVER THAMES

Cock
Marsh

Tumuli

Marlow Lock

M

R

Noah's
House

Patches

Coney
Copse

Stone
House

73

Winterhill
Farm

Harvest
Moon

Greythatch

CH

The
Grange

88

Dial
Close

Winter
Hill

NT

Winter
Lodge

Hillgrove
Farm

Halloween

Lea
Farm

Hillgrove
Wood

Bredon
House

Quarry Wood

Dry Cottage

King's
Coppice
Farm

NT

NT

NT

NT

Cookham Dean

Hardings
Farm

Sch.

All Seasons

Bigfrith
Common

P

Woodlands
Farm

93

Mount
Hill

The
Mount

Cookhamdean
Common
(NT)

81

Mount
Farm

Butlers
Gate

BS

reconstructed, retaining its original width, in
1966. The main street is dominated by the
Crown Hotel, built 1807 and formerly the
Town Hall. Holy Trinity Church is by

Gilbert Scott, 1852, and the Roman Catholic
church is a surprisingly uninspired design by
Pugin. The town's most ancient building is
the Old Parsonage, once part of a great
14thC house and containing panelled rooms
and beautifully decorated windows. West
Street, at the top of the High Street, has
great literary associations – Thomas Love

Peacock wrote *Nightmare Abbey* at no 47,
Shelley wrote *Revolt to Islam* in Albion
House, while his wife Mary Godwin created
Frankenstein there. T. S. Eliot also lived in
West Street for a while after World War I.
The Royal Military Academy was also here –
it moved to Sandhurst in 1812. Marlow's
shops are excellent. Down by the lock, the
new white clapboard houses are striking –
their angular roofline was inspired by
traditional mill buildings. They were
designed by J. Seymour Harris.

Cookham Dean

Berks. Large parts of Cookham Dean are
owned by the National Trust, standing
above steep beech woods by the river.
Winter Hill has one of the best views over
the Thames Valley, and is well worth the
steep walk. Kenneth Grahame, who wrote
The Wind in the Willows, published 1908,
lived at Mayfield between 1906–10. It is
thought that Quarry Wood may have been
the 'wild wood' mentioned in the story.

BOATYARDS

Ⓑ**Harleyford Marine** Harleyford Manor, nr
Temple Lock. (Marlow 71361). Ⓡ Ⓢ Ⓦ Gas,
long-term mooring, winter storage, slipway,
chandlery, provisions, books and maps, boat
and engine sales and repairs, toilets,
showers. Licensed club for members in
Harleyford Manor. Ⓜ

Ⓑ**Wooten's Boatyard** Gibraltar Lane,
Winter Hill, Cookham Dean. (Marlow
4244). Ⓡ Ⓢ Ⓦ Pump-out, long-term
mooring, winter storage, slipway, boat
building, boat and engine sales and repairs,

98 Marlow

toilets, fishing boat hire. *Closed winter weekends.* M(limited).

BOAT TRIPS

MV Dorothy This superb 1923 Edwardian beaver stern day launch operates a variety of luxury cruises. Details from River Days, Bridge Close, Riverside, Marlow (72805).

MOORING

Higginson Park Marlow (fee), and by a small park below the lock.

PUBS AND RESTAURANTS

Bull High Street, Bisham. (Marlow 2675). Wethered's real ale, restaurant with a wide range of international dishes, snacks and garden.

Compleat Angler By Marlow Bridge, Marlow (4444). Restaurant and hotel with riverside terrace, by the famous suspension bridge. Popular stop on the tourist circuit. Used to be 'The Anglers Rest'; now the name commemorates Izaak Walton's famous book, published in 1653. The Valaisan Restaurant serves French cuisine in a romantic atmosphere. Sometimes there is a pianist. *L & D* (must book). Very expensive à la carte menu.

George & Dragon The Causeway, Marlow (3887). Large pub and restaurant serving Wethered's real ale. Bar meals and a good set dinner *at 19.00 (not Sun).*

Burgers The Causeway, Marlow (3389). Continental confectioners with wide range of breads. Morning coffee and teas. *Closed Sun & Mon afternoon.*

Chequers High Street, Marlow (2053). Brakspear's real ales in a 17thC inn facing the old Wethered brewery. Restaurant serves steaks, seafood, and chicken dishes. *Closed Sun.*

Coach & Horses West Street, Marlow. Good town pub. Bar meals.

Ship West Street, Marlow. 15thC pub with nautical theme. Wethered's real ale, bar meals, garden.

Red Lion West Street, Marlow. Wethered's real ale.

Prince of Wales Mill Road, Marlow. Wethered's real ale in a local pub opposite the excellent 'Jolly Frier' fish & chip shop.

Marlow Donkey Station Road, Marlow. Wethered's real ale and bar lunches (*not Sun*) in a Victorian pub near the station. The 'Donkey' was a famous local train, as the sign indicates.

Cavaliers 24 West Street, Marlow (2544). French and continental food under oak beams. *Open for L & D (closed Mon L).*

Mad Hatter Bistro 47 West Street, Marlow (72653). *Closed Sun D & Mon.* This was once 'Peacock's Restaurant', where Thomas Love Peacock wrote *Nightmare Abbey* (1818). The poet Percy Bysshe Shelley also stayed here.

Two Brewers St Peter Street, Marlow. Near the river. Wethered's real ale, bar meals and garden. Apparently Jerome K. Jerome wrote part of *Three Men in a Boat* here.

Spade Oak Coldmoorholme Lane, Bourne End (20090). (Off map – north of Spade Oak Farm). Excellent array of real ales in a popular hotel. Wide range of bar meals, garden.

Jolly Farmer Church Road, Cookham Dean. Courage real ales, bar meals and garden.

Chequers Dean Lane, Cookham Dean. Courage real ale, garden.

Hare & Hounds Cookham Dean Common. Wethered's real ale, and a collection of chamber pots.

'Swan Uppers' at Marlow Lock

This is an excellent and therefore popular stretch of the Thames, commencing at Bourne End, where the water is very wide and favoured for sailing. Below Cookham Bridge the river splits into four – make sure you take the clearly marked lock cut, which was opened on 1 Nov 1830. Formosa Island lies to the south, Hedsor Wharf to the north. Emerging from the cut one is confronted with a steep hillside thickly wooded with beech – this is Cliveden, owned by the National Trust. These woods continue to Taplow and Boulter's Lock, where a main road skirts the river on the Maidenhead side, and the bridge by the lock is packed with 'gongoozlers' on a sunny summer's day.

NAVIGATIONAL NOTES

Cookham Lock (Bourne End 20752). 183ft 0in × 25ft 0in. Fall 4ft 3in.
Boulter's Lock (Maidenhead 24205). 199ft 6in × 21ft 3in. Fall 7ft 10in. W
Max draught: 4ft 6in.

Holy Trinity Church, Cookham

NOTES FOR WALKERS

The towpath keeps to the west of the river throughout this section, with only a small detour through Cookham village, to rejoin the river by Formosa Place. The ferry at Bourne End is for hotel patrons only. An excellent section, full of contrasts – the preserved 'prettiness' of Cookham, the handsome beech woods of Cliveden, and the bustle of Boulter's Lock.

Bourne End
Bucks. EC Wed. PO, shops. A riverside commuter village, famous for 'Bourne End Sailing Week'. Cock Marsh opposite, 132 acres, is owned by the National Trust.
Cookham
Berks. EC Wed. PO, no food shops. A self-consciously pretty village of pubs, antique shops, restaurants and boutiques, with bijou cottages filling the gaps in between. BMWs and Porsches line the kerbs. Cookham is famous as the home of the artist Stanley

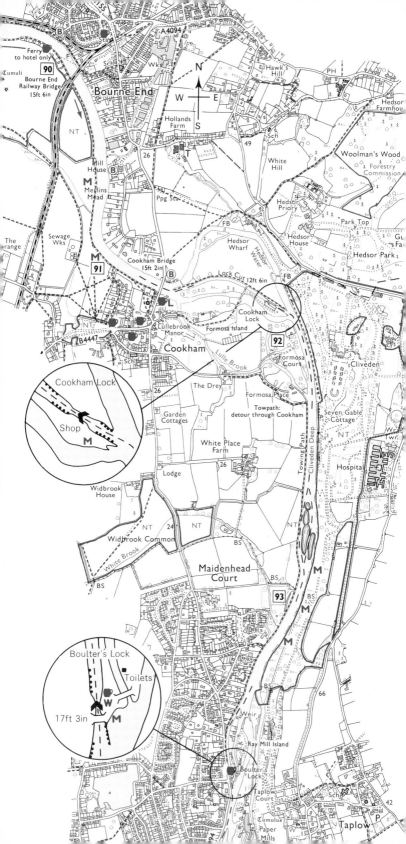

Spencer – his work is exhibited in the old Wesleyan Chapel, *open daily from 10.30*. His *Last Supper*, painted in 1920, hangs in the splendid square-towered Holy Trinity Church, built by the Normans in 1140 on the site of a Saxon building. There are fine 16thC monuments, and the church is floodlit after dark. The bridge, an iron structure, was built in 1867. John Turk, of Turks Boatyard, is Her Majesty's Swan Keeper – a unique appointment. In the *third week of July* he takes to his boat with a supply of 'tea' (an intoxicating mixture of dark rum and milk) to mark the swans, together with representatives of the Vintners' and Dyers' Companies, in their double sculling skiffs. This colourful event is known as 'Swan Upping.'

Hedsor
Bucks. A priory and an over-restored church on the hill. It is worth the walk up for the splendid views over the beech woods. Hedsor House was rebuilt in 1862 in an Italianate style. Lord Boston's Folly, an 18thC structure, faces the church from the opposite hill.

Hedsor Wharf An important shipping point for timber, paper and coal for over 500 years until the lock cut by-passed it in 1830. At the lower end of Hedsor Water there was once a lock – the original cottage still stands, a single room cut from the chalk and fronted with brick. Hedsor Water is private.

Cliveden Taplow, nr Maidenhead, Berks. (Burnham 68561). A most marvellous stretch of beech woods from Hedsor to Taplow surrounds the house. Built in 1862 for the Astor family, it was the background to many 20thC political intrigues and scandals, ending with the Profumo affair in

1963. Fine tapestries and furniture, and a theatre which heard the first performance of *Rule Britannia*. It is now a hotel, leased from the National Trust. B&B will cost between £200–£400 per night.

BOATYARDS

Ⓑ **Bourne End Marina** Wharf Lane, Bourne End (22813). Ⓡ Ⓢ Ⓦ Ⓟ Ⓓ Pump-out, gas, hire craft (several companies based here), day hire boats, long-term mooring, crane, chandlery, boat and engine repairs, boat sales, toilets.

Ⓑ **DB Marine** Cookham Bridge. (Bourne End 26032). Day hire boats.

Ⓑ **Turks Boatyard** Cookham. (Bourne End 20110/28413). Ⓦ Gas, hire craft, day hire boats, long-term mooring, winter storage, slipway, boat building, boat and engine repairs, engine sales, toilets. *Closed Sat afternoon & Sun in Winter.*

MOORING

Excellent free moorings by the meadows above Cookham Bridge, and beautiful quiet moorings below Cookham Lock at Cliveden. There are very limited moorings below Boulter's Lock.

PUBS AND RESTAURANTS

ⓦ✗ **Moorings** Bourne End (20056). Free house, bar food, children's playground, crazy golf, restaurant. Ferry to Bourne End. Ⓜ

ⓦ **Firefly** Station Approach, Bourne End. Ind Coope real ale and bar meals (*not Sun*). Garden.

ⓦ **Ferry** By the bridge, Cookham. Fine low-ceilinged pub behind newer extension. Good food (children's menu), Young's, Marstons and Ruddles real ales, regular entertainment.

ⓦ **Bel & the Dragon** High Street, Cookham. Attractive pub dating from 1417 serving Brakspear's, Wethered's and Young's real ales. Food.

ⓦ✗ **King's Arms** High Street, Cookham. (Bourne End 20146). Very smart red plush old coaching inn with a good restaurant. The fixed price set menus are excellent. Wethered's real ales, bar meals and superb garden.

ⓦ **Royal Exchange** High Street, Cookham. Ind Coope and Benskins real ales, food, children's room, garden.

ⓦ **Crown** The Moor, Cookham. Courage real ales, garden. Food *Mon–Fri*.

✗♥ **Le Radier** 19–21 Station Hill Parade, Cookham. (Bourne End 25775). Excellent but not over-priced French bourgeois cooking. *D Tue–Sat*, must book.

✗♥ **Two Roses** High Street, Cookham. (Bourne End 20875). Cottage restaurant, home cooking. Reasonable prices. *Open D & Sun L.*

✗ **Copper Kettle** High Street, Cookham. (Bourne End 20900). Cakes, scones, flapjacks, all home made, with coffee and tea. Meals at *lunchtime*. *Closes 17.45; Sun morning & all day Mon.*

✗♥ **Boulter's Inn** Boulter's Lock Island, Maidenhead (21291). Right by the lock in the Old Ray Flour Mill, built 1726 and converted in 1950. Smart restaurant serving French and English cuisine. Interesting green phone box outside.

ⓦ✗ **Taplow House Hotel** Berry Hill, Taplow. (Maidenhead 70056). Two Berni restaurants and two bars serving Courage and McEwans real ales in a Georgian mansion, standing in 6½ acres of grounds. Many functions held here.

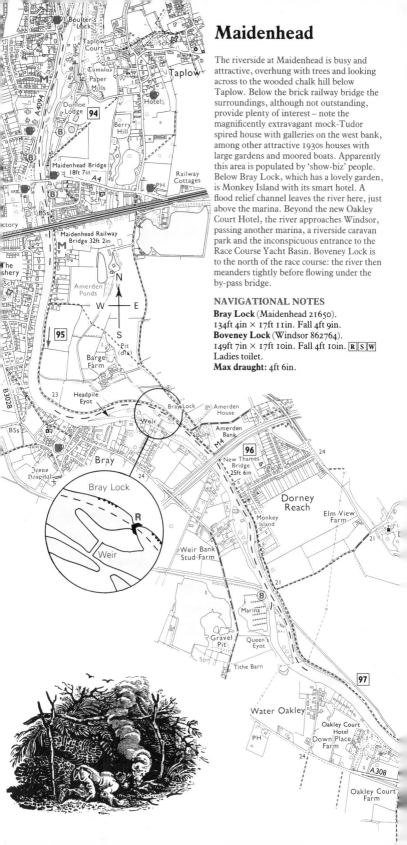

Maidenhead

The riverside at Maidenhead is busy and attractive, overhung with trees and looking across to the wooded chalk hill below Taplow. Below the brick railway bridge the surroundings, although not outstanding, provide plenty of interest – note the magnificently extravagant mock-Tudor spired house with galleries on the west bank, among other attractive 1930s houses with large gardens and moored boats. Apparently this area is populated by 'show-biz' people. Below Bray Lock, which has a lovely garden, is Monkey Island with its smart hotel. A flood relief channel leaves the river here, just above the marina. Beyond the new Oakley Court Hotel, the river approaches Windsor, passing another marina, a riverside caravan park and the inconspicuous entrance to the Race Course Yacht Basin. Boveney Lock is to the north of the race course: the river then meanders tightly before flowing under the by-pass bridge.

NAVIGATIONAL NOTES

Bray Lock (Maidenhead 21650).
134ft 4in × 17ft 11in. Fall 4ft 9in.
Boveney Lock (Windsor 862764).
149ft 7in × 17ft 10in. Fall 4ft 10in. R S W
Ladies toilet.
Max draught: 4ft 6in.

NOTES FOR WALKERS

Below Maidenhead Bridge, the towpath is continuous on the east side to Windsor Bridge. The riverside road at Maidenhead is the best part of the town, so a walk into the centre is not recommended. A detour through Dorney and Boveney would prove rewarding although there is much of interest on the river.

Maidenhead

Berks. EC Thur. MD Fri, Sat. All services. A dormitory suburb of London, close to the M4 motorway, and remarkable only for the architectural sterility of new development. All character has effectively been destroyed. Fortunately, the best part of the town is the riverside, especially around the beautifully balustraded bridge built in Portland stone by Sir Robert Taylor 1772–7. The town centre and shopping precinct (Nicholson's Walk) is about ¾ mile to the west of the bridge.

Tourist Information Centre Central Library, St Ives Road, Maidenhead (25657).

Maidenhead Railway Bridge The two beautiful arches, each 123ft long, are reputedly the largest brickwork spans in the world. Built 1839 by Brunel.

Bray

Berks. EC Wed. PO, stores. Although there is much commuter development, Bray still retains its village centre. The well-preserved largely 13thC church is approached via a fine brick gatehouse of 1450. Simon Alwyn, the 16thC vicar of Bray who changed his creed three times to hold the living under Henry VIII, Edward VI, Mary and Elizabeth I, was immortalised in song, and now lies buried in the churchyard. Just outside the village is the Jesus Hospital, founded in 1627.

Ockwells Manor About a mile south west of Bray. Built by Sir John Norreys, 1446–66, it is one of the most elegant and refined timber-framed buildings in England. A careful 20thC restoration has left much original work. It contains a famous set of armorial stained glass. Private.

Monkey Island *Berks.* On the island are the fishing lodge and pavilion of the 3rd Duke of Marlborough, built in 1744 and now a hotel. In the restaurant rooms there are monkey paintings on the ceiling, by Clermont. The name of the island, however, is a derivation of Monk's Eyot. M for patrons.

Down Place A pretty 18thC riverside mansion, once the meeting place of the Kit Kat Club. Steele, Addison, Walpole and Congreve were members. It now houses Bray Studios. Nearby is Oakley Court, a magnificent Victorian Gothic 'castle' of 1859. All the elements of romantic medievalism are present. Now a hotel.

Dorney Court and Church (Burnham 4638). A gabled and timbered house built with soft pink Tudor brick around 1500, it has been occupied by the present family for 400 years. Many restorations have not altered the original feeling of the house which contains fine furniture and paintings. The church forms a perfect unit with the court, and contains a Norman font, 17thC woodwork and a Garrard monument. Cream teas and shop. *Open Easter, mid Apr–mid Oct Suns & B. Hols, also Mon & Tue Jun–Sep. Charge.*

Boveney

Bucks. A village scattered round a green. There are some over-restored Tudor buildings, which still remain attractive. The pretty flint and clapboard church nestles in trees by the river.

BOATYARDS

Ⓑ **Andrews Bros** Mill Lane, Taplow. (Maidenhead 24056). W Long-term mooring, winter storage, chandlery, boat and engine sales and repairs, crane, toilets.

Ⓑ **Bray Boats** Ray Mead Road, Maidenhead (37880). W Pump-out, gas, hire craft, day hire boats, long-term mooring, boat and engine sales and repairs. Large trip boat with bar for charter.

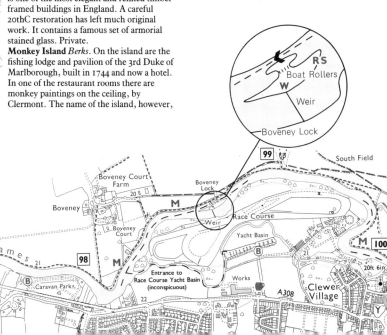

Ⓑ**Bray Marina** Monkey Island Lane, Bray. (Maidenhead 23654). Ⓢ Ⓦ Ⓟ Ⓓ Gas, long-term mooring, chandlery, provisions, books and maps, boat sales, boat and engine repairs, toilets, showers. Ⓜ
Ⓑ**Windsor Marina** Maidenhead Road, Oakley Green, Windsor (853911). Ⓢ Ⓦ Ⓟ Ⓓ Pump-out, gas, long-term mooring, winter storage, slipway, chandlery, provisions, books and maps, boat building, boat and engine sales and repairs, crane, toilets, showers. Ⓜ
Ⓑ**Race Course Yacht Basin** Maidenhead Road, Windsor (851501). Ⓡ Ⓢ Ⓦ Ⓟ Ⓓ Gas, long-term mooring, winter storage, slipway, dry dock, chandlery, boat and engine sales and repairs, toilets, showers. Ⓜ

MOORING

On the towpath side below Boulter's Lock, and below Maidenhead Railway Bridge (fee), where there is a pleasant grassy area. There are free moorings on the towpath side above Boveney Lock, good for the walk through Boveney to Dorney. The three large marinas also have overnight moorings.

PUBS AND RESTAURANTS

See previous section for Boulter's Inn and Taplow House Hotel.
🍺✕ **Thames Hotel** Ray Mead Road, Maidenhead (28721). A modernised riverside hotel and restaurant with an imaginative French/English menu. Wethered's real ale in the River Bar. *D & Sun L.*
✕🍷 **La Riva** Ray Mead Road, Maidenhead (33522). By the bridge. Intimate Italian restaurant. *L & D* (must book). *Closed Sat L & Sun.*

🍺✕ **Skindles Hotel** Above Maidenhead Bridge (23366). Riverside complex with three restaurants and a health club. (*Closed Sun–Tue.*) Wine bar and 'Orkney Arms' with pub snacks. Live rock and roll *on Mon.*
🍺 **Riviera Hotel** (River Bar). Overlooking the Thames below Maidenhead Bridge. Wethered's real ale, food, garden.
✕🍷 **Thames Curry Centre** Ray Mead Road, Maidenhead (20116). Curries and tandooris. Take-away service. *L & D.*

Maidenhead town centre where you will find more pubs and eating places, lies about ¾ mile south west of the bridge.

🍺 **Old Station** Bath Road, Taplow. Known locally as the 'Tin Shack', it serves Ind Coope real ale and bar meals *on weekdays.*
🍺 **Hind's Head** High Street, Bray. An elegant and expensive Tudor inn, where the Queen entertained foreign royalty on 23 Apr 1963. Courage real ale straight from the cask. Children's room, garden.
✕🍷 **Waterside Inn** Ferry Road, Bray. (Maidenhead 20691). Faultless French cuisine presented by Messrs Roux. A very smart riverside restaurant in a beautiful setting. Exciting menu, attentive waiters, expensive wine. *Closed Mon, Tue L & Sun D in winter.* Must book.
🍺 **Crown** High Street, Bray. Beamy old pub with good, but not cheap, food, Courage real ale, and a sheltered courtyard with vines.
🍺 **Windsor Lad** Maidenhead Road, Windsor. Very handy for those moored in the Race Course Yacht basin, this large pub serves Courage real ale and food *at lunchtime.*

Maidenhead Railway Bridge

The river at Windsor is, as you would expect, busy with trip boats, rowing and motor boats, walkers and children feeding the ducks. On the north bank is the smart Eton College Boat House, while magnificent Windsor Castle dominates the river for miles around. Leaving Windsor, the Thames winds around the Home Park, passing the playing fields of Eton, and the famous college, on the north bank. There are fine views across the park to Windsor between the Victoria and Albert Bridges – HM's former boat house can be seen standing by a private dock. Datchet is to the east. Below Albert Bridge the navigation channel passes through the New Cut (built 1822 and creating Ham Island, now a bird sanctuary) to Old Windsor Lock, and on past moored boats and bungalows towards Runnymede.

NAVIGATIONAL NOTES

Romney Lock (Windsor 860296).
257ft 7in × 24ft 5in. Fall 6ft 7in. |W| Ladies toilet.
Old Windsor Lock (Windsor 861822).
179ft 0in × 24ft 2in. Fall 5ft 9in. |W|
Max draught: 5ft 6in.

NOTES FOR WALKERS

Crossing Windsor Bridge from Eton, walkers may skirt the Home Park as far as Victoria Bridge, then follow the B470 to rejoin the towpath at Albert Bridge, then on to Runnymede. An amble around Windsor and Eton, and a visit to the castle, should be on every itinerary.

Windsor

Berks. EC Wed. All shops and services. A clean and tidy town demonstrating that if you are going to be a tourist attraction, you can at least do it well. The castle is a splendid fairy tale edifice, and the changing of the guard ceremony in the morning is conducted with a uniquely British mixture of military authority and showmanship. The main street curves around the castle, and is full of pubs, restaurants and souvenir shops. There are many fine buildings in the town, most of them 19thC. The Church of St John the Baptist in the High Street, built 1820–2, has three galleries supported by delicate cast iron piers. The town hall, built by Wren in 1689–90 after a design by Sir Thomas Fitch, has the usual open ground floor. The ceiling is supported by four Tuscan columns which stop two inches short: a private joke of the architect's at the expense of a doubting mayor. To the west of the town there is a fine riverside park. Theatre at the Theatre Royal (Windsor 853888).
Tourist Information Centre Central Station, Windsor (852010).
Windsor Castle
The largest inhabited castle in the world, first built by Henry II, 1165–79. Most succeeding monarchs have left their mark, notably Charles II, and Queen Victoria who spent over £1 million on modernisation. The building falls into three sections:
Lower Ward St George's Chapel, the finest

example of Perpendicular architecture in the country. The Albert Memorial Chapel, originally built by Henry VII and then turned into a Victorian shrine.
Middle Ward The Round Tower, with a panoramic view over 12 counties.

Changing the Guard, Windsor Castle

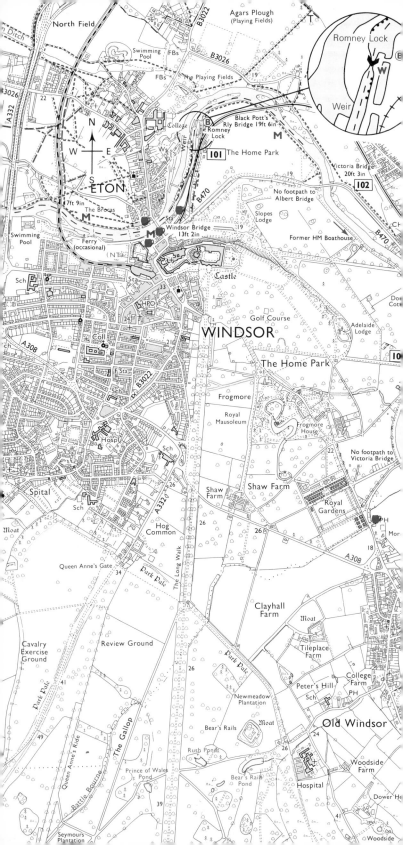

Upper Ward The Private Apartments and the State Apartments, containing a collection of paintings. The castle is surrounded by parks; Home Park borders on the river and contains Frogmore House, built by Wyatt in 1792 out of an earlier house, and the Royal Mausoleum. *The castle precincts are open daily – other parts of the castle are open to the public but times vary (details: Windsor 868286). Charge.*

Windsor Great Park
A total area of 4800 acres between the Thames and Virginia Water. There has been a starling roost in the park for over 100 years, and a heronry at Fort Belvedere.

Eton
Berks. PO, shops. Windsor Bridge is now used by pedestrians only, and the lack of through traffic has made the long and rambling High Street a very pleasant place to walk. The famous college is very much the heart and soul of Eton. It was founded by Henry VI in 1440 and the buildings date from 1441 to the present day. The magnificent 15thC Eton College, chapel and cloisters are *open to the public daily 10.00– 12.00 & 14.00–16.00.*

Datchet
Berks. EC Wed. PO, shops, fish & chips. At its best around the green, where there is still a village feeling. The rest is a large dormitory suburb.

Old Windsor
Berks. PO, shop. A great expanse of suburban houses with no sign of the 9thC village, built around the site of a Saxon royal palace. The 13thC church, hidden among trees, was restored by Gilbert Scott in 1863. To the south of the village lies Beaumont College (now owned by ICL), established in 1861. The mansion was built by Henry Emlyn in 1790.

BOATYARDS
Ⓑ **Tom Jones (Boat Builders)** Romney Lock Boat House, Windsor (860699). Gas, long-term mooring, winter storage, books and maps, boat building, boat and engine sales and repairs, toilets.
Ⓑ **John Hicks Boat Yard** The Waterfront, Datchet. (Slough 43930). Ⓢ Ⓦ Ⓓ Pump-out, gas, hire craft, books and maps, boat building, boat and engine repairs, toilets. *Closed in winter.* Ⓜ
Ⓑ **Crevalds Services** 105 Straight Road, Old Windsor. (Windsor 860393). Ⓡ Ⓢ Ⓦ Ⓟ Ⓓ Gas, winter storage, slipway, chandlery, books and maps, boat building, boat and engine sales and repairs, toilets.

BOAT TRIPS
Salter Bros 1 Thames Side, Windsor (865832). A company synonymous with the Thames – their trip boats are still referred to as 'Salters Steamers'. Scheduled *summer* services from Marlow, Windsor, Cookham and Reading.
French Brothers Runnymede Boathouse, near Runnymede House, Windsor Road, Old Windsor. (Windsor 851900). Trips to Hampton Court, Windsor and intermediate places. Also private charter for functions. Tea room close by.

MOORING
There are good moorings on both sides of the river above Windsor Bridge, and on the Windsor side below Black Pott's Bridge. The moorings at Runnymede, Old Windsor are pleasant and grassy, but you will be made very aware of the close proximity of Heathrow Airport.

PUBS AND RESTAURANTS
🍺 **Thames Hotel** Barry Avenue, Windsor. Riverside pub serving Ind Coope real ales. Food, garden.
🍺✕ **Old House** Thames Street, Windsor (861354). An elegant and exotic Thames-side hotel, with a pleasant courtyard and sub-tropical bamboo room. Restaurant with excellent French/English menu, bar snacks. Free house.
Windsor has many fine pubs, the following are those nearest the river:
🍺 **Royal Oak** Datchet Road, Windsor.

Courage real ales, garden, food. Fine panelling.

🍺 **Adam & Eve** Thames Street, Windsor. Bass Charrington real ales in this pub which has close associations with the Theatre Royal. Food and covered courtyard with an old pear tree.

🍺 **William IV** Thames Street, Windsor. Courage real ales in a beamy pub. Occasional Morris dancers. Food, garden.

🍺 **Carpenters Arms** Market Street, Windsor. Old pub near the castle serving Bass Charrington real ales.

🍺 **Horse & Groom** Castle Hill, Windsor. Courage real ales, *lunchtime* food.

In Thames Street, opposite the castle, there are a number of places to eat – McDonald's, Berni Steak House, Henekey's Steak House, London Steak House, Summerfields Pizza and Pasta, and the Curry Garden Restaurant, so you should find something suitable. Also recommended are:

✗🍷 **Don Peppino** 30 Thames Street, Windsor (860081). Excellent Italian food and wine. *Open L & D (closed Sun)*. Must book.

✗ **Country Kitchen** 3 King Edward Court, Windsor (868681). Salads, quiches and savoury pies. *Open 10.00–17.00 Mon–Sat*. Carvery *Sun lunch 12.00–15.00*.

The following five pubs are easily found in Eton High Street, straight up from the bridge:

🍺 **Three Tuns** Eton. Wethered's real ale.

🍺 **Crown & Cushion** Eton. Courage real ale, food, garden.

🍺 **College Arms** Eton. Courage real ale, food, garden.

🍺 **George** Eton. Wethered's real ale, food.

🍺 **Christopher** Eton. Brakspear's and Courage real ales.

✗🍷 **House on the Bridge** By Windsor Bridge, 71 High Street, Eton. (Windsor 860914). International restaurant with own moorings. Riverside terrace. *Open L & D*. M

🍺 **Watermans Arms** Bridge Street, Eton. Near the Eton College Boat House. An Eton skiff is suspended in one of the bars, and there is a notable collection of rude postcards. Courage real ales are served, and meals *at lunchtime*.

The following three pubs in Datchet are off the map, to the east, by the Green:

🍺 **Manor Hotel** Datchet. Charrington and Brakspear's real ales, garden, children's room.

🍺 **Royal Stag** Datchet. Ind Coope and Friary Meux real ale. Food at *lunchtime*.

🍺 **Morning Star** Datchet. Courage real ale, food, garden. This 14thC pub is supposedly haunted.

🍺 **Lord Nelson** 4 Datchet Road, Old Windsor. Courage real ales, garden.

🍺✗ **Bells of Ouzeley** Straight Road, Old Windsor. (Windsor 861826). Busy red plush pub near the river. Courage real ales, food, garden. M

Romney Lock

During the summer Runnymede and the river throng with trippers and visitors, against the backdrop of Cooper's Hill, richly wooded and topped by the RAF Memorial. The Magna Carta Memorial can be seen from the river – the Kennedy Memorial is hidden in the trees. To the north are the remains of Ankerwyke Priory. Passing Holm Island, the London Stone stands by the river: this marked the former limit of the jurisdiction of the City of London over the Thames. There is some smart and mellow new housing on the north bank above Staines Bridge, but for the most part the riverside is lined with a wonderful, and sometimes ludicrously eccentric, array of holiday chalets and bungalows, houseboats and moored craft of indiscriminate vintage. At Penton Hook a large marina has been established in flooded gravel pits – it is approached from below the lock. Below here is Laleham where the bungalows disappear and Laleham Abbey and park provide a breathing space before Chertsey.

Laleham Sailing Club

NAVIGATIONAL NOTES

Bell Weir Lock (Egham 32333).
257ft 7in × 24ft 5in. Fall 6ft 0in. R Ladies toilet.
Penton Hook Lock (Staines 52657).
266ft 8in × 24ft 10in. Fall 4ft 0in. R W
Max draught: above Staines 5ft 6in; below Staines 6ft 6in.
Note that Penton Hook Marina is approached from *below* the lock.

NOTES FOR WALKERS

Change from the south bank to the north at Staines Bridge; after a short detour along Clarence Street and Thames Street you will rejoin the towpath. In the summer Runnymede is thick with visitors and their parked cars – a noisy respite before Staines is tackled.

Runnymede
Surrey. Beside the river on the south bank – a stretch of open parkland backed by the wooded slopes of Cooper's Hill. The paired

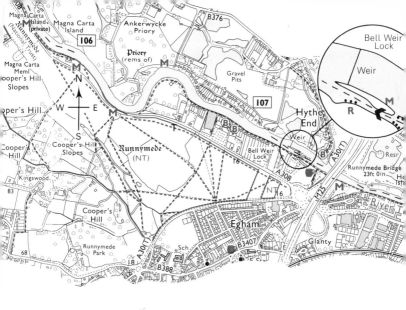

gatehouses, by Lutyens, introduce an area of memorials. The inspiration is the sealing of the Magna Carta in 1215. On top of the hill is the Commonwealth Air Forces Memorial. This quadrangular structure, built by Sir Edward Maufe, 1953, perfectly exploits its situation. Below are the Magna Carta Memorial and the Kennedy Memorial, the latter built on an acre of ground given to the American people. There are many good walks. The area is owned by the National Trust.

Ankerwyke Built on the site of a Benedictine nunnery is Ankerwyke Priory, a low, early 19thC mansion surrounded by trees, among which is the Ankerwyke Yew whose trunk is 33ft in circumference.

Staines
Surrey. EC Thur. All services, launderette, fish & chips. A commuter town which has expanded hugely over the last 30 years. However, the area around the pleasantly situated church has remained virtually unchanged. Clarence Street, which culminates in Rennie's stone bridge, built 1829–32, still has the feeling of an 18thC market town. To the north are huge reservoirs.

Laleham
Surrey. PO, stores. The first impression of Laleham is one of bungalows and houseboats. The village does not exploit the river at all, and the centre lacks the riverside feeling of some other towns hereabouts. The 18th and 19thC church is well placed in a wooded graveyard, which contains the tomb of Matthew Arnold. In the church, note the Norman arcades on both sides of the nave, and the expressionist window by W. Geddes, 1926. To the south of the town is Laleham Park. Formerly the grounds of Laleham House, built about 1805, it is now a wooded public park reaching down to the river.

Thorpe Park Staines Road, Chertsey (562633). A popular theme park with plenty of water activities – Thunder River, Water Gardens, pedalos, Water Bus trips and Farm Ferry – as well as Space Station Zero, Treasure Island Railway and Phantom Fantasia. All worth trying! *Open Easter–end Sep. Charge.*

BOATYARDS

(B) Runnymede Boatyard (Eurocruisers) Yard Mead, Windsor Road, Egham (62914). [R][W][D] Pump-out, hire craft, boat building and sales, boat and engine repairs, toilets. [M]

(B) Nicoles Boatyard Yard Mead, Windsor Road, Egham (32342). [R][S][W][D] Pump-out, hire craft, day hire boats, long-term mooring, winter storage, dry dock, crane, boat building, boat and engine sales and repairs (specialists in steam craft), toilets.

(B) J. Tims & Sons Timsway, Staines (52093). [R][S][W][D] Gas, long-term mooring, winter storage, boat building, boat and engine sales and repairs. *Closed Sun.*

(B) Penton Hook Marina Staines Lane, Chertsey (566771). A vast marina in flooded gravel pits. [M]

(B) Chertsey Marine Penton Hook Marina, Chertsey (565195). [R][S][W][P][D] Pump-out, gas, hire craft, long-term mooring, winter storage, two mobile cranes, slipway, chandlery, provisions, books and maps, boat and engine sales and repairs, toilets, showers.

(B) Harris Boatbuilders Laleham Reach, Chertsey (563111). [R][S][W][D] Pump-out, gas, hire craft, long-term mooring, winter storage, slipway, boat building, boat and engine repairs, some boat sales.

MOORING

There are free moorings by grass and trees at Runnymede, but the idyll is tempered rather by the jets from Heathrow (good for plane-spotters). There are short stay moorings at Ankerwyke and on the north bank below Staines Bridge. Longer stays are made on the south side. The moorings at Laleham are very attractive: a grassy bank with willows.

PUBS AND RESTAURANTS

🍺✕ **Runnymede Hotel** Windsor Road, Egham (36171). Very smart hotel with riverside gardens and conference facilities. International restaurant and bar. M

🍺 **Crown** High Street, Egham. Courage real ale, garden, snacks. Good local pub.

🍺 **King's Arms** High Street, Egham. Courage real ale, snacks and meals. Good plain local.

🍺 **Red Lion** High Street, Egham. 17thC inn serving Ind Coope real ale, snacks and meals.

🍺 **Halfway House** The Causeway, Egham. Courage real ale, garden, snacks and meals.

🍺✕ **Swan** The Hythe, by Staines Bridge. (Staines 52494). Fuller's real ales. Bar meals, international restaurant and carvery. Riverside terrace. *Open L & D.*

✕🍷 **Barnaby's Carving Rooms** 1 Clarence Street, Staines (57546). Children welcomed here. *Open L & D.* M

🍺✕ **Thames Lodge** Thames Street, Staines (54221). Bar food and mainly English restaurant meals. *Open L & D.* M

🍺 **Ship** The Causeway, Staines. Wood panelled pub serving Ind Coope real ale, snacks and meals.

🍺 **Bells** Church Street, Staines. Close to the (haunted) churchyard. Courage real ale.

🍺 **Phoenix** Church Street, Staines. Courage real ales, snacks and meals. Frequent live jazz and folk music.

🍺 **Feathers** The Broadway, Laleham. Courage real ales, *lunchtime* food, garden.

🍺 **Turk's Head** The Broadway, Laleham. Small pub serving Courage real ale. Snacks at *lunchtime.*

🍺 **Three Horseshoes** Shepperton Road, Laleham. Attractive and comfortable pub, once patronised by Sir Arthur Sullivan and Marie Lloyd. Watney's and Websters real ales, excellent snacks and meals (*not Sun or B. Hols*). Garden.

112 Weybridge

Passing the attractive seven-arched stone bridge at Chertsey, the river loops round Chertsey Meads. The riverside bungalows reappear above Shepperton Lock – many are wooden and painted in lemon-yellow or eau-de-Nil. Built between the wars for weekend use they are now in great demand, many being permanently occupied. The names are

Shepperton Lock (Walton 221840). 174ft 5in × 19ft 10in. Fall 6ft 8in. R S W Ladies toilet.
Sunbury Lock (Sunbury 782089). Old lock: 154ft 8in × 19ft 3in; New lock: 206ft 0in × 24ft 4in. Fall 6ft 2in. R W Ladies toilet.
Max draught: 6ft 6in.
The River Wey joins the Thames *below* Shepperton Lock. The old course of the river north of Desborough Island is navigable – it may be shallow in places.

NOTES FOR WALKERS

Nauticalia runs a ferry service below Shepperton Lock, so walkers can enjoy this ancient crossing, noting that 'droves of sheep

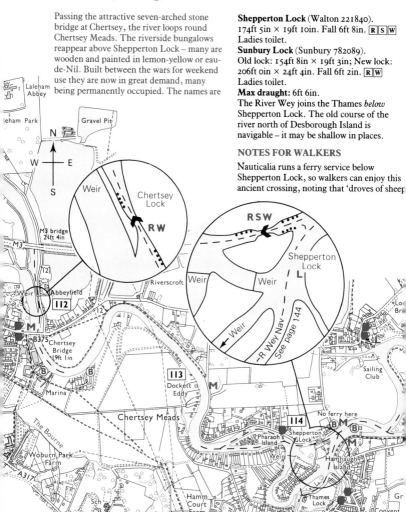

wonderful – 'Petit Paradis' and 'Near-a-Weir' can enliven even the dreariest day on the river. The River Wey (see page 143) joins by Shepperton Lock, with Weybridge to the south. The tree-lined Desborough Cut isolates Lower Halliford although with care you can, if you wish, navigate the original course, to visit Shepperton.
Sunbury is more attractive: there is a very pretty lock cottage by the locks.

NAVIGATIONAL NOTES

Chertsey Lock (Chertsey 562208). 200ft 8in × 21ft 0in. Fall 4ft 0in. R W

will be carried at the fare of one shilling per score (shepherd to clean up afterwards)'.
Chertsey
Surrey. EC Wed. All shops and services. From the river the first sight of Chertsey is James Paine's stone bridge, built 1780–2. Chertsey just manages to retain a feeling of the 18thC, especially around Windsor Street, which runs past the site of the abbey. Today nothing remains of what was one of the greatest abbeys in England. Founded in AD666, rebuilt during the 12thC, it was finally destroyed during the Reformation. It is thought likely materials from the abbey

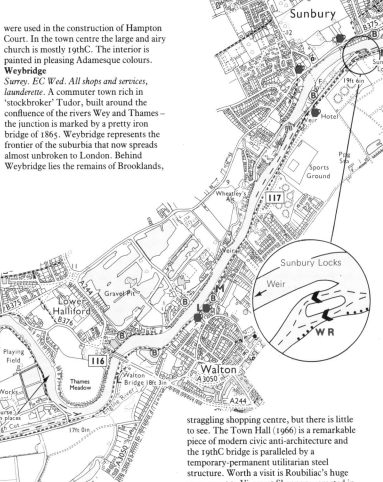

were used in the construction of Hampton Court. In the town centre the large and airy church is mostly 19thC. The interior is painted in pleasing Adamesque colours.

Weybridge
Surrey. EC Wed. All shops and services, launderette. A commuter town rich in 'stockbroker' Tudor, built around the confluence of the rivers Wey and Thames – the junction is marked by a pretty iron bridge of 1865. Weybridge represents the frontier of the suburbia that now spreads almost unbroken to London. Behind Weybridge lies the remains of Brooklands,

the doyen of motor racing circuits in the early 20thC. Part of the legendary banking of the track can still be seen from the London–Portsmouth railway.

Shepperton
Surrey. All shops and services, launderette. Recognisable from the river by the lawns of the 19thC Manor House, Shepperton is a surprising example of village survival. The square contains a number of relatively intact 18thC inns. The church, with its fine brick tower, was built in the 17th and 18thC – note the box pews. To the north of the church is the rectory, which has an excellent Queen Anne front of about 1700. The famous film studios are to the north, near the vast Queen Mary Reservoir.

Walton-on-Thames
Surrey. EC Wed. All shops and services, launderette, fish & chips. There is much new development here, including a huge

straggling shopping centre, but there is little to see. The Town Hall (1966) is a remarkable piece of modern civic anti-architecture and the 19thC bridge is paralleled by a temporary-permanent utilitarian steel structure. Worth a visit is Roubiliac's huge monument to Viscount Shannon – erected in 1755 it wholly dominates the church. Thames Meadow, to the west, is an area of parkland, much favoured by courting couples.
Tourist Information Centre Town Hall, New Zealand Avenue, Walton (228844).

Sunbury
Surrey. EC Thur. Shops and launderette. A welcome respite after Walton – perhaps Sunbury is more socially desirable. There is a pleasant village feeling, but the parish church is a 19thC disaster. Sunbury Court, the grand mansion of the town, was built in 1770 and is now a Salvation Army Youth Centre.

BOATYARDS

ⓑ**W. Bates & Son** Bridge Wharf, Chertsey (562255). Ⓡ Ⓢ Ⓦ Ⓟ Ⓓ Pump-out, gas, day hire boats, long-term mooring, winter storage, provisions, books and maps, boat and engine repairs, boat sales, toilets, showers. Ⓜ
ⓑ**Chertsey Meads, Marina** Mead Lane, Chertsey (564699). Ⓡ Ⓢ Ⓦ Ⓓ Gas, hire craft, day hire boats, winter storage, slipway, books and maps, boat building and sales, boat and engine repairs.

114 Weybridge

Ⓑ **Nauticalia** Ferry Lane, Shepperton. (Walton 244396). Ⓦ Gas (Calor & Shell), long-term mooring, winter storage, slipway, brassware, books and maps, boat building, boat and engine repairs and sales, toilets.

Ⓑ **Eyot House** D'Oyly Carte Island, Weybridge (848586). Long-term mooring, winter storage, slipway, boat building, boat and engine repairs and sales.

Ⓑ **Kenneth M. Gibbs** Sandhills, Russell Road, Shepperton. (Walton 220926). Gas, long-term mooring, slipway, chandlery, books and maps, boats and engine repairs, toilets.

Ⓑ **Walton Marine Sales** Walton Bridge, Walton (226266). Ⓡ Ⓢ Ⓦ Long-term mooring, winter storage, slipway, chandlery, books and maps, boat and engine sales and repairs, toilets, showers. *Closed Tue.*

Ⓑ **Shepperton Marina** Felix Lane, Shepperton. (Walton 243722). Ⓦ Gas, long-term mooring, chandlery, provisions, toilets, showers. Ⓜ

Ⓑ **DBH Marine** Angler's Wharf, Manor Road, Walton (228019). Ⓡ Ⓦ Ⓓ Gas, day hire boats, long-term mooring, overnight mooring, dry dock, books and maps. *Closed Sun in winter.* Ⓜ

Ⓑ **Geo Wilson & Sons** Sunbury (782067). Gas, day hire boats, long-term mooring, winter storage, slipway, chandlery, books and maps, boat building, boat repairs (traditional craft). *Closed Mon in winter.*

Ⓑ **Turk's of Sunbury** Thames Street, Sunbury (782028). Ⓡ Ⓢ Ⓦ Ⓓ Pump-out, gas, hire craft, day hire boats, slipway, books and maps, boat building, boat and engine repairs, toilets, showers. *Closed winter weekends.* Ⓜ

MOORING

24hr moorings opposite Dockett Eddy, Chertsey Meads; also below Penton Hook Lock; on the towpath side at Walton; and below Sunbury Locks.

BOAT TRIPS

JGF Passenger Boats Cowley Sale, 300yds above Walton Bridge (01-543 0607). River trips and private hire.

PUBS AND RESTAURANTS

🍺✗ **Bridge Hotel** Chertsey (563175). A choice of real ales in a busy riverside pub with nautical theme. Galleon restaurant has a good varied menu (*Closed Sun D & Mon*). Buffet, garden. Ⓜ

🍺 **Cricketers** Chertsey Bridge. Free house.

🍺✗ **Thames Court Hotel** Shepperton (Walton 221957). Oak panelled and balconied free house with French restaurant (*Closed Sun D & Mon*) and *lunchtime* buffet. Ⓜ

✗ **Dorney Tea Gardens** On South Bank below Shepperton Lock. Breakfast *from 07.30 daily.*

🍺 **King's Head** Church Square, Shepperton. Snug 14thC tavern near the river. Real ale. *Lunchtime* food, snacks, patio.

🍺✗ **Anchor** Church Square, Shepperton (Walton 221618). A fine wood-panelled pub with an à la carte restaurant (*L & D*). Eldridge Pope, Ruddles and Young's real ales. Bar food, snacks.

✗🍴 **Blubecker's Eating House** Church Square, Walton (243377). Wide range of medium and substantial dishes in a 300-year-old cottage. *L & D* (Reserve).

🍺 **Old Crown** 83 Thames Street, Weybridge. A rambling weatherboard pub by the old course of the River Wey. Nautical decor. Courage real ales, snacks, garden.

🍺 **Lincoln Arms** 104 Thames Street, Weybridge. Bass, Young's and Courage real ales in a large riverside pub with garden.

🍺✗ **Ship** Russell Road, Shepperton (Walton 227320). Real ale, snacks, patio with river view. Excellent restaurant. *Open L & D.*

🍺 **Swan** Manor Road, Walton. An imposing riverside pub, licensed since 1770. Young's real ales, buffet and garden. Ⓜ

🍺✗ **Anglers Inn** Anglers Wharf, Manor Road, Walton (227423). A Chef & Brewer Tavern, serving real ale, bar food. River-view restaurant *open Wed–Sat in summer.*

🍺 **Old Manor House** 113 Manor Road, Walton. Courage real ales in pub with fine floral display. Snacks and meals, garden.

✗🍴 **Angelo's** 70 Terrace Road, Walton (241964). Good pasta, seafood and excellent sweets. Children's helpings. *L & D.* (Reserve D). *Closed Sun.*

🍺 **Flower Pot Hotel** Thames Street, Sunbury. 14thC pub. Snacks.

🍺 **White Horse** Thames Street, Sunbury. Bar meals, garden.

🍺 **Magpie** Thames Street, Sunbury. Choice of real ales, bar food and snacks, garden. Ⓜ

🍺 **Weir** Towpath opposite Sunbury Weir. Large modernised pub with garden. Courage real ale, snacks and meals.

Sunbury Court Island is lined with immaculate chalets: opposite and to the east is a vast area of reservoirs and waterworks behind green grassy banks. Below Platt's Eyot is Hampton, where the ferry still survives under the care of George Kenton, and the church stands right by the river. Bushy Park stretches away to the north east: in the river are Tagg's and Ash Islands, lined with smart moored craft and eccentric houseboats. The large Swiss chalet behind Tagg's Island is part of Hucks Boatyard. Below Hampton Bridge is the Palace, standing close to the river, but separated from it by an extremely long red brick wall. Thames Ditton Island is absolutely packed with bungalows and chalets. The river becomes very wide as it curves past Thames Ditton and the floating pontoons of a large boatyard.

NAVIGATIONAL NOTES

Molesey Lock (01-979 4482).
268ft 4in × 24ft 10in. Fall 6ft 1in. R S W
Pump-out (coin-operated), ladies toilet.

NOTES FOR WALKERS

Walkers on this stretch may have the rare pleasure of using a ferry, to cross from Hurst Park to visit Hampton village. If you stand and wave, George Kenton's will come to bring you across. You may then follow the A308 to Hampton Court. The towpath is continuous to Hampton Court Bridge, but not nearly such fun. Below the bridge, the towpath continues on the north bank.

Hampton

Middx. Shops, launderette. An attractive late 18thC village, still linked by ferry to the south bank, whose heart remains intact despite much new development. The riverside is dominated by the church, built in 1831 by Lapidge. It contains a good modern window by Eric Fraser. Despite the proximity of Hampton Court, the village

Hampton Court

owes its existence to Hampton House. Bought by David Garrick in 1754, the house was subsequently altered by Adam. By the river is Garrick's Temple, built to house Roubiliac's bust of Shakespeare. Nearby, the large and incongruous Swiss chalet owned by Hucks really is Swiss – it was brought over in 1899. To the west of the town the river bank is taken up by a vast waterworks. The buildings range in style from impressive official Italianate to plain 20thC brick. Facing Hampton across the river is Hurst Park, compact new housing on the site of the former race course.

East Molesey

Surrey. EC Wed. PO, shops, launderette. A not unattractive town facing the river and Hampton Court. The riverside is good, and Molesey Lock is a natural magnet for strollers. The name derives from 'Muleseg' – Mūl's Island.

Hampton Court Palace

Middx. (01-977 8441). Probably the greatest secular building in England. Cardinal Wolsey, son of an Ipswich butcher, was graced by ambition and ability to such an extent that at the age of 40 he had an income of £50,000 a year. He was thus able to build the grandest private house in England. Work began in 1514. Henry VIII was offended by the unashamed ostentation of his lieutenant and in 1529, following Wolsey's downfall and his failure to secure the annulment of Henry VIII's first marriage, the king took over the house. Henry spent more on Hampton Court than on any other building, establishing it as a Royal Palace. Subsequently Wren added to it, but little work has been done since. Unlike Windsor, Hampton Court survived the 19thC relatively intact. Today it is occupied by

116 Hampton Court

Grace and Favour residents and people who work at the palace. In the formal gardens (at their best in *mid-May*) are the Great Vine, planted in 1789, and the Maze where Harris, one of Jerome K. Jerome's *Three Men in a Boat*, got hopelessly lost along with 20 followers and a keeper. *Open daily. Closed Christmas, Boxing Day and Jan 1. Charge for house, grounds free.* Teas in the grounds. Boat trips from Westminster Pier *Jun–Sep* (01-930 4721). Behind the palace is Bushy Park, enclosing 2000 acres. A formal design reminiscent of Versailles, it is famous for deer. The Palace Boathouse by the bridge hires out rowing boats by the hour.

toilets. Port Hampton, also on Platt's Eyot, provides long-term mooring, winter storage, slipway and dry dock.
Ⓑ**Constable's Boat House** 15 Thames Street, Hampton. (01-941 4858). Day hire, boat and engine repairs, welding.
Ⓑ**George Kenton** Hampton Ferry Boatyard, Thames Street, Hampton. (01-979 4712). Ⓦ Gas, hire craft, long-term mooring, winter storage, some boat sales, toilets. Also operates Hampton Ferry.
Ⓑ**Thames Voyages** Hampton Court Road, Hampton. (01-941 2676). ⓇⓌ Gas, hire craft, long-term mooring, winter storage, slipway, chandlery, books and maps, boat building,

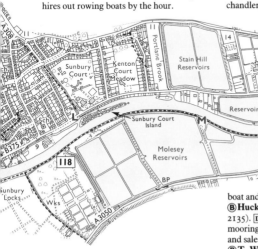

Hampton Green
Middx. A fine series of buildings round the green. Most are 18thC, but some are earlier. By the green is Hampton Court Bridge, built by Lutyens in 1933.
Thames Ditton
Surrey. EC Wed. PO, shops, launderette. The centre of this unspoilt riverside village has somehow kept at bay the usual careless development of the Surrey bank. The church is in the midst of an excellent graveyard and garden where the peace is only broken by the eternal jets from Heathrow. Inside are several good brasses. The huge pendulum of the tower clock swings exceedingly slow and loud, guaranteed to throw any vicar out of his stride. By the river are some pretty whitewashed houses around the suspension bridge to Thames Ditton Island.

BOATYARDS

Ⓑ**Hampton Marine** Platt's Eyot, Lower Sunbury Road, Hampton. (01-979 3447). ⓌⒹ Gas, chandlery, provisions, books and maps, boat and engine sales and repairs,

boat and engine repairs and sales, toilets. Ⓜ
Ⓑ**Hucks & Co** Hampton Court. (01-979 2135). Ⓓ Gas (Calor & Shell), long-term mooring, slipway, dry dock, boat building and sales, boat and engine repairs, toilets.
Ⓑ**T. W. Allen & Son (Yachts)** Ash Island, Hampton Court. (01-979 1997). ⓇⓈⓌ Pump-out, gas, hire craft, day hire boats, long-term mooring, winter storage, slipway, books and maps, boat building, boat and engine sales and repairs, toilets, showers. *Closed winter weekends.* Ⓜ
Ⓑ**Maidboats** Ferry Yacht Station, Thames Ditton. (01-398 0271). ⓇⓈⓌⒹ Pump-out, gas, hire craft, slipway, books and maps, boat building, boat and engine sales and repairs, toilets. Ⓜ

MOORING

Free moorings on the towpath side about a mile below Sunbury Lock by Molesey Reservoirs and on the towpath at West Molesey Wharf, opposite Platt's Eyot. Below Hampton Bridge there are moorings for visitors to Hampton Court Palace, plus 24hr moorings close by (enlivened, until about 23.00, by the thumping 'disco boats').

PUBS AND RESTAURANTS

🍺 **Bell** 8 Thames Street, Hampton. Right by the church and overlooking the river, this small pub serves Taylor Walker real ale.

White Hart 70 High Street, Hampton.
Single bar pub with a wide range of real ales.
Cardinal Wolsey The Green, Hampton
Court. Fuller's real ales and bar meals in a
pub by the stables and the green.
King's Arms Lion Gate, Hampton Court
Road. Good choice of real ales and excellent
food in a superbly situated pub adjoining the
Palace wall. Fine interiors. Children
welcome.
Mitre Hotel Hampton Court Bridge.
(01-979 2264). A Berni Inn serving Bass and
Truman's real ales in 'the Toye Inn'.
Restaurant *open L & D*. Garden.
Crown Inn Summer Road, Thames
Ditton. Watney's real ales and excellent bar
food in a friendly pub just over the river
from Hampton Court.
Bistro Etoile 41 Bridge Road, East
Molesey. (01-979 2309). French and English
food in a nice old fashioned atmosphere.
Open L & D (closed Sat L).
Lantern 20 Bridge Road, East Molesey.
(01-979 1531). Excellent authentic French
food and mouthwatering sweets. Realistic
wine lists. *Open L & D (closed L Mon & Sat,*

L & D Sun). Reserve. Children's helpings.
Albany Queen's Road, Thames Ditton.
Bass Charrington's real ales in a distinctive
riverside pub, which was once a farmhouse.
This part of the river is called 'Albany
Reach'. Garden. M
Swan Hotel Summer Road, Thames
Ditton. (01-398 1814). Riverside pub behind
Thames Ditton Island serving Truman's real
ale. Carvery restaurant *(closed Sat L, Sun D
& Mon)* and snacks.

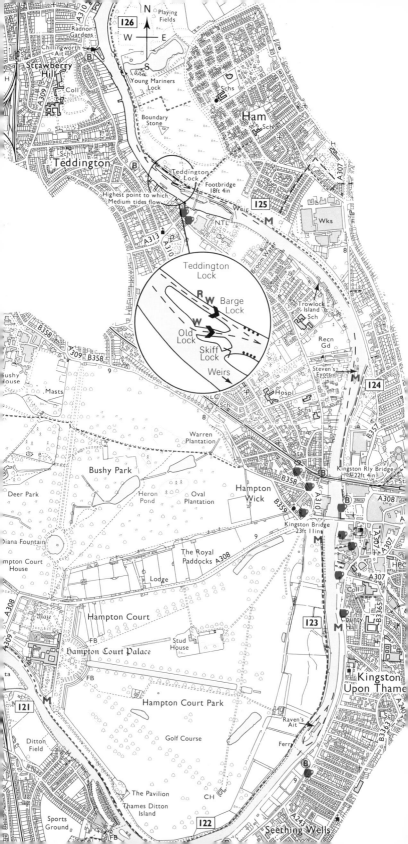

As the river turns north it bisects the parkland of Hampton Court and the housing and industry of Surbiton and Kingston. Queen's Promenade, Kingston, is busy with walkers and sunbathers during the summer, and rowing boats can be hired by the hour from here. Above the five-arched Kingston Road Bridge and the railway bridge the Thames is dominated by the twin chimneys of Kingston Power Station. Approaching Teddington there is a profusion of rowing, sailing and canoe clubs, resulting in a good deal of activity on the water. Teddington Lock and Weir, the lowest on the river controlled by Thames Water, is particularly attractive, with a tree-lined east bank, and the long and dramatic weir stretching round to the west side. It is here that the flow of the River Thames can be monitored precisely (up to 15,000 million gallons per day in times of flood). By the weir are Thames Television studios. 265yds below Teddington Lock, on the east bank, an obelisk marks the boundary of the jurisdiction of Thames Water and the Port of London Authority.

NAVIGATIONAL NOTES

Teddington Locks (01-940 8723). *Barge:* 650ft 0in × 24ft 9in. *Old:* 177ft 11in × 24ft 4in. *Skiff:* 49ft 6in × 5ft 10in. *Fall:* 8ft 10in. R W Traffic moving upstream must observe the light signals at the end of the lock island.
1. Central red lights – Barge and Old Lock closed.
2. Flashing red arrow pointing left – Barge Lock not ready.
Flashing white arrow pointing left – Barge Lock ready.
3. Flashing red arrow pointing right – Old Lock not ready.
Flashing white arrow pointing right – Old Lock ready.
4. Those using the Skiff Lock should follow the lock keeper's instructions.
Max draught: 6ft 6in.
The river is tidal below Teddington Lock for 2 hours each side of high water.

NOTES FOR WALKERS

Walkers should keep to the Hampton Court side, following Pavilion Terrace and the Barge Walk to Kingston Bridge. Unfortunately not much of the park can be seen, due to a very long brick wall and thick trees. There is, however, usually plenty of activity on the river, and parts of the Kingston waterfront are attractive. Those who would like to walk through Kingston may take the ferry above Raven's Ait, operated by Hart's Boatyard. At Kingston Bridge walkers must cross to the east and make a short detour by road to join the path before the railway bridge. Passing to the front of the massive power station the path continues on the east to Teddington and on to Richmond. Access to Teddington is via the footbridge at the lock.

Kingston upon Thames
Surrey. EC Wed. All shops and services. A Royal Borough where seven Saxon kings were crowned. The coronation stone is displayed outside the Guildhall. There is a good river frontage, centred round the stone bridge built 1825–8 by Lapidge. Away from the river the market place is the centre of the town, which suffers badly from traffic but still looks pretty, containing buildings of all periods, the Italianate Town Hall, 1838–40, being the most striking. London Road includes good 18thC buildings and the largely Tudor Lovekyn chapel. Note also the five conduit houses built by Cardinal Wolsey to supply water to Hampton Court. Coombe, to the east, was the home of John Galsworthy (1867–1933), author of *The Forsyte Saga*. One of his houses, Coombe Leigh, in George Road, is now a school – it is thought Forsyte House was modelled on this building and its (then) surroundings.

Teddington
Middx. PO, shops, launderette. An unremarkable town where R. D. Blackmore (1825–1900), author of *Lorna Doone* lived from 1860. The site of his house, Gomer House, is at the end of Doone Close, near the station. The tiny parish church, largely 18thC, is dwarfed by the incomplete bulk of St Alban's, a church of unnecessary size. The riverside, viewed from the Surrey bank, is one of Teddington's most pleasing aspects. The Thames Television studios stand in Broom Road, near the weir.

BOATYARDS
Ⓑ **Maidboats** – see page 116.
Ⓑ **Thames Marina** Portsmouth Road, Thames Ditton. (01-398 6159). R S W P D Gas, long-term mooring, winter storage, slipway, crane, chandlery, books and maps, clothing, boat building, boat and engine repairs and sales, toilets. *Closed winter Sun.* M

120 Kingston upon Thames

ⒷRacing Sailboats Hart's Boatyard, Portsmouth Road, Surbiton. (01-399 2113). W Pump-out, long-term mooring, slipway, boat and engine repairs, toilets. Ferry to Home Park. *Closed Sun and winter afternoons.*

ⒷTurks of Kingston Thames Side, Kingston. (01-546 2434). R S W D Pump-out, long-term mooring, boat building and repair, toilets. *Closed winter weekends.* M

ⒷTough Bros Teddington Wharf, Teddington. (01-977 4494). R W Long-term mooring, winter storage, slipway, crane, boat building and sales, boat and engine repairs, toilets. *Closed weekends.* M

ⒷSwan Island Harbour 1 Strawberry Vale, Twickenham. (01-892 2861). R S W D Gas, winter storage, long-term mooring, slipway, boat and engine sales and repairs, toilets, showers. *Closed Sun.* M

MOORING

There are good moorings on the Kingston waterfront, at Stevens Eyot, and on the towpath side above Teddington Lock.

BOAT TRIPS

Turks of Kingston Thames Side, Kingston. (01-546 2434). Several craft available for party hire, carrying up to 175 passengers. Also a regular *summer* service to Hampton Court.

PUBS AND RESTAURANTS

✕❢ **Ayudhya** 14 Kingston Hill, Kingston. (01-549 5984). Authentic Thai food in tropical atmosphere and comfortable surroundings. *Open L & D, closed Mon.*

🍺 **Fox & Hounds** 60 Portsmouth Road, Surbiton. Courage real ales and *lunchtime* bar food. Near Hart's boatyard.

🍺 **Kingston Mill** High Street, Kingston. Choice of real ales, and *lunchtime* bar meals in pub overlooking the Thames.

🍺 **Ram** 34 High Street, Kingston. Courage real ales and *lunchtime* bar meals. This comfortable pub also has a garden.

🍺 **Bishop out of Residence** Bishop's Hall, Thames Street, Kingston. A modern Young's pub overlooking the Thames. *Lunchtime* bar food.

✕❢ **Deep Pan Pizza** 149 Clarence Street, Kingston. (01-546 1469). Wide choice of pizzas – original or deep pan – and good selection of salads. *L & D.*

✕ **Clouds** 6 Kingston Hill, Kingston. (01-546 0559). A cheerful café with a wide ranging menu. Good sweets. *Open daily to 23.00.*

🍺 **Swan** High Street, Hampton Wick. Courage real ale and *lunchtime* bar meals.

🍺 **Foresters** High Street, Hampton Wick. Large pub serving Ind Coope and Taylor Walker's real ales. *Lunchtime* bar meals.

🍺 **Anglers** Broom Road, Teddington. Next door to Thames Television. Choice of five real ales, riverside garden and bar food. M

🍺 **Tide End Cottage** 8 Ferry Road, Teddington. Mann's real ale, bar meals and a pleasant patio.

As the river passes Eel Pie Island and enters Horse Reach, Richmond Hill can be seen rising gently from the east bank, with the large Star & Garter Home dominating the view. To the west lies Marble Hill Park. The

Teddington Lock

river is the focal point of Richmond – indeed the view of the river from Richmond Hill is dramatic and much photographed.

Richmond Bridge is an elegant and slightly humped 18thC structure, one of the prettiest bridges on the river.

Beyond the railway bridge is Richmond half-tide lock, the movable weir and footbridge, built in 1894 (see 'Navigating the Tidal Thames' page 127) – its gaily painted arches belie its more serious function of tide control. Curving around the Old Deer Park, Isleworth Ait is passed, with the old village and church close by the river to the north. Behind wooded and muddy banks is Syon Park, and opposite are the Royal Botanic Gardens, Kew, a mass of trees when seen from the river. Immediately below Brentford Dock Marina is the entrance to the Grand Union Canal, a direct link with Birmingham. On the north bank at Kew is Strand-on-the-Green, a cluster of desirable houses and fashionable pubs facing the towpath. It may be possible to moor opposite the Kew Toll House, by prior arrangement with the Assistant Harbour Master who is based here (01-940 8288). The Oxford and Cambridge Boat Race finish is below Chiswick Bridge, the line being marked by piles and the University Stone. The handsome Barnes Railway Bridge marks the start of Corney Reach. There are two pubs below the bridge and some shops. Landing may be possible here.

NOTES FOR WALKERS

An absolutely splendid section for walking. The path keeps to the south side throughout, with only a short detour from the river at Richmond. There is a ferry link with Marble Hill Park. No one should miss the opportunity to climb Richmond Hill to enjoy one of the classic views of the river, and Richmond village is very rewarding. Kew Gardens should also be visited. Across the river is Strand-on-the-Green, with its fine houses and pubs. Barnes Railway Bridge is accompanied by a foot crossing, and walkers can choose which bank they take to reach Hammersmith – those who enjoy pubs will prefer the north.

Ham

Surrey. Built round the common, Ham has houses of all periods, but, apart from Ham House the most interesting are 20thC. Parkleys Estate, by Eric Lyons, 1954–6, is one of the most striking housing developments in Surrey.

Ham House (01-940 1950). A superb 17thC riverside mansion, the exterior largely by Sir John Vavassour. Inside, the 17thC plasterwork is remarkable. It contains a collection of period furniture. *Open 11.00–17.00 Tue–Sun. Charge.*

Twickenham

Middx. All shops and services. One of the most elegant and desirable areas in the 18thC, Twickenham has since disappeared under waves of suburbia. However, the area around St Mary's Church remains relatively intact. The vigorous church, with its three-storey tower, dates largely from 1714. Alexander Pope has many connections with Twickenham. In the church there are monuments to him and to his parents. The surviving glory of Twickenham is

Richmond Bridge

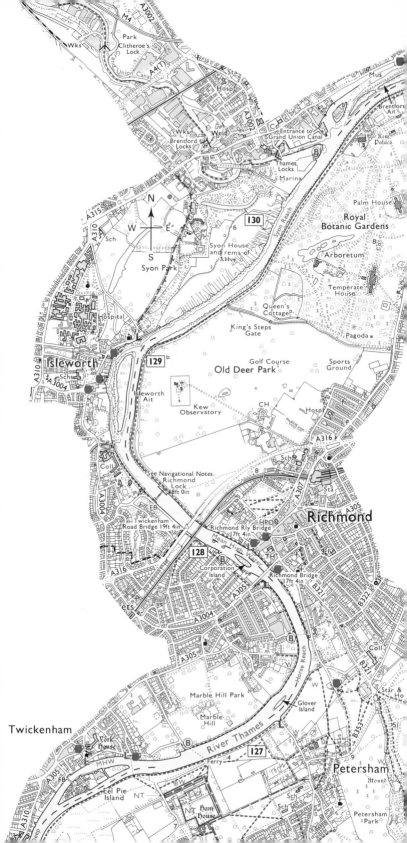

Strawberry Hill, Walpole's Gothic fantasy, and one of the earliest examples of the 18thC Gothic revival. It is still as charming and convincing a case for the revival as when it was built. Designed first by John Chute and Richard Bentley between 1753–63, and later by Thomas Pitt, the house has a strong feeling of unity. It well expresses Walpole's appreciation of Gothic forms and spirit. The interior is the most successful part. It now houses St Mary's Training College and can be viewed only by appointment.

Tourist Information Centre District Library, Garfield Road, Twickenham (01-892 0032).

Marble Hill House Restored Palladian mansion, built by George II for his mistress, Henrietta Howard. Fine collection of early Georgian furniture and pictures. The house stands in parklands which run down to the river. *Open daily. Charge.* Open-air concerts on *summer Sun evenings.*

In the grounds are York House, built about 1700, and the Octagon of Orleans House. York House is now the Municipal Offices. Nearby is a rather astonishing group of statuary: a life representation of either the Birth of Venus or the Pearl Fishers.

Eel Pie Island Twickenham. In Edwardian days the hotel on the island ran tea dances. In the 1960s it housed a noisy night club which featured popular rock groups, including the Rolling Stones.

Petersham
Surrey. But for the traffic, this would be one of the most elegant village suburbs near London. It is exceptionally rich in fine houses of the late 17th and 18thC. These are not visible from the river, but Douglas House, 1700, close to the east drive of Ham House, and Rutland Lodge, 1740, both in River Lane, are not far away from the Thames.

Richmond upon Thames
Surrey. EC Wed. All shops and services. One of the prettiest riverside towns in the London area. Built up the side of the hill, Richmond has been able to retain its Georgian elegance and still has the feeling of an 18thC resort.

Richmond Green is the centre, both aesthetically and socially. Perhaps the most beautiful green in any town in England, it is surrounded by early 18thC houses. Only the brick and terracotta theatre, built in 1899, breaks the pattern; so deliberately that it is almost refreshing. By the green is the site of Richmond Palace, a Royal residence built by Henry VII after 1497 out of the earlier Sheen Palace. It was largely derelict by the mid 17thC and today nothing survives but the gateway. Behind the gate, in Old Palace Yard, is The Trumpeter's House. This magnificent building with 11 bays is c1708 and shows a strong Wren influence. Richmond Hill continues the 18thC tradition. Dominated by the neo-Georgian bulk of the Star & Garter Home, the hill has marvellous views over the river and the scenery around. Richmond Theatre, The Green, Richmond (01-940 0088) shows productions from London's West End and touring companies.

Tourist Information Centre Central Library, Little Green, Richmond (01-940 9125).

Richmond Park 2000 acres in area, the park was first enclosed by Charles I. Stocked with deer, it remained a favourite hunting ground till the 18thC. Private shooting stopped in 1904 but hunting lodges can still be seen. White Lodge, built for George II in 1727, now houses the Royal Ballet School. Today the park is a recreation area, famous for walking and riding. *Open 07.00–dusk.* The Observatory, 1729 by William Chambers, in the Old Deer Park is a building of scientific interest. The three obelisks nearby were used to measure London's official time.

Richmond Bridge This fine stone bridge with its five arches and parapet is one of the most handsome on the Thames and was frequently the subject for paintings in the 18th–19thC. Built in the classical style by James Paine, 1777, it replaced the earlier horse ferry and was a toll bridge until 1859. In 1937 it was skilfully widened without loss of character.

Richmond Railway Bridge Typical of the early railway period, this iron and concrete bridge by Locke was built in 1848 as part of the Richmond–Staines–Windsor line. It should be compared with Barnes Railway Bridge by the same designer.

Twickenham Bridge This wide concrete structure by Maxwell Ayrton carries the Chertsey Arterial Road and was opened in 1933.

Isleworth
Middx. This village with its 17th and 18thC houses is at its prettiest from the river before Syon House is reached. Church Street, with the 15thC tower of All Saints' Church, the London Apprentice Inn and a few Georgian houses, makes a charming setting.

Syon Park Park Road, Brentford, Middx. (01-560 0881). Built on the site of a 15thC convent, the present square structure with its corner turrets is largely 16thC, although the house was entirely refaced in 1825. It is mainly of interest on account of the interior decoration by Robert Adam, 1761. Close to the house is the Garden Centre, whose only contribution aesthetically has been to fill the fine 18thC glasshouse by Fowler with exotic plants. The grounds of the house extend to the river where there is an elegant boat house with Ionic columns, attributed to Capability Brown. Also of interest in the grounds are the Vintage Motor Museum and the Butterfly House which has a huge variety of live butterflies and insects from all over the world. *Open 12.00–17.00 G. Fri to Sep, closed Fri & Sat. Charge. Gardens open daily throughout the year. Charge.*

Royal Botanic Gardens Kew Road, Richmond. (01-940 1171). Apart from their exceptional botanic interest, the gardens are of historic importance, being the consecutive work of two ages, the mid 18th and the mid 19thC. As a national institution, they originated when part of the gardens of Richmond Lodge, 1700, by Capability Brown, and of Kew Palace, mid 18thC by

Chambers, were taken over by the State and enlarged under Sir William and Sir Joseph Hooker in 1841. A large part of the charm of the gardens today lies in the presence of the 18thC temples and 19thC glasshouses, the Orangery and Kew Palace. The Palace, or

Dutch House, built by the merchant, Samuel Fortry, 1631, is a gabled brick house close to the river and typical of the style favoured by London merchants at this period. The new Princess of Wales Glasshouse, opened in 1987, contains herbaceous plants from the tropics. *Open daily. Small charge.*

Kew Bridge The bridge was opened by Edward VII in 1903 and is officially called the King Edward VII Bridge. Designed by Sir John Wolfe Barry and Cuthbert Brereton, it replaced the earlier 18thC bridge and is a fine stone structure with three spans.

Kew Railway Bridge When it was opened in 1869 this five-span lattice girder bridge was part of the London and South-Western Railway extension. It was designed by W. R. Galbraith.

Kew
Surrey. Old Kew centres round the green with its 18thC houses and the entrance to the Botanic Gardens at one end. The church of St Anne is partly 18thC but greatly altered in the 19thC.

Grand Union Canal
Leaving the Thames at Brentford, this is the 'backbone' of the English canal system – an amalgamation of no less than eight separate canals. The original course, built at the turn of the 18thC, was the Grand Junction Canal. Built to a wide (14ft 0in) gauge, it was profitable until the 1930s. Extensively used by pleasure craft, there is still barge traffic at the London end. See 'Navigating the Tidal Thames', p127.

Musical Museum St George's Church, High Street, Brentford (01-560 8108). A fascinating collection of automatic, old and odd musical instruments. A conducted tour during which many of the instruments are played lasts approximately 1½ hours and starts at *14.30 on Sat & Sun Apr–Sep. Donation.*

Kew Bridge Steam Museum Green Dragon Lane, Brentford (01-568 4757). Working beam engines, the oldest being built in 1820, are fired up at weekends. *Open daily 11.00–17.00. Charge.*

Chiswick
West London. Chiswick stretches between Kew Bridge and Hammersmith Terrace and provides some of the most picturesque scenery anywhere on the river near London. Its Georgian houses extend along Strand-on-the-Green and again at Chiswick Mall. Between these points the grounds of three large 18thC mansions originally extended to the river: Grove House, Sutton Court and Chiswick House. Only Chiswick House remains. The site of Grove House has been built over. Duke's Meadows, part of the grounds of Chiswick House, is now a recreation ground by the river. Chiswick Cemetery backs on to St Nicholas Church where Lord Burlington and William Kent are buried.

Chiswick Bridge Built in 1933, this bridge has the longest concrete arch of any bridge on the Thames. The centre span measures 150ft. Designed by Sir Herbert Baker, it was opened by the Prince of Wales.

Chiswick House Burlington Lane W4. (01-994 3299). Lord Burlington so admired Palladio's Villa Capra at Vicenza that he modelled Chiswick House on it when it was built 1725–9. The interior decoration is by Kent. The gardens, by Bridgeman and Kent, still have fine statuary. *Open daily. Closed Mon all year and Tue in winter. Charge.*

Mortlake
London. In the 17thC Mortlake was famous for its tapestry works of which little remains. But some of the tapestries can be seen in the Victoria & Albert Museum. The riverside is picturesque along Thames Bank where there is a fine group of 18thC houses.

Barnes Railway Bridge This light and elegant iron bridge by Locke was opened in 1849 to connect with the Richmond line. Its design is similar to Richmond Railway Bridge.

Oxford v Cambridge Boat Race On a *Saturday in March or April* this famous annual event is held over a 4-mile course from Putney to Mortlake. Get to the riverside early for a good view.

Richmond Lock

BOATYARDS

Ⓑ **W. Hammerton** Ferry Boat House, Marble Hill Park, Twickenham. (01-892 9620). Rowing boat hire, long-term mooring, chandlery, boat sales. Ⓜ

Ⓑ **Brentford Marine Sales** The Boathouse, Justin Close, Brentford. (01-568 0287). Ⓡ Ⓢ Ⓦ Long-term mooring, winter storage, chandlery, provisions, books and maps, boat and engine repairs, boat sales, outboard sales.

Ⓑ **Richmond Slipways** 1 Ducks Walk, Twickenham. (01-892 5062). Ⓡ Ⓦ Long-term mooring, winter storage, slipway, boat sales. Ⓜ

Ⓑ **Petersham Boat Services** Petersham Road, Richmond. (01-940 0173). Ⓦ Ⓟ Rowing boat hire, long-term mooring, second-hand books and some chandlery, boat building, boat and engine sales and repairs. *Closed Mon.* Ⓜ

Ⓑ **Bason & Arnold** 76 Grove Park Road, Chiswick W4. (01-994 2431/2100). Ⓦ Ⓟ Ⓓ Slipway, chandlery, books and maps, boat and engine sales and repairs. *Closed Sun.*

BOAT TRIPS

See special section on page 18.

PUBS AND RESTAURANTS

🍺✕ **Pope's Grotto** Cross Deep, Twickenham. (01-892 3050). Young's real ale in a comfortable modern pub by the river. Restaurant, bar food and courtyard at the back.

🍺 **Eel Pie** 9 Church Street, Twickenham. Plain low-ceilinged pub with a wide choice of real ales, excellent *lunchtime* bar food.

🍺 **White Swan** Riverside, Twickenham. A startlingly attractive black and white balconied pub, bright with geranium and lobelia in summer. Plain and comfy inside, it stands right on the river edge. Choice of real ales, good *lunchtime* bar food and occasional music.

🍺 **Rose of York** Petersham Road, Richmond. Sam Smith's real ale, bar meals and garden. This pub used to be the Tudor Close.

🍺 **Christies Tavern** 1–3 Hill Rise, Richmond Bridge. Choice of real ales in modern Victorian-style pub. Bar food, disco upstairs.

🍺 **Waterman's Arms** 12 Water Lane, Richmond. A small cosy pub in a cobbled riverside street. *Lunchtime* food, garden.

🍺✕ **White Cross** Riverside, Richmond. (01-940 0909). Young's real ales, *lunchtime* bar meals and separate restaurant in a friendly riverside pub with a garden.

✕🍷 **Red Lion** 18 Red Lion Street, Richmond. (01-940 2371). Competent and friendly Chinese restaurant. *D* (Reserve).

✕🍷 **The Refectory** 6 Church Walk, Richmond. (01-940 6264). Good, tasty and filling English fare in a pretty restaurant, with tables in the garden in summer. (*Closed Mon*).

✕🍷 **Pizza Express** 20 Hill Street, Richmond. (01-940 8951). A wide choice of pizzas at reasonable prices. *L & D.*

✕🍷 **Mrs Beeton's** 58 Hill Rise, Richmond.

(01-940 9561). Home-baked cakes, soups and salads, and more substantial food in the evenings.

🍺 **Castle** 18 Upper Square, Isleworth. Large Young's pub serving *lunchtime* bar food.

🍺 **Inn on the Square** Lower Square, Isleworth. Good choice of real ales.

🍺✕ **London Apprentice** 62 Church Street, Isleworth. (01-560 1915). 15thC riverside pub with Elizabethan and Georgian interiors, and prints of Hogarth's 'Apprentices' on the walls. English restaurant. *Closed Sun, D Mon, L Sat.*

🍺✕ **Orange Tree** 45 Kew Road, Richmond. (01-940 0944). Good value European food plus additional attraction of theatre upstairs. *L & D. Performances Mon–Sat Sep–Apr.*

🍺 **Royal Tar** 3 High Street, Brentford. A very large range of real ales in a very small pub. Bar food.

🍺 **Plough** 24 Kew Bridge Road, Brentford. Courage real ale and excellent bar meals.

🍺 **Rose & Crown** 79 Kew Green, Kew. Large 20thC mock-Tudor pub with garden. Courage real ale and *lunchtime* food.

🍺 **Greyhound** 82 Kew Green, Kew. Small 20thC mock-Tudor pub. Courage real ale and *lunchtime* food.

🍺✕ **Coach & Horses** 8 Kew Green, Kew. (01-940 1208). Large Young's pub with an à la carte restaurant (*L daily, D Wed–Sat*) and garden. *Lunchtime* bar meals and *evening* snacks.

✕ **Original Maids of Honour Shop** 288 Kew Road, Kew Green. (01-940 2752). Long established tea shop serving delicious cream cakes and maids of honour, along with a substantial set lunch. *Open daily (closed Sun & Mon afternoons & evenings).*

✕🍷 **Le Provence** 14 Station Parade, Kew. (01-940 6777). Good French provincial food. *Closed Sun, Mon, mid Aug–mid Sep.*

🍺 **Steam Packet** 85 Strand-on-the-Green, Chiswick, W4. Courage real ale, *lunchtime* food and garden. Overlooks the river.

🍺✕ **City Barge** 27 Strand-on-the-Green, Chiswick, W4. (01-994 2148). A popular old pub of great character dating from 1484, right on the towpath, serving Courage real ales and *lunchtime* food in the downstairs restaurant.

🍺 **Bulls Head** 15 Strand-on-the-Green, Chiswick, W4. Riverside pub serving Watney's and Websters real ales.

🍺 **Ship** 10 Thames Bank, Mortlake, SW14. At high water spring tides, the water laps at this riverside pub, which has suitably nautical decor. Watney's real ale, *lunchtime* food and outside drinking. The boat race finishes near here.

🍺 **White Hart** The Terrace, Riverside, Barnes SW13. Riverside Young's pub. *Lunchtime* bar meals and garden.

🍺 **Waterman's Arms** 375 Lonsdale Road, Barnes SW13. Small riverside pub serving Watney's real ale.

🍺✕ **Bull's Head** 373 Lonsdale Road, Barnes SW13. (01-876 5241). Attractive, large Young's pub famous worldwide for its jazz (*every evening and lunchtime on Sat & Sun*). Separate restaurant serving English food (*L & D*) and bar lunches.

From **Richmond** to **Limehouse** navigation on the Thames is far more complex than on the upper reaches. The river here is a commercial waterway first and foremost and pleasure craft must take much greater care. The River Thames below Teddington is controlled by the Port of London Authority which produces a useful set of free notes, *The Pleasure Users' Guide to the Tidal Thames*.

For general navigational enquiries about the river contact the Assistant Harbour Master, Tower Pier, London EC3N 4DT (01-481 0720).

While hire companies do not allow their craft to be taken below Teddington Lock, there may be many owners of pleasure boats who wish to make the passage from the Thames to the canal system via Brentford or Limehouse, and with proper planning this should present no particular difficulties. Obviously the short Teddington to Brentford passage is the simpler of the two.

DO NOT, HOWEVER, UNDERTAKE THE JOURNEY IF:

1. You have any doubts regarding your boat handling ability in tidal waters.
2. Your boat is underpowered, unreliable or unseaworthy.

THOSE WHO DO WISH TO MAKE THE JOURNEY SHOULD NOTE THE FOLLOWING:

1. High water at Teddington and Brentford is 1 hour later than London Bridge.
2. Spring tides are best avoided. Choose neap tides.
3. Choose a calm, clear day.
4. Make sure your boat has an anchor and warp, a reliable engine, adequate fuel and reserve fuel.
5. Know the sound signals, and keep to the right.
6. Wear lifejackets.
7. Study the tide tables.

TEDDINGTON TO BRENTFORD

Phone the lock keeper at Brentford (01-560 1120) to let him know you are coming. Leave Teddington shortly before or at high water to gain the benefit of the ebbing tide. Arrive at Brentford within 2–2½ hours of high water to pass through the lock. Beware of barge traffic.

BRENTFORD TO TEDDINGTON

Leave Brentford as soon as the lock opens, 2–2½ hours before high water, to gain the benefit of the flood tide.

TEDDINGTON TO LIMEHOUSE BASIN

Leave Teddington at high water to gain the benefit of the ebb tide. Tie up at the holding off moorings outside Limehouse Basin and wait for the lock to open, which will be 3½ hours before the next high water. Phone Limehouse Basin (01-790 3444) and inform them of your intentions.

LIMEHOUSE BASIN TO TEDDINGTON

Pass through the entrance lock at Limehouse as early as possible, 3½ hours before high water, to gain the benefit of the flood tide. *In all the above cases the tidal barrier at Richmond will be open.*

MOORING

There are few opportunites for pleasure craft to moor between Teddington and Limehouse. During the *summer* the piers are generally too busy with trip boats to accommodate casual visitors. If you do wish to stop, you are advised to contact one of the boatyards or marinas listed with the relevant map, to see if they have room for you. The PLA may have certain moorings available – details from the Assistant Harbour Master.

RICHMOND LOCK

(01-940 0634). The only lock on the river operated by the PLA. For 2 hours either side of high water the weirs are lifted and the river up to Teddington is fully tidal. When any of the weirs are down a red disc or light is displayed under each of the three arches but any arch not displaying a red disc or light may be used. If all are red, the half-tide lock must be used (charge). The size of the lock is 250ft 0in × 26ft 8in. There are rollers for small craft.

HEADROOM

On the tidal river the clearance at bridges is given as the maximum at mean high water springs – this is less than the headroom at chart datum (lowest astronomical tide). In practice this means that there will usually be more headroom than that indicated.

DRAUGHT

The depth at the centre span of Westminster Bridge is approximately 2ft 8in at chart datum (about 4ft 0in at mean low water springs). In practice there is usually a greater depth than this – full details are given in the aforementioned PLA publication. The depth at all the other bridges is greater than Westminster.

CANALS

Those who wish to navigate on the adjoining British Waterways Board's canals will require a licence, available from:

Craft Licensing Office
Willow Grange
Church Road
Watford WD1 3QA.
Watford 26422

and a copy of the *Nicholson/OS Guide to the Waterways 1. South*, which gives all navigational details.

The river is flanked by elegant houses at
Hammersmith and Chiswick, but further
downstream it becomes grimy and
industrial, especially in the area of Fulham
Power Station. There is, however, as always
on the lower Thames, plenty of interest. One
of the most bizarre buildings on the whole
river must be Harrod's Depository. A
cupola'd building in the same terracotta as
the main store, it stands proudly near
Hammersmith Bridge. There is a small
wharf in front where a light railway ran
directly into the building. Parkland around
Putney Bridge soon gives way to industry,
relieved at Battersea by the splendid St
Mary's Church at the riverside, opposite
Lots Road Power Station. Albert Bridge,
getting weaker, received support in the form
of a solid pier under its span. Thus was its
light elegant appearance destroyed.

NOTES FOR WALKERS

After the splendid walk around Barnes to
Putney, the Thames towpath terminates,
giving way to road as far as Putney Bridge.
The course of the river can best be followed
through London by keeping to the north
side, and purchasing a *Nicholson's London
Streetfinder* to guide you when detours are
necessary.

NORTH BANK

Hammersmith Terrace

W6. These 16 identical houses with their
gardens running down to the river were built
as a block in 1750. The historian of the
Thames, the late Sir Alan Herbert, lived in
the Terrace.

Upper Mall

W6. Some fine 18thC houses and the 17thC
Ship Inn. William Morris lived in Kelmscott
House between 1878–96.

Lower Mall

W6. This is prettier than the Upper Mall and
characterised by the Rutland and Blue
Anchor pubs, 18thC cottages and a
dilapidated Victorian boat house with a
wrought-iron balcony.

Hammersmith Bridge

Sir Joseph Bazalgette's suspension bridge,
1887, has a distinct personality of its own.
This flows from the partly gilt iron pylons
crowned with fussy pavilion tops, all of
which bestow a sense of frivolity upon it.

Fulham

In the 18th and 19thC Fulham was the fruit
and kitchen garden north of the Thames, but
today little of the fertile village with its great
houses is left and most of Fulham is a sprawl
of buildings. The river bank with Fulham

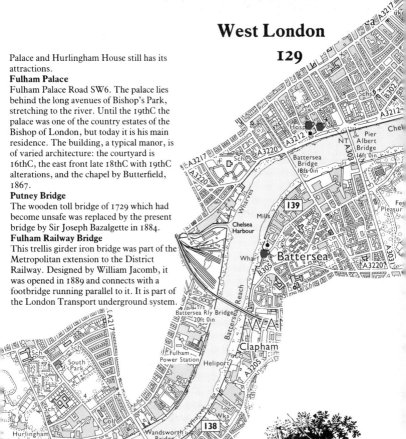

Palace and Hurlingham House still has its attractions.

Fulham Palace

Fulham Palace Road SW6. The palace lies behind the long avenues of Bishop's Park, stretching to the river. Until the 19thC the palace was one of the country estates of the Bishop of London, but today it is his main residence. The building, a typical manor, is of varied architecture: the courtyard is 16thC, the east front late 18thC with 19thC alterations, and the chapel by Butterfield, 1867.

Putney Bridge

The wooden toll bridge of 1729 which had become unsafe was replaced by the present bridge by Sir Joseph Bazalgette in 1884.

Fulham Railway Bridge

This trellis girder iron bridge was part of the Metropolitan extension to the District Railway. Designed by William Jacomb, it was opened in 1889 and connects with a footbridge running parallel to it. It is part of the London Transport underground system.

Hurlingham House

Ranelagh Gardens SW6. This is the only large 18thC residence still surviving in Fulham. The house has a fine river front with Corinthian columns and is now the centre of the Hurlingham Club. Members play tennis, golf and croquet in the grounds.

Wandsworth Bridge

In 1938 the 19thC bridge was replaced with the existing structure by E. P. Wheeler.

Fulham Power Station

SW6. This four-chimneyed edifice by G. E. Baker & Preece, Cardew & Rider, 1936, is a striking landmark.

Chelsea Harbour

A new, expensive development dominated by The Belvedere tower block. The golden ball on its roof slides up and down with the level of the river. The development is still under construction and the offices, restaurants, penthouses and classy moorings will soon be joined by a luxury hotel. Chelsea Wharf, just along the bank, is a collection of business units, mostly involved with the media.

Battersea Railway Bridge

The West London Extension Railway, of which this bridge was a part, was opened in 1863 to connect the south of England directly with the north. The line was the only one which did not end at a London terminus and was therefore a target for bombing in the Second World War.

Lots Road Power Station

Lots Road SW10. This huge and dominating structure was built in 1904 to provide electricity for the new underground railway.

Battersea Bridge

The old Battersea Bridge of 1772 was a picturesque wooden structure much painted by Whistler and Turner. But this bridge of 1890 by Sir Joseph Bazalgette is a grimy iron structure without aesthetic pretension.

Crosby Hall

Cheyne Walk SW3. (01-352 9663). The hostel of the British Federation of University Women is of interest for its hall. Once part of the residence of Sir John Crosby, a 15thC wool merchant in Bishopsgate, the hall, 1466–75, was brought here from Bishopsgate almost in its entirety. It has a sumptuous painted roof and is hung with tapestry and a painted cloth screen. The leather emblazoned chairs are Spanish. *Open 10.00–12.00 and 14.00–16.00, although often closed due to private functions. Free.*

Chelsea Old Church
Cheyne Walk SW3. The church was bombed during the war and rebuilt in 1964. Its interior is of great interest on account of Sir Thomas More's private chapel, 1528, and the many 17thC monuments, all of which escaped destruction.

Cheyne Walk
SW3. The walk is characterised by the houseboats and the 18thC houses of riverside village type, nos 46–48, and terraced architecture, nos 19–26.

Carlyle's House
24 Cheyne Row SW3. (01-352 7087). Once the haunt of writers such as Dickens and Tennyson, and the home of Thomas and Jane Carlyle 1834–81. *Open 11.00–16.30 Wed–Sun, Apr–Oct. Charge.*

Albert Bridge
A delightful 100-year-old suspension bridge connecting Chelsea and Battersea. The bridge was closed during 1972 and 1973 by the GLC, who had it strengthened by a huge solid support under the main span, unfortunately showing scant regard for the original structure. It's a pity it could not have been left as a footbridge.

SOUTH BANK

Barnes Terrace
SW13. Close to the river an attractive village atmosphere pervades. The 18thC houses with their cheerful iron verandas and balconies contrast with the iron railway bridge, 1849, crossing the river at this point. Near the Church of St Mary, Church Road, are more good early 18thC houses.

Castelnau
Barnes is rich in Victorian houses and some of the best are to be seen in Castelnau. Remarkably standardised, they are largely semi-detached and typical of Early Victorian villa architecture with their arched windows.

Barn Elms Park
Barn Elms was originally the mansion of Sir Francis Walsingham, Secretary of State to Elizabeth I. Nothing remains of the house apart from the ornamental pond and the ice house. Until recently the park was used by the Ranelagh Polo Club, but it is now used exclusively as school playing fields.

Putney
The Embankment is picturesque. The London Rowing Club and Westminster School have their boat houses here and the eights and sculls can be seen practising in the afternoon amidst the swans. Each *spring* the Oxford and Cambridge boat race is rowed between Mortlake and Putney. The first race was held at Henley in 1829. Beside Putney Bridge, the badly sited ICL building entirely dwarfs the Church of St Mary, rebuilt by Lapidge in 1836 and damaged by fire some years ago. It is now functioning again.

Wandsworth
Until the 19thC Wandsworth was a village oasis on the River Wandle – a good fishing river – and was noted for a local silk and hat industry. The course of the Wandle can still be traced near the Church of All Saints. The Surrey Iron Railway, whose wagons were drawn by horses, stretched beside the river.

The windmill, which was part of the pumping station for the railway, was sited at the corner of Windmill Road. Today, little remains to point to the past. There are a few Georgian houses in Church Row, but the river bank is a grimy industrial scene. Wandsworth is famous throughout the Home Counties as the home of Young's Brewery.

Battersea
Many of the old riverside warehouses are now gone, leaving the tall tower blocks dominant. Redevelopment is under way.

St Mary's Church
Church Road SW11. The church is one of the few relics of Battersea's 18thC village. Built in 1775 by Joseph Dixon, it is strangely Dutch in character. Inside is some good 17thC glass. From the porch is an outstanding view of Lots Road Power Station and the industrial Thames.

BOATYARDS

Ⓑ **Alan See** Barge Elsie, 21 Lower Mall, Hammersmith W6. (01-748 7738). Long-term mooring, boat and engine sales and repairs. Ⓜ

BOAT TRIPS
See special section on page 18.

PUBS AND RESTAURANTS

🍺 **Black Lion** 2 South Black Lion Lane W6. A lovely 400-year-old riverside pub with a super paved garden. Bar meals.

🍺 **Old Ship** 25 Upper Mall W6. A comfortably modernised large 18thC pub, with lots of red plush and three rowing skiffs as decor. A veranda overlooks the Thames. Watney's real ales, excellent bar meals with changing menu – roast beef, fish, pies and various salads.

🍺 **Dove** 19 Upper Mall W6. A mellow old riverside tavern dating from the reign of Charles II with wooden settles and low ceilings. There is a small terrace with views of the river. Fuller's real ales (since 1796) and good *lunchtime* bar meals.

🍺✕ **Rutland** 15 Lower Mall W6. (01-748 5586). A Watney's pub with a river-view restaurant upstairs (*L & D*).

🍺 **Blue Anchor** 13 Lower Mall W6. Courage real ales and bar meals in a pub overlooking the river, right by Hammersmith Bridge.

🍺 **Ship** Jews Row SW18. Comfortable 19thC pub overlooking the river, just off Wandsworth Bridge. Large garden, barbecues in *summer*. A Young's pub serving bar snacks.

🍺 **Star & Garter** 4 Lower Richmond Road SW15. Large pub near the Putney Bridge slipway, serving Courage real ales and bar meals.

🍺 **Cross Keys** 2 Lawrence Street SW3. 18thC pub on Chelsea Embankment. Courage real ales and bar food. Garden.

🍺✕ **Kings Head & Eight Bells** 50 Cheyne Walk SW3 (01-352 1820). Large smart 400-year-old Chelsea pub overlooking the river. Fremlin and Wethered's real ales, excellent bar meals.

St Mary's Church, Battersea

132 Central London

The River Thames, squeezed between embankments, curves through the heart of the capital, a water highway plied by many trip boats. A voyage on one is the best way of seeing London: no traffic, no fumes and an informative commentary. It is fascinating by day and magical by night. A common sight along the embankments is young boys fishing for dace, roach and eels.

NORTH BANK

Chelsea Embankment
SW3. Chelsea Embankment was made in 1871. No 17 is Norman Shaw's famous Swan House.

Physic Garden
Royal Hospital Road SW3. (01-352 5646). Founded in 1673 by the Apothecaries Society this is the second oldest botanical garden in the UK. There is a replica of the statue of Sir Hans Sloane by Rysbrack, 1733, here. *Open Apr–Oct 14.00–17.00 Wed & Sun. Charge.*

Royal Hospital
Royal Hospital Road SW3. (01-730 0161). The Hospital was founded by Charles II as an institution for invalid and veteran soldiers and built by Wren. Alterations were made in the 18thC by Robert Adam and Sir John Soane. The 200 in-pensioners and the many out-pensioners wear scarlet frock coats in the summer and dark blue overcoats in the winter – a uniform dating from the 18thC.

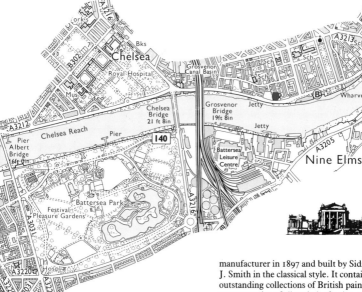

On *Sundays* the pensioners parade at *10.30* in the forecourt in Royal Hospital Road. Visitors may attend the chapel service at 11.00. The museum, hall and chapel are *open 10.00–12.00, 14.00–16.00 Mon–Sat all year; 14.00–16.00 Sun Apr–Sep. Free.*

Tate Gallery
Millbank SW1. (01-821 1313). The gallery was founded by Sir Henry Tate, the sugar manufacturer in 1897 and built by Sidney R. J. Smith in the classical style. It contains outstanding collections of British painting, representative of all periods, foreign painting and British and foreign sculpture dating from 1880 until the present day. Popular exhibitions are arranged regularly. *Open daily. Closed Sun morning. Free.*

Millbank Tower
Millbank SW1. The traditional balance of the river bank has been overturned by this office building by Ronald Ward and Partners, 1963. Whereas the Houses of Parliament originally dominated the Thames, the Millbank Tower – 34 storeys

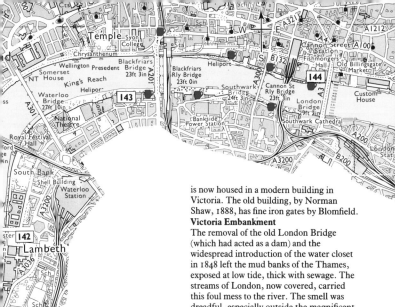

and 387ft high – now rules the north bank as the Shell building rules the south.

Victoria Tower Gardens

Abingdon Street SW1. The gardens are memorable for their sculpture. Rodin's *Burghers of Calais*, 1895, is close to the river and near the entrance stands a monument to Mrs Emmeline Pankhurst and Dame Christabel Pankhurst, champions of the women's suffragette movement in the early 1900s.

Houses of Parliament

Parliament Square SW1. (01-219 3000). Despite their authentic medieval appearance, the Houses of Parliament were

in fact completed in 1860. Attributed to Charles Barry, it is certain that his assistant, Pugin, had a strong influence on the designs. The medieval Palace of Westminster, seat of the Norman kings, once stood on the site. Of this only Westminster Hall remains.

Westminster Abbey

Broad Sanctuary SW1. (01-222 5152). The Abbey has been the burial place of the Kings and Queens of England since the 10thC, but the existing Gothic building dates from the 13thC. It has been greatly restored. It is so rich in architectural and historic interest that the visitor should buy a guide at the door. *Open 08.00–18.00 Mon–Sun.*

Old Scotland Yard

Victoria Embankment SW1. Scotland Yard

is now housed in a modern building in Victoria. The old building, by Norman Shaw, 1888, has fine iron gates by Blomfield.

Victoria Embankment

The removal of the old London Bridge (which had acted as a dam) and the widespread introduction of the water closet in 1848 left the mud banks of the Thames, exposed at low tide, thick with sewage. The streams of London, now covered, carried this foul mess to the river. The smell was dreadful, especially outside the magnificent new Houses of Parliament. In 1863 Joseph Bazalgette started his scheme to clear up this intolerable stench. Three new west–east sewers would intercept the streams running north–south and carry the sewage away. The lowest of these formed part of the new Victoria Embankment, with the District Line Railway incorporated at the same time. It was completed in 1870, Bazalgette was knighted, and his bust is incorporated into the parapet by Hungerford Bridge.

Victoria Embankment Gardens

WC2. *Summer lunchtime* concerts and plays are performed here. Of considerable interest in the gardens is the York Water Gate by Nicholas Stone, 1625. The Water Gate was

the entrance from the Thames to York House, London residence of the Duke of Buckingham in the 17thC.

Cleopatra's Needle

Victoria Embankment SW1. One of a pair erected about 1500BC at Heliopolis, the ancient Egyptian centre of sunworship. The Needle was presented to Britain by Mohammed Ali in 1819 and erected here in 1878 after almost being lost at sea.

Savoy Hotel

Strand WC2. (01-836 4343). The hotel was founded by Richard D'Oyly Carte and built to the designs of T. E. Colcutt. When it opened in 1889 it represented a revolution in comfort and had 70 bathrooms. The builder is reputed to have inquired whether the guests were amphibians! The name was taken from the fact that it was built on part of the site of the old Savoy Palace.

Somerset House

Strand WC2. Built in 1776 by Sir William Chambers on the site of Protector Somerset's house, this magnificent building with its arches, terrace and river entrances decorated with lions and Tuscan columns, was intended to compete with the splendour of

Adam's Adelphi. Once occupied by the General Register Office whose records of birth and death go back to 1836, it now houses the Register of Divorce, Wills and

Probate, and the Inland Revenue. In the east wing is King's College, part of the University of London. On the corner of the gardens following the building on the Embankment is a bronze statue of Brunel by Marochetti, 1866. Brunel was the engineer in charge of the building of the Great Western Railway. His ship, the *Great Eastern*, was launched on the Thames, at Millwall.

The Temple
EC4. The name derives from the Order of Knights Templar who occupied the site from 1160–1308. In the 17thC the Temple was leased to the benchers of the Inner and Middle Temple, two Inns of Court. These inns, together with Lincoln's Inn and Gray's Inn, hold the ancient and exclusive privilege of providing advocates in the courts of England and Wales. To appreciate the Temple Buildings, only a few of which are visible from the river, a visit should be made on foot. On the Embankment, Sir Joseph Bazalgette's arch and stairs mark the 19thC access to the Temple from the river.

City of London
Blocks of offices stretch between Blackfriars, whose name recalls the 13thC monastery of the Dominicans, and London Bridge. In Upper Thames Street there are a number of Wren churches: St Benet's, St Mary's Somerset (tower only), St James Garlickhythe and St Michael Paternoster Royal.

Mermaid Theatre
Puddle Dock EC4. (01-236 5568). The original theatre, the first in the City since the 16thC, was opened in a converted warehouse in 1959 following energetic campaigning by Lord Bernard Miles. It was rebuilt on a new site and reopened in 1981. Bar/buffet.

Vintners Hall
EC4. Built in 1671, but altered in 1870 and 1910, the fine wrought-iron entrance bears two swans. The swans reflect the ancient privilege the Vintners' Company shares with the Dyers' Company of each possessing a game of swans on the Thames. Each *July* a census of the swans on the reaches up to Henley is made. This is known as the 'Swan Upping'. The cygnets are marked with one nick for the Dyers' Company and two nicks for the Vintners'. The Queen's swans are unmarked. Occasionally a swan feast is held. The Swan Warden, with a retinue of officials and musicians playing woodwind instruments, presents roast cygnets to the Master.

Cannon Street Station
EC4. Only the murky red-brick arched train sheds with their monumental towers remain of the great Victorian station by J. Hawkshaw and J. W. Barry. These extend into the river at the railway bridge. The rest of the station has been rebuilt further inland.

Fishmongers' Hall
EC4. Built in the grand classical manner in 1831–4 by Henry Roberts, the Fishmongers' Company administers the annual Doggett's Coat and Badge Race for Thames Watermen. This race, the oldest annual contested sporting event and the longest rowing race in the world (1 furlong short of 5 miles), was introduced in 1715. Doggett, an Irish comedian and staunch Hanoverian, who used the services of the watermen to ferry him to and from the theatres, decided to mark the anniversary of the accession of George I to the throne by instituting an annual race for watermen. The race is from London Bridge to Cadogan Pier, Chelsea, and is usually held *at the end of July*. The victor is presented with a red coat, breeches and cap, and a silver arm badge bearing the words 'The Gift of the late Thomas Doggett'.

The Monument
EC4. (01-626 2717). A 17thC hollow fluted column by Wren, built to commemorate the Great Fire of London. It marked the northern end of the original London Bridge and gives a magnificent view over the city. *Open daily, closed Sun in winter. Charge.*

St Magnus the Martyr
Lower Thames Street EC3. This Wren church, 1687, has an imaginatively detailed steeple, added in 1706 and reaching 185ft high. This contrasts with the sheer modern wall of Adelaide House. The ornate black and gold clock dates from 1709. In the churchyard, once part of the approach to old London Bridge (destroyed in 1831), can be seen stones from the old bridge and also the remains of a Roman wharf. The interior of the church has some of the most sumptuous woodwork to be seen anywhere in the city.

Old Billingsgate Market
Lower Thames Street EC3. The yellow-brick Victorian building with arcaded ground floor was built by Sir Horace Jones, 1875. The first reference to a market at Billingsgate was made in AD870. A free fish market was established by statute in 1699, but until the 18thC coal, corn and provisions were also sold. The fish-porters wore curious leather hats with flat tops and wide brims, formerly known as 'bobbing hats'. Bobbing was the charge made by the porter to carry fish from the wholesaler to the retailer. These hats enabled the porter to carry about a hundredweight of fish on his head. The market moved down river to new premises on the Isle of Dogs in 1982.

The Custom House
Lower Thames Street EC4. A custom house has stood beside Billingsgate since AD870. The present building is by Laing, 1813–17, but the river façade was rebuilt by Smirke in 1825. Badly bombed in the war, the building has been restored. It is suitably official and all of Portland stone and yellow brick.

SOUTH BANK

Battersea Park
SW11. The park was laid out by Sir James Pennethorne as a public garden and opened

by Queen Victoria in 1858. There is a boating lake, a subtropical garden, a children's zoo and sculptures by Moore, Hepworth and Epstein. The famous Easter Parade is held on *Easter Sunday* and sometimes, depending on the venue of the Royal Tournament, there is a march-past of performers (*July*). The London Peace Pagoda was completed in 1983.

Battersea Power Station
SW8. One of the most potent buildings on the river bank, this vast oblong of brick with its four chimneys was designed by Sir Giles Gilbert Scott, 1932–4, and was one of the finest examples of contemporary industrial architecture. Redundant as a power station, it is presently being converted, at vast expense, into a sports and leisure complex.

Albert Embankment
SE1. Designed as a broad footwalk by Sir Joseph Bazalgette, 1867, the Embankment stretches between Vauxhall and Westminster Bridges. The upper Embankment was the site of the 18thC Vauxhall Gardens, whose Chinese pavilions and walks were the envy of Europe, but today it is mainly a display of 20thC commercial architecture.

Lambeth Palace
Lambeth Palace Road SE1. The Palace is probably the most important medieval building in London and has been the site of the Archbishop of Canterbury's residence since the 12thC. The red-brick gatehouse, 1495, and the Great Hall, rebuilt about 1660 and now housing the library, can be seen from the road.

County Hall
Westminster Bridge SE1. Once the imposing headquarters of the Greater London Council but now possibly to become a hotel. It was designed by Ralph Knott, 1921–3, and reflects the architect's admiration for Piranesi. The central feature is the concave giant colonnade and the niches filled with sculpture. The magnificent lion beside County Hall was formerly the trademark of a brewery. Erected in 1837, the lion is made of Coade stone, an artificial stone impervious to weather. For many years it stood outside Waterloo Station and was moved to its present position on Westminster Bridge in 1966.

Shell Centre
SE1. Part of the area known as the South Bank, the Shell Centre was designed by Sir Howard Robertson, 1962. Of greyish white concrete with monotonous little square windows, the flat surface is totally unrelieved – it seems more in character to view it as a

physical feature rather than as architecture. The central 351ft-high skyscraper rises like a huge grey mountain. On the top is a public viewing gallery with magnificent views of London. The Centre covers 7½ acres and is a self-contained empire of shops, garages, cinemas, squash courts and swimming pool. Long corridors make the interior as dead as the exterior.

The South Bank Arts Complex
SE1. (01-921 0682). The Festival Hall, the Queen Elizabeth Hall, the National Theatre, the National Film Theatre, the Hayward Gallery and the Museum of the Moving Image are the buildings included in the complex which originated with the Festival of Britain in 1951. The Festival Hall, completed in 1951 and built by Sir Robert Matthew and Sir Leonard Martin, has seating for 3400. The Queen Elizabeth Hall by Hubert Bennett, 1967, is much smaller and intended for recitals. Bennett also designed the Hayward Gallery, opened in 1968. The Arts Council exhibit travelling exhibitions and their own collection of sculpture and paintings here. The overall social conception for the South Bank is admirable, and architecturally the best use is made of the river position through raised terraces, but the buildings are dreary and the visitor can be overwhelmed by the maze of tunnels and winding staircases which lead to the terrace area, and by the blind corners to the buildings which in many instances block the view and lead to a sense of isolation. Nevertheless, the range of cultural activities, both organised and spontaneous, can be enjoyed by everyone.

Upper Ground
SE1. The decrepit warehouses that used to line the bank have been demolished, and replaced by the impressive London Weekend Television building, beyond which is the Coin Street development – look out for the fine art deco 'OXO' tower – illuminated by night – and for Sea Containers House with its distinctive real gold leaf balls dominating the vista.

Bankside
SE1. Until the 19thC Bankside was the site of amusement gardens and theatres. In the 16thC the Rose Theatre, the Swan and the Globe were all around Bankside and it was also the scene of bear-baiting. Close to the theatres were the inns, Spurre, Christopher and Bull. Today the area has been developed and almost all is changing apart from Bankside Power Station and the few remaining 17th and 18thC houses (Wren

lived in no 49 and watched the building of St Paul's). At the far end of Bankside is the delightful 17thC Anchor Inn. The Globe theatre is now being rebuilt on its original site.

Bankside Power Station
SE1. This predatory one-chimneyed brick edifice by Sir Giles Gilbert Scott, 1935, may be compared with Battersea Power Station by the same architect.

Winchester Square
Clink Street SE1. The site of the old Clink Prison, burnt down in the Gordon Riots of 1780, leads to the square. This was once the main courtyard of Winchester Palace, seat of the Bishops of Winchester. The 13thC house was burnt down in 1814. A wall of the old Clink chapel stands amidst the redevelopment.

Southwark Cathedral
Borough High Street SE1. (01-407 2939). Built by Augustinian Canons in 1206 and greatly restored. The tower was built c1520 and the nave, by Blomfield, 1894-7. In the Middle Ages the cathedral was part of the Augustinian Priory of St Mary Overie. Despite its 19thC additions, it is still one of the most impressive Gothic buildings in London. Apart from the wealth of monuments, the model in the retro-choir showing the priory and Winchester Palace in 1540 is of special interest, as is the collection of carved wooden bosses from the 15thC roof. *Open 09.00–18.00 Mon–Sun.*

BRIDGES

Chelsea Bridge
The suspension bridge of 1858 was replaced in 1934 by this concisely designed structure by G. Topham Forrest and E. P. Wheeler.

Victoria Railway Bridge
When it was opened in 1859, this was the widest railway bridge in the world – 132ft wide and 900ft long – and it provided 10 separate accesses to Victoria Station. It has now been widened further to meet the demands of modern transport.

Vauxhall Bridge
By 1900 when this bridge was built, J. Walker's iron bridge which it supplanted had become the most hazardous on the river. This structure is by Sir Maurice Fitzmaurice and W. E. Riley.

Lambeth Bridge
The site was first occupied by a horse ferry, then the ugly suspension bridge of 1862, and finally in 1932 by this steel bridge by G. Topham Forrest. It has been attractively painted in red and brown.

Westminster Bridge
Westminster Bridge by Thomas Page, 1862, is at its best at high tide. At low tide the lanky piers are drab with mud. It was built when the stone bridge of 1749 was demolished.

Charing Cross Railway Bridge
This bridge is also known as the Hungerford Bridge. Its ugliness holds a certain curiosity when seen against the palatial splendour of Whitehall Court. It replaced the 19thC suspension bridge. A separate footbridge runs alongside to Waterloo Station.

Waterloo Bridge
Sir Giles Gilbert Scott's concrete bridge, faced with Portland stone, 1945, is plain and elegant. It replaced John Rennie's early 19thC bridge, a beautiful design of Greek columns and nine elliptical arches.

Blackfriars Bridge
Although the general outline is bold, it has rather a dwarfed and stunted look. It was built by William Cubitt in 1899 from the designs of Thomas Page and took the place of the 18thC bridge by Robert Mylne. Note the 'pulpits', a reminder of the religious significance of its name.

Blackfriars Railway Bridge
Built in 1886 for the London, Chatham and Dover Railway, this elegant iron bridge, with its high parapet and decorative coat of arms at each end, can best be seen from the road bridge.

Southwark Bridge
This bridge, which is rather lifeless, replaced Rennie's early 19thC iron bridge, considered one of the finest on the river. It is by Sir Ernest George, 1919. The steps on the south side, Southwark Causeway, were used by Wren when he travelled across the river to supervise work on St Paul's.

Cannon Street Railway Bridge
Built in 1866 as part of the extension of the South-Eastern Railway, the bridge's engineers were J. Hawkshaw and J. W. Barry. It is a prominent structure on account of the 19thC train shed which juts out on one side of the bridge. The shed's monumental towers and gloomy brick edifice lend character to the whole.

London Bridge
Until 1749 London Bridge was the only bridge over the river in London. The first wooden bridge recorded was built by the Saxons, but it is possible that the Romans may also have had a bridge here. In 1176 the wooden bridge was replaced by a stone structure. This had houses, shops and a church built along it and was very similar in appearance to the Ponte Vecchio in Florence. The heads of traitors were displayed on the spikes of the fortified gates at either end. In 1831 this bridge was demolished and a new bridge by John Rennie replaced it. This granite bridge with its five arches had, in its turn, to be rebuilt. It had become too narrow to meet the additional demands of modern traffic and because of structural faults could not be widened. The new bridge, constructed under the direction of the City Engineer, is built of concrete. It has an elegant flat-arched profile in three spans carried on slender piers. It was opened to traffic in 1973. The McCulloch Corporation of Arizona paid 2,460,000 dollars for the facing materials of Rennie's bridge, which has been reconstructed spanning Lake Havasu.

BOAT TRIPS

See special section on page 18.

PUBS AND RESTAURANTS

🞄 **King William IV** 110 Grosvenor Road SW1. A small survival of tradition in an area

Westminster Bridge and the Houses of Parliament

of redevelopment. Ind Coope and Taylor Walker real ales and *lunchtime* bar meals.

✗♥ **Villa dei Cesari** 135 Grosvenor Road SW1. (01-828 7453). The Roman Empire lives on in this restaurant in a converted riverside warehouse. *D only. (Closed Mon).* The Chelsea Yacht and Boat Company is next door.

☞✗ **Rivers** 35 Albert Embankment SE1. (01-735 3723). Busy pub and French restaurant with good river views. Flowers and Wethered's real ales, bar food. *L & D (not Sun or L Sat).*

☞✗ **PS Tattershall Castle** Victoria Embankment, Hungerford Bridge SW1. (01-839 6548). A Trumans paddle steamer pub with an excellent fish bar and buffet. The ship is good fun to explore, with plenty of exposed machinery, and the river views are excellent. You can drink and eat in the open or under cover but be warned – it sways. *L & D.*

✗♥ **Hispaniola** Victoria Embankment, Hungerford Bridge WC2 (01-839 3011). A floating restaurant serving French and English dishes. *L & D (Reserve). Closed Sun & L Sat.*

✗♥ **National Theatre Restaurant** Upper Ground, South Bank SE1 (01-928 2033). Reserve a table with a river view, and enjoy the predominantly English food. *D only. (Reserve). Closed Sun.*

☞ **Blackfriar** 174 Queen Victoria Street EC4. A wonderful marble and bronze Art Nouveau pub, where you can drink a choice of Bass, Courage or Wethered's real ales in the company of (sculptured) goblins, fairies and animals. Bar food. *Closed Sat & Sun.*

☞✗ **Founders Arms** Bankside SE1. (01-928 1899). A new Young's pub in a superb position by the power station. Glass walls, which slide open when the sun shines. Capitalise on the view across to St Paul's. Vast terrace and good bar meals *(not Sat L or Sun D).* English-style restaurant *open L & D, closed Sat L & Sun D.*

☞✗ **Samuel Pepys** 48 Upper Thames Street EC4. (01-248 3048). A large converted warehouse with a riverside terrace and balcony. English food, as you would expect, is served in the restaurant *L & D (Reserve).* Bass and Charrington real ale is served and there is bar food in the downstairs bar, 6ft 0in below high water level.

☞✗ **Anchor** Bankside SE1 (01-407 1577). Near Southwark Bridge. A riverside tavern dating from 1750, on the site of an earlier building where Samuel Pepys took refuge during the Great Fire of London. Five small bars and three restaurants cater for coach loads of tourists during the *evenings*. Enjoy Courage real ales on a wooden settle, your head under beams and feet on bare boards. Good bar food. *L & D.*

☞✗ **Regalia London** Swan Pier, Swan Lane EC4 (01-623 1805). Near London Bridge. Another gently swaying pub and restaurant, this one in the City. French and English food in the restaurant, *L Mon–Fri only.*

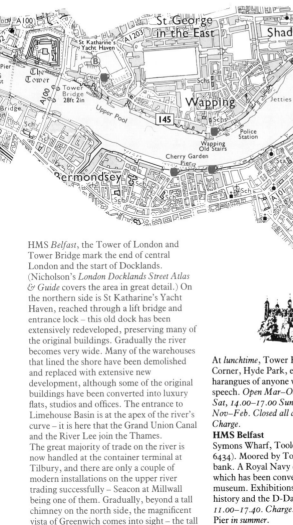

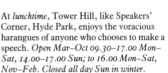

HMS *Belfast*, the Tower of London and Tower Bridge mark the end of central London and the start of Docklands. (Nicholson's *London Docklands Street Atlas & Guide* covers the area in great detail.) On the northern side is St Katharine's Yacht Haven, reached through a lift bridge and entrance lock – this old dock has been extensively redeveloped, preserving many of the original buildings. Gradually the river becomes very wide. Many of the warehouses that lined the shore have been demolished and replaced with extensive new development, although some of the original buildings have been converted into luxury flats, studios and offices. The entrance to Limehouse Basin is at the apex of the river's curve – it is here that the Grand Union Canal and the River Lee join the Thames.

The great majority of trade on the river is now handled at the container terminal at Tilbury, and there are only a couple of modern installations on the upper river trading successfully – Seacon at Millwall being one of them. Gradually, beyond a tall chimney on the north side, the magnificent vista of Greenwich comes into sight – the tall masts of the *Cutty Sark* and the pillared elegance of the Royal Naval College. A little over 3 miles downstream (not shown on the map) stands the magnificent Thames Barrier, which is intended to protect the city from possible flooding in the years to come.

Tower of London
Tower Hill EC3. (01-709 0765). Although greatly restored and altered over the centuries, the Tower of London is probably the most important work of military architecture in Britain and has been used as a palace, a fortress and a prison since William the Conqueror built the White Tower in 1078. Apart from the historic and architectural interest of the building, there are the Crown Jewels and the Museum of Armaments to see. The uniformed yeoman warders who act as guides lend colour to the scene. On the riverside, Gun Wharf displays trophy guns and there is a children's beach.

At *lunchtime*, Tower Hill, like Speakers' Corner, Hyde Park, enjoys the voracious harangues of anyone who chooses to make a speech. *Open Mar–Oct 09.30–17.00 Mon–Sat, 14.00–17.00 Sun; to 16.00 Mon–Sat, Nov–Feb. Closed all day Sun in winter. Charge.*

HMS Belfast
Symons Wharf, Tooley Street SE1. (01-407 6434). Moored by Tower Bridge on south bank. A Royal Navy cruiser, launched 1936, which has been converted into a floating museum. Exhibitions deal with cruiser history and the D-Day landings. *Open daily 11.00–17.40. Charge.* Ferry from Tower Pier *in summer.*

Tower Bridge
This bridge with its two Gothic towers was built by Sir John Wolfe Barry and his assistant Isambard Brunel, the younger, in 1894. The towers are not purely ornamental. Inside is part of the machinery which operates the bascules or drawbridges and there are also stairs to the upper lattice-work footbridge which is open to visitors. The bascules, which also provide a roadway, separate in the middle and are lifted upwards to allow a headway of 140ft. Only on a few occasions has the system failed. In 1952 a bus was trapped on the bridge as the bascules rose and had to leap several feet, but there were no serious injuries. In 1968 during hot weather, the pistons swelled and it was not possible to operate the bridge. At the moment, all the original steam-powered machinery is on display and the bridge is operated electrically. The bridge was opened to the public in 1982, and is worthy of a visit,

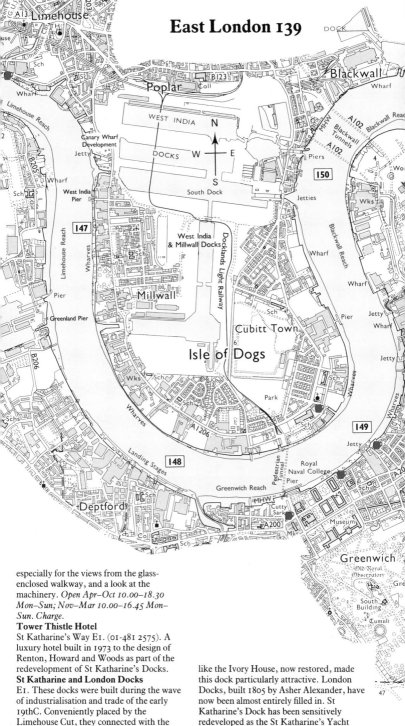

especially for the views from the glass-enclosed walkway, and a look at the machinery. *Open Apr–Oct 10.00–18.30 Mon–Sun; Nov–Mar 10.00–16.45 Mon–Sun. Charge.*

Tower Thistle Hotel
St Katharine's Way E1. (01-481 2575). A luxury hotel built in 1973 to the design of Renton, Howard and Woods as part of the redevelopment of St Katharine's Docks.

St Katharine and London Docks
E1. These docks were built during the wave of industrialisation and trade of the early 19thC. Conveniently placed by the Limehouse Cut, they connected with the national canal system. Until their closure in 1968 they were mainly associated with long-term storage, especially of wine and wool. Both docks are of architectural value. St Katharine's, built in 1828, was designed by Thomas Telford, the engineer of the Menai Straits Bridge and the Holyhead Road with Philip Hardwick as his architect. Buildings

like the Ivory House, now restored, made this dock particularly attractive. London Docks, built 1805 by Asher Alexander, have now been almost entirely filled in. St Katharine's Dock has been sensitively redeveloped as the St Katharine's Yacht Haven. Converted warehouses now contain pubs, restaurants and shops.

Hay's Wharf
Hay's Lane SE1. The wharf was built in 1931 by H. S. Goodhart-Rendel and shows a strong Scandinavian influence with its figure of St Olave. The reliefs are by Frank Dobson. Now part of London Bridge City

and developed as shops, pubs and restaurants.

Cherry Garden Pier
Turner sat here to paint *The Fighting Temeraire* as she returned from the battle of Trafalgar and this is where ships sound their signal if they want Tower Bridge to be raised.

Rotherhithe Tunnel
The circular air vents of this road traffic tunnel connecting Rotherhithe and Stepney can be seen on either side of the river. The tunnel was opened in 1908. 6278ft long, it carries two lanes of traffic.

Surrey Commercial Docks
These docks have been closed since 1969 and many have been filled in, with the land now used mostly for housing. Built in 1807, later enlarged by the addition of Greenland Dock, they were the only docks on the south side of the river. There were berths for 53 ships. The docks dealt mainly with timber, and at one time 200,000 tons of cargo were handled annually.

Royal Naval Victualling Yard
Grove Street SE8. The site of the Victualling Yard, an army supply depot till 1961, indicated the importance of Deptford as a naval and ship building centre from the 16th to the 19thC. Founded in 1513 the yard became the principal naval dockyard in the kingdom, rivalling Woolwich. Sir Francis Drake was knighted at the yard after his world voyage on the *Golden Hind*.

Limehouse Basin
E14. (01-790 3444). This used to be called the Regent's Canal Dock, and forms part of the Grand Union Canal system, which was opened in 1820 to allow barges to trade between London and Birmingham. The Limehouse Cut also provides access to the River Lee. There is still a good deal of barge traffic here, and visiting pleasure craft should take care. An extensive redevelopment scheme is under way.

Canary Wharf
A £3–4 billion development planned around an 800ft tall skyscraper, topped by a pyramid. The ultimate bizarre example of Docklands vernacular architecture?

Isle of Dogs
Until the industrialisation of the early 19thC the Isle of Dogs was mainly pastureland and marshes. Windmills stood by the river. By 1799 the Port of London had become so overcrowded that Parliament authorised the building of a new dock on the Isle of Dogs, under the auspices of the West India Company. Built by William Jessop, the two West India Docks were opened in 1802. In 1870 the South Dock was added. It was built on the site of the City Canal which had connected Limehouse Reach and Blackwall Reach between 1805 and 1829. The Millwall Docks, the most southern, were completed

in 1864. For many years these docks had a monopoly of all West India goods. Now they have been superseded by the container port at Tilbury, and the area is at the heart of the great Docklands redevelopment.

Island Gardens
Saunders Ness Road E14. This small park at the south tip of the Isle of Dogs was opened in 1895 to commemorate the spot which Wren considered had the best view of Greenwich Palace across the water.

Greenwich
SE10. The splendour of Greenwich's royal and naval past is witnessed by the magnificent riverside grouping of the Queen's House and the Royal Naval College. Their perfection is frozen, missing the environment for which they were originally conceived. Once a fishing village, Greenwich grew in stature after the building of the Palace of Placentia, favoured by the Tudor sovereigns. Little remains of the medieval period, and the Queen's House and Naval College reflect the glories of the 17th and 18thC. Inland, Greenwich is crowded and busy with traffic. There are some good antique shops.

Royal Naval College
Greenwich SE10. (01-858 2154). The college was once the site of the medieval Palace of Placentia. Mary II decided not to live in the palace, then already partly rebuilt by Webb. Instead she commissioned Wren to rebuild it as a hospital for aged and disabled seamen. Designed in the Baroque style, it was completed in 1705. The Painted Hall, or Dining Hall, has a swirling Baroque ceiling by Thornhill, one of the finest of its period. The chapel with details in the neo-classical spirit dates from 1789. In 1873 the hospital became the Royal Naval College to provide for the higher education of naval officers. *Closed Thur. Free.*

Queen's House
Romney Road, Greenwich SE10. (01-858 4422). Framed and dominated by the Naval College, this delightful white house in the

Palladian style was built for Queen Anne of Denmark by Inigo Jones, 1618. It is now part of the National Maritime Museum. *Closed Sun morning. Charge.*

National Maritime Museum
Romney Road, Greenwich SE10. (01-858 4422). The museum is devoted to the history of the sea and is of exceptional maritime interest. There is an unrivalled collection of seascapes, many of which bring the naval battles they depict vividly alive. Naval charts, magnificent model ships of all

periods, uniforms and navigational instruments are all here. *Closed Sun morning. Charge.*

Greenwich Pier
SE10. The *Cutty Sark*, one of the old 19thC tea and wool sailing clippers, stands in dry dock. Many hardships were endured by the crew in the clipper races between England and China or Australia. The history of the *Cutty Sark* is displayed in drawings and photographs. Close by, *Gipsy Moth IV*, the yacht in which Sir Francis Chichester made his solo circumnavigation of the world, is also open for public viewing. *Both closed Sun morning. Charge.*

Greenwich Tunnel
The Blackwall Tunnel which had opened in 1897 was designed as a road traffic tunnel. In 1902 it was therefore decided to build a pedestrian subway to link Greenwich with the Isle of Dogs. There was opposition from the watermen and lightermen who feared that their services would no longer be required. The southern entrance to the footway is in Cutty Sark Gardens, Greenwich, and the northern in Island Gardens, Isle of Dogs. Fascinating walk.

Greenwich Park
SE10. The park was laid out for Charles II by Le Notre. It commands a magnificent view of the Royal Naval College and of the river. It contains 13 acres of wooded deer park, a bird sanctuary and archaeological sites. To the west of the park is Crooms Hill, whose 18thC houses flank the road up to Blackheath. At the foot of the hill is Greenwich Theatre.

Old Royal Observatory
Greenwich Park SE10. (01-858 1167). The original observatory, still standing amidst the group of 17th, 18th and 19thC buildings, was built by Wren for Flamsteed, first Astronomer Royal, in the 17thC. Astronomical instruments and exhibits relating to the history of astronomy are displayed in the old observatory buildings and the time ball which provided the first public time signal in 1833 still operates. The Caird Planetarium in the south building has educational programmes for schools in the term time and public programmes in the holidays. *Closed Sun morning. Charge.*

BOATYARDS

Ⓑ **St Katharine's Yacht Haven** 52 St Katharine's Way E1. (01-488 2400). Ⓡ Ⓢ Ⓦ Ⓓ (nearby). Pump-out, hire craft, long-term mooring, chandlery, provisions, books and maps, visitor's and seasonal moorings, toilets, showers. Ⓜ *Access from the river is only possible between 2 hours before and 1½ hours after high water at London Bridge, between 06.00–20.30 Apr–Aug, 08.00–18.00 Sep–Mar.*

BOAT TRIPS

See special section on page 18.

PUBS AND RESTAURANTS

✕♥ **Princes Room** Tower Hotel, St Katharine's Way E1. (01-481 2575). Inventive international menu in a comfortable, but expensive restaurant overlooking the river. *L & D* (Reserve). *Closed L Sat.*

✕ **Dickens Inn** St Katharine's Yacht Haven E1. (01-488 2208). Lots of exposed timbers in a converted warehouse, which was moved *en masse* 300yds to its present situation overlooking the dock. Arkell's, Fuller's and Ruddles real ales, and bar meals. There are two restaurants upstairs, *open for L & D.* (Reserve).

☛ **Old Justice** 94 Bermondsey Wall East SE16. (01-237 3452). A well hidden riverside pub, serving Charrington real ale.

☛✕ **Angel** 101 Bermondsey Wall East SE16. (01-237 3608). A very fine unspoilt 16thC pub built partly on piles sunk into the river bed, giving sweeping views up and down river from the balcony. Courage real ale is served along with good bar food – upstairs restaurant has an English menu, with plenty of fish. *L & D. Closed D Sun, L Sat.*

☛ **Town of Ramsgate** 62 Wapping High Street E1. (01-488 2685). A 17thC riverside tavern serving Charrington real ale and bar ⚔ meals, standing alongside Wapping Old Stairs. Here it is reputed that pirates were taken and tied to the piles at low tide, after receiving the summary justice of the infamous Judge Jeffreys. The unfortunate victims were not removed until they had suffered the 'Grace of Wapping' – three tides. It is also said the judge used to watch the drownings from the Angel, across the river, although other pubs also claim this dubious distinction. Now the execution dock is used by pub patrons in happier circumstances.

☛✕ **Prospect of Whitby** 57 Wapping Wall E1. (01-481 1095). A historic riverside pub with a spacious courtyard, on the coach tour circuit. In the beamy flagstoned bar you can sup Watney's real ale, and sample hearty bar food. There is also a separate French restaurant, and live music in the bar. Judge Jeffreys is said to have also used this pub. *L & D* (Reserve). *Closed L Sat.*

☛✕ **Mayflower** 117 Rotherhithe Street SE16. (01-237 4088). Once the Shippe this partially rebuilt Tudor inn overlooking the river was renamed to commemorate the Pilgrim Fathers' ship which set off from a dock here and is notable as perhaps the only pub permitted to sell stamps, a right granted as an aid to seamen. In the cosy bar with high backed settles you can enjoy Charrington real ale and good *lunchtime* bar meals. Restaurant *open L & D (not Sun).* Good river views.

☛✕ **Grapes** 76 Narrow Street E14. (01-987 4396). A Thames-side local which Dickens is reputed to have called The Six Jolly Fellowship Porters in *Our Mutual Friend.* Whistler apparently came here to paint the river. Taylor Walker and Ind Coope real ales and *lunchtime* bar food. A separate restaurant serves fine fish dishes, and is *open for L & D* (Reserve). *Closed Sun, L Sat.*

✕♥ **Le Papillon** 57 Greenwich Church Street SE10. (01-858 2668). Opposite the *Cutty Sark.* Excellent and inventive menu in a Victorian setting. Good wine list. *L & D* (Reserve). *Closed L Sat & Sun.*

142 East London

Trafalgar Tavern Park Row SE10. (01-858 2437). Watney's and Young's real ales in a pub with fine river views, close to the Naval College. One of the bars resembles a ship, and Lord Nelson features in many of the pictures. Excellent restaurant with varied menu. *Open for L & D* (Reserve). *Closed D Sun, D Mon.*

Cutty Sark Ballast Quay, Lassell Street SE10. (01-858 3146). A Georgian riverside pub, dating from 1695, and with a nautical theme. Bass and Charrington real ales, whitebait suppers in the bar and a separate English restaurant. *Open L Mon–Fri, D Thur–Sat.*

Waterman's Arms 1 Glenaffric Avenue E14. (01-538 0712). Decorated along maritime lines with oars, barrels and pictures of ships. Bar snacks and Taylor Walker real ale.

The Cutty Sark, Greenwich

RIVER WEY AND GODALMING NAVIGATION

Boats have used the River Wey since medieval times, but the present navigation dates from the 17thC. In 1651 Sir Richard Weston was authorised to make the river navigable for 15 miles from Weybridge to Guildford. This involved the building of 12 locks and 10 miles of artificial cut. This early navigation had the usual battles with mill owners, but gradually trade developed, predominantly local and agricultural in character. More unusual were the extensive Farnham Potteries, who shipped their wares to London along the Wey. In 1760 the Godalming Navigation was opened, adding another 4 miles to the waterway, and by the end of the 18thC considerable barge traffic was using the river. This was greatly increased by the building of the Basingstoke Canal in 1796, and the Wey & Arun Junction Canal in 1816; the latter offered a direct route from London to Portsmouth and the south coast. This canal closed in 1871, but trade continued to thrive on the Wey and as late as the 1960s barges were still carrying timber to Guildford.

Hopes were raised in 1981 of a revival in commercial carrying, when two motor barges began bringing grain to Coxes Mill from the Tilbury Grain Terminal. Unfortunately this traffic was short-lived, and at present there is no commercial traffic. In 1964 the Wey Navigation was given to the National Trust and in 1968 the Godalming section was also handed over.

The navigation authority is: The National Trust Navigation Office, Dapdune Lea, Wharf Road, Guildford GU1 4RR. Telephone: Guildford 61389. Annual or visitor's licences are issued here, or at Thames Lock. Rules and by-laws are issued with each licence.

Speed limit is 4 knots – in practice, slower. Watch your wash. Use only the special Wey lock handles, available from Thames Lock, the NT Navigation Office or Guildford and Godalming hire craft companies. When leaving the locks, exit gates may be left open, with all the paddles *down* (except New Haw Lock, which should always be left empty).

As a river navigation, the Wey is subject to flood water, increasing the speed of the current and pull of the weirs. When conditions are very bad, locks may be padlocked. Moor up in a sheltered place and seek advice if you are in any doubt regarding your safety.

There are no particular problems with mooring on the river, apart from frequent changes in the water level. Respect private property.

Maximum dimensions

Length:	73ft 6in
Beam:	13ft 10in
Draught:	3ft 0in to Guildford
	2ft 6in above Guildford
Headroom:	7ft 0in to Guildford
	6ft 0in to Godalming (at normal levels)
Locks:	16 (including Worsfold and Walsham Flood Gates)

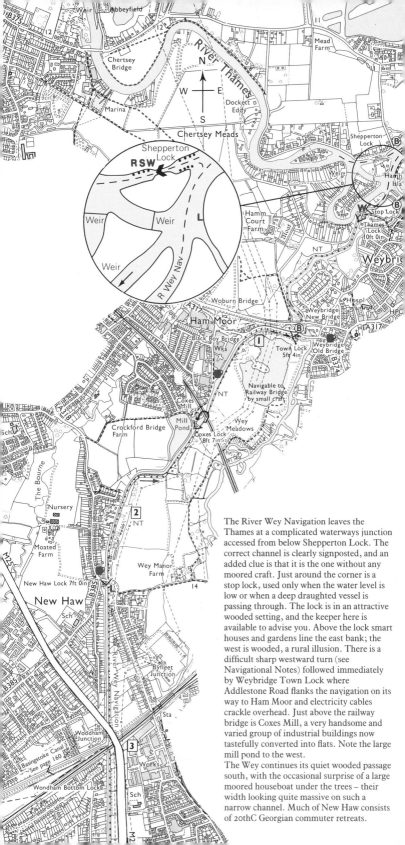

Weir · Abbeyfield

River Thames

Chertsey Bridge

Chertsey Meads

Marina

Dockett Eddy

Mead Farm

Shepperton Lock

N
W · E
S

RSW

Weir · Weir

L

Weir

R Wey Nav

Shepperton Lock

Hamm Isla

Stop Lock

W

Thames Lock 10ft 0in

Hamm Court Farm

Trout

NT

Weybri

Woburn Bridge

Weybridge New Bridge

Ham Moor

Hospl

A317

Black Boy Bridge
Wks

B

I

Town Lock 5ft 4in

Weybridge Old Bridge

NT

Navigable to Railway Bridge by small craft

Coxes Mill

Crockford Bridge Farm

Mill Pond

Coxes Lock 8ft 7in

Wey Meadows

The Bourne

Nursery

2
NT

Moated Farm

Wey Manor Farm

14

New Haw Lock 7ft 0in

New Haw

Sch

Byfleet Junction

Woodham Junction

3

Basingstoke Canal
See page 160

Works

Woodham Bottom Lock

Sch

River Wey Navigation

Sta

The River Wey Navigation leaves the Thames at a complicated waterways junction accessed from below Shepperton Lock. The correct channel is clearly signposted, and an added clue is that it is the one without any moored craft. Just around the corner is a stop lock, used only when the water level is low or when a deep draughted vessel is passing through. The lock is in an attractive wooded setting, and the keeper here is available to advise you. Above the lock smart houses and gardens line the east bank; the west is wooded, a rural illusion. There is a difficult sharp westward turn (see Navigational Notes) followed immediately by Weybridge Town Lock where Addlestone Road flanks the navigation on its way to Ham Moor and electricity cables crackle overhead. Just above the railway bridge is Coxes Mill, a very handsome and varied group of industrial buildings now tastefully converted into flats. Note the large mill pond to the west.

The Wey continues its quiet wooded passage south, with the occasional surprise of a large moored houseboat under the trees – their width looking quite massive on such a narrow channel. Much of New Haw consists of 20thC Georgian commuter retreats.

Moored craft line the banks above the partly turf-sided New Haw Lock as the cut makes a bee-line for Byfleet, cowering under massive concrete structures and earth embankments of the M25 motorway. There is no longer any peace to be had here. The Basingstoke Canal (see page 160), leaves the Wey in the midst of a flurry of bridges.

NAVIGATIONAL NOTES

Thames Lock (Weybridge 843106). Attended. Licences and visitor passes, lock handles for sale or hire. Craft of deeper draught than 1ft 9in coming up from the Thames should consult the lock keeper before entering the lock – he may then use the stop lock to increase the water level. [W]
Weybridge Old Bridge The navigation channel is the most westerly arch (furthest right) when coming upstream, thus involving some tight turns. The lock is immediately above the bridge. The original course of the river is navigable for a short distance by small craft.
New Haw Lock. Leave this lock empty. Slipway.

NOTES FOR WALKERS

The towpath can be joined from Weybridge by taking the footpath alongside the Old Crown pub, crossing the footbridge and bearing left by the poultry pen to reach Thames Lock. The towpath is in excellent shape as far as Send, beyond which it becomes a little less well defined in places, but still quite walkable. Pleasant wooded stretches are intermingled with factories and smart Surrey riverside gardens. House and boat names provide endless amusement, with hundreds of awful 'Wey' puns to spot ('Under Wey', 'This Wey Up', 'Anchors-a-Wey' and so on).

Weybridge
See page 113 for information.
Coxes Mill *Surrey*. Overlooking Coxes Lock is a magnificent group of mostly 19thC mill buildings, partly brick, partly concrete and partly weatherboard, the best industrial architecture on the river. As recently as 1981 there was a short-lived revival of water-borne transport to the mill, with the motor barges *Anny* and *Clinton* bringing grain from the Tilbury Grain Terminal, but this has now ceased and the buildings have been converted into flats.

BOATYARDS

Ⓑ**Weybridge Marine** 91 Thames Street, Weybridge (847453). Long-term mooring, winter storage, slipway, boat building, boat and engine repairs.
Ⓑ**Weybridge Boat House** Weybridge Old Bridge, Weybridge (842131). Gas, winter storage, slipway, boat building, boat sales, toilets.

PUBS AND RESTAURANTS

🍺 **Old Crown** 83 Thames Street, Weybridge. A rambling weatherboard pub by the old course of the River Wey. Nautical decor. Courage real ales, snacks, garden.
🍺 **Lincoln Arms** 104 Thames Street, Weybridge. Bass, Young's and Courage real ales in a large riverside pub with garden.
🍺 **Pelican** Ham Moor Lane, Ham Moor. Attractive brick and tile riverside pub with a garden and mooring for customers. Watney's real ale, snacks. Unfortunately no towpath access.
🍺 **White Hart** by New Haw Lock. Courage real ales and good home-cooked food (*L, not Sun*) in a plain modern pub with a fine riverside garden. Coffee and snacks.

146 Pyrford

Approaching Parvis Bridge a lookout should be kept on the west bank for the craft *Under Wey*, which has brought fresh meaning to the term 'short boat'. Above the bridge the Wey becomes more rural – breaks in the riverside trees reveal open meadows and farmland. The popular Anchor pub is close to the bridge at Pyrford, with Pyrford Marina opposite; just beyond is Pyrford Lock and many moored craft, including two large houseboats. The navigation now passes Pyrford Place, its presence revealed by a charming little riverside terrace with statuettes. Except in times of flood, Walsham Flood Gates are left open, and you can pass uninterrupted through the partially turf-sided square chamber, overlooked by the quaintly business-like lock cottage. There is a large weir to the east. The river splits to form a trio of islands at Newark, where the remains of a priory can be seen at the water's edge. The lock cut can be found without difficulty. The river now makes an uncertain course for Papercourt Lock, arguably the prettiest on the river, with its stepped weir – however, watch out for the cross current caused by this structure.

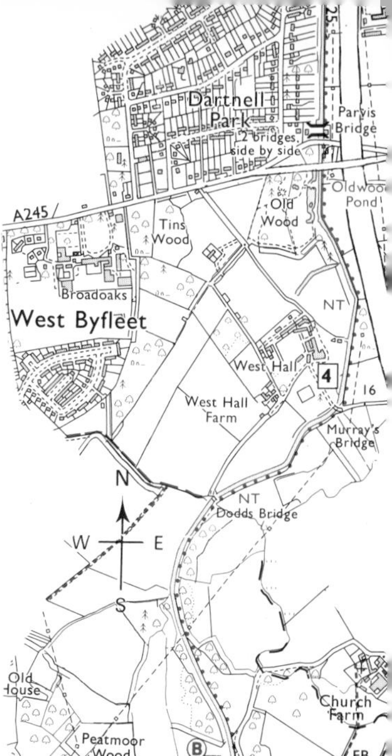

NAVIGATIONAL NOTES

All the locks on this section are unattended.
Walsham Flood Gates are left open except in
times of flood when the gates should be
closed with one paddle at each end left up.
Be wary of the cross current below
Papercourt Lock.

NOTES FOR WALKERS

The towpath throughout this section is in
good condition. After Murray's Bridge
housing and motorway are left behind and
the river becomes pleasantly rural. Just
below Pigeon House Bridge a path leads to
the tall, handsome Ockham Mill, to the east
of which are the Royal Horticultural
Society's Gardens at Wisley. At Walsham
the towpath crosses the weir, which is
popular with canoeists. Less than a mile to
the south is Ripley, a village with many
pubs. The path crosses to the north side for a
short way at Newark Lock, then back to the
south at Newark New Bridge, only to cross
again at the lovely Papercourt Lock.

Byfleet

Surrey. EC Wed. PO, shops. Although
buried by modern commuter housing, parts
of the old village can be found. The church
with its bellcote is mostly late 13thC, and the
17thC brick manor house is an elegant
delight in the midst of so much dreariness.
To the north are the remains of the old
banked Brooklands Race Track.

Pyrford Village

Surrey. Surrounded by water-meadows and
trees, Pyrford is still a real village, an oasis in
the ever-spreading suburban web. Brick
cottages overlook the church, an almost
intact Norman building; such a thing is rare
in the Home Counties and is thus an even
greater pleasure. Inside is a 17thC pulpit.
There are many attractive 18thC houses.

Royal Horticultural Society's Gardens

Wisley. (Woking 224234). By footpath south
east of Pigeon House Bridge to Ockham
Mill, then north east towards Wisley. A 200-
acre botanic garden acquired by the RHS in
1904 and famous for its trials and
improvements of new varieties. Notable
collections of old fashioned and new roses,

rhododendrons, camelias, heathers and rock
garden plants. *Open daily (members only
Sun). Charge.*

Newark Priory The tall broken flint walls of
the 12thC Augustinian priory stand in a
meadow at the river's edge, an enticing and
romantic ruin. Unfortunately there is no
right of navigation up to the walls.

Ripley

Surrey. PO, shops. A village on the old
Portsmouth Road now by-passed by the A3.
Worth a visit if you are interested in pubs.

BOATYARDS

ⓑ**Pyrford Marina** Lock Lane, Pyrford,
Woking. (Byfleet 40739). Ⓡ Ⓢ Ⓦ Ⓓ Pump-
out, long-term mooring, winter storage,
slipway, dry dock, books and maps, boat
and engine repairs (by outside contractors
and DIY), boat sales, toilets, showers.
Manager resident on site. Ⓜ

PUBS AND RESTAURANTS

🍺 **Queen's Head** 2 High Road, Byfleet.
¼ mile east of Parvis Bridge. Ind Coope real
ale, *lunchtime* snacks and a garden.

🍺 **Plough** 104 High Road, Byfleet (off map
to east). Courage real ales in a pub on the
edge of the village green. Garden.

🍺 **Anchor** Pyrford Lock. A beautifully sited
pub with a comfortable interior and a vast
riverside terrace. Courage real ale is served
along with excellent *lunchtime* food.

🍺 **Seven Stars** Newark Lane, Ripley. An
ivy-covered road house serving Friary Meux
real ale and *lunchtime* snacks. Garden.

🍺 **Half Moon** High Street, Ripley. A wide
choice of real ales and *lunchtime* food.

🍺 **Talbot** High Street, Ripley. A beamy
coaching inn with a fine antique beer engine.
Bass real ale, *lunchtime* snacks and *evening*
meals.

🍺 **White Hart** High Street, Ripley. A local
pub serving Ind Coope real ale and *lunchtime*
food. Garden.

🍺 **Anchor** High Street, Ripley. A Tudor
brick half-timbered coaching inn, with a
lovely old fashioned rambling interior.
Friary Meux and Ind Coope real ales and
excellent *lunchtime* food (*not Sun*). Children
welcome.

Thames Lock, Weybridge

Triggs Lock

Factories and offices line the south bank, followed by a sand and gravel works as the navigation passes under the quaint laddered High Bridge and approaches Cart Bridge, to the west of Send. As you pass Worsfold Flood Gates, note the unique peg arrangement on the paddles. Just above here is the National Trust workshop. Once again the Wey resumes its rural course, passing Triggs Lock, with its very pretty asymmetrical lock cottage. To the south east lies Send Church. The navigation now begins to sweep around Sutton Place, and comes very close to the A3 with its constant traffic rumble. Care should be exercised at Broadoak Bridge and Bower's Lock (see below). The approach to Stoke Lock is tree-lined, a blessing in that it alleviates some of the noise pollution of the nearby trunk road, but now Guildford is being approached and the scene is increasingly urban. A few willows overhang by Stoke Bridge – the mill to the south, a handsome and functional building, houses Guildford Marine, which deals in boats and chandlery. Now all is back gardens, roads and factories: the approach to Guildford town centre from downstream is not particularly attractive.

NAVIGATIONAL NOTES

All locks in this section are unattended.
Worsfold Flood Gates In normal conditions these gates are left open. In times of flood, leave the gates closed with one paddle fully up at each end.
Broadoak Bridge The approach from downstream is very narrow. After a sharp turn to the south west to avoid the weir, pass through the arch closest to the towing path.
Bower's Lock When approached from downstream the lock is to the left before the footbridge. When locking down, take the sharp blind turn to the right with care.

NOTES FOR WALKERS

A ½ mile section of the towpath around High Bridge can become overgrown – this could be avoided by leaving the river at Tanyard Bridge to walk through Send and rejoin at Cart Bridge – a useful detour for

supplies. Send is left along a crunchy gravel drive, and beyond Worsfold Flood Gates the surroundings are again rural. Send Church can be reached from Wareham's Bridge, but it looks better at a distance. Above Send Church Bridge the path is again rough, and the noise of the A3 is a nuisance. Gradually Guildford looms ahead and, against all expectations, the towpath deteriorates, and the river seems sadly ignored.

Send

Surrey. EC Wed. PO, shops, launderette. An unremarkable linear village but a useful supply centre. The church, a muddled affair of all periods, lies close to the old course of the river and well to the south west of the main centre. Although nicely sited amongst trees and 18thC houses, it all looks better from the river than close to, so stay on the water and leave illusions intact.
Sutton Place *Surrey.* One of the most important early Tudor houses in England, Sutton Place was built by Sir Richard Weston, who also constructed the Wey Navigation. It is a brick house, with terracotta ornamentation, built originally round a square; one side was demolished in the 18thC leaving the plan more open. The house is an interesting mixture of Renaissance and English styles, and was once owned by the late Paul Getty. Private.

PUBS AND RESTAURANTS

🍺 **New Inn** Cart Bridge, Send. A well situated pub with pleasant riverside gardens where barbecues are held in the *summer*. Friary Meux and Ind Coope real ales are served, along with bar meals *lunchtime &*

evening. There are plenty of shops and a launderette further east.

🍺 **Fox & Hounds** Sutton Green, Surrey. A typical village inn, tastefully modernised. Ind Coope real ale and snacks *lunchtime & evening.*

🍺 **Bell** Woking Road, Guildford. A straightforward pub serving Friary Meux and Ind Coope real ales. *Lunchtime* meals and *evening* snacks.

🍺 **Row Barge** Riverside at Stoke Bridge. Pleasant garden and mooring, close to the Guildford Waterside Centre. Courage beers, coffee and bar food.

150 Guildford

Approaching Guildford from the north, one would believe the town wished to ignore entirely the opportunities offered by the River Wey. Scruffy and overgrown, it creeps behind factories, strewn with rubbish and forgotten by all but a few anglers. However, at Friary Bridge there is an abrupt change: the town turns to face the water – and what a jolly scene it is – riverside walks, a handsome mill, the theatre, a busy boatyard, pubs and restaurants, all overlooked by the castle. Note especially the rare treadmill crane standing by Town Wharf, where the Wey Navigation becomes the Godalming Navigation and leaves Guildford in an ideal setting with parkland to the east and pleasant private gardens glimpsed over high walls to the west. A jetty marks the site of the old St Catherine's Ferry on the Pilgrims' Way. A small stream spills into the river here through an inauspicious metal pipe below a pretty grotto where those who pass are 'treading the path trod by Geoffrey Chaucer's Canterbury Pilgrims in the reign of King Edward the Third'. Just beyond is Sandy Corner, where any young children on board will want to moor up and play. The river passes Shalford through flat meadowland, with riverside fibre mills above the low Broadford Bridge. There are usually some interesting craft moored here and at Guns Mouth, the entrance to the unnavigable Wey & Arun Canal. A fine wooded stretch below Unstead Lock ends abruptly at a frozen food depot, an indication that the main roads are closer than you might think.

NAVIGATIONAL NOTES

Take care approaching Mill Mead Lock – the channel is very narrow. The old course of the river above Sandy Corner is navigable for a short way by small craft.
Keep well clear of the weir above St Catherine's Lock.
Broadford Bridge is low, with only 6ft 0in headroom. In exceptional circumstances the water level can be lowered by prior arrangement, phone Guildford 66565.

NOTES FOR WALKERS

As mentioned, the approach to Guildford from the north is disappointing, but all improves after Friary Bridge. The towpath changes sides at Wood Bridge, involving a very hazardous road crossing, with traffic everywhere. Cross the backwater but keep to the west side at Mill Mead Lock. Shops and town centre pubs are to the east of Town Bridge.
The walk to the south along the Godalming Navigation is extremely pleasant. The North Downs Way proper, a 140-mile walk from Farnham to Dover, should cross at St Catherine's Ferry – since this is now defunct, a detour through Guildford is necessary. Up the path by the streamlet, on a knoll to the south, are the remains of St Catherine's Chapel. There is no particularly rural feeling any more – railway and roads are never far away. Interest is provided at Shalford, where the old Wey & Arun Canal leaves the Godalming Navigation at Guns Mouth.
The Wey & Arun Canal Trust have devised a

Dapdune Wharf, Guildford

36-mile walk along or beside this canal, details of which are given in an excellent guide *The Wey–South Path*, available from The Hon Secretary, 24 Griffiths Avenue, Lancing, West Sussex, for which there is a charge.

Guildford
Surrey. EC Wed. All shops and services. The town is built on the steep sides of the Wey valley and so its centre is very compact, overlooked on the west by the bulk of the cathedral, and on the east by the castle ruins. The best parts of the town are around the cobbled High Street, which leads steeply down to the river where there are interesting mill and wharf buildings, including one of the few treadle-operated cranes still in existence. The High Street is particularly attractive, and is rich in good buildings of all periods; facing each other at the top, the Baroque splendour of the 17thC Guildhall and the 18thC simplicity of Holy Trinity Church determine a rich diversity that characterises the street. Also in the High Street is the Tudor grammar school. The University of Surrey has been developed on the slopes of the cathedral hill; the buildings show a better feeling for architecture than many modern universities. The strength of Guildford as a cultural centre is shown by the modern Yvonne Arnaud Theatre, standing on an attractive riverside site, surrounded by trees but still in the town centre. Guildford seems to have been by tradition a popular and self-contained town, and this feeling still survives.
Guildford Cathedral The brick mass of the cathedral overlooks the town from many directions. It is an uncompromising and unsubtle thing, the last debased fling of the Gothic revival. Designed by Edward Maufe in 1932, it was only completed in 1966, and sadly reveals its period all too clearly. From the outside it is a mixture of cinema, power station and church; the inside is a complete contrast – a wealth of detail, and delicate use of shape and form, far more genuinely Gothic in feeling. Interesting furniture, fittings, glass and statuary.
Guildford House 155 High Street, Guildford (505050). Art exhibitions in a 17thC town house. Note the fine staircase and ceilings. *Open Mon–Sat.*
Tourist Information Centre Civic Hall, London Road, Guildford (67314/505050).
Shalford
Surrey. EC Wed. A meandering village built loosely along the main road, rustic and cottage in parts, but disappointing round the green. It is at its best by the river, which is flanked by old wharf and warehouse buildings.
Wey & Arun Canal
This navigation linked London with the south coast at Littlehampton, and Portsmouth, between 1816 and 1871, and has been lately romanticised as 'London's lost route to the sea'. The first 100yds or so is still in water and used for moorings. Much of the rest of the route is still intact, although dried up and overgrown. The Wey & Arun

Canal Trust are working towards restoration, a dream that may well become reality. Meanwhile the canal makes a very attractive walk, linking the North and South Downs Way (see 'Notes for Walkers').

BOATYARDS

Ⓑ**Plancraft Marine** Dapdune Wharf, Wharf Road, Guildford (62213). Ⓡ Ⓦ Long-term mooring, winter storage, chandlery, books and maps, boat building, boat and engine sales and repairs. *Closed Sun.*
Ⓑ**Guildford Boat House** Millbrook, Guildford (504494). Ⓡ Ⓢ Ⓦ Ⓓ Pump-out, gas (Super), hire craft, day hire boats (rowing and canoes), slipway, books and maps, boat building, boat and engine sales and repairs, toilets. A very friendly and helpful company. Ⓜ

BOAT TRIPS

Guildford Boat House (Guildford 504494). Regular *summer* trips on *Harry Stevens* (69 passengers), and restaurant cruises on *Alfred Leroy* (56 passengers).

PUBS AND RESTAURANTS

🍺 **Greyhound** South of Onslow Bridge on the towpath side. A comfortable corner pub serving Courage real ale and bar food.

Many pubs, restaurants and shops can be found to the east of Town Bridge.
🍺 **Bulls Head** 123 High Street, Guildford. A superbly old fashioned and beamy 16thC pub saved from the ravages of the developers and beautifully restored. A fine choice of real ales is offered, along with very good bar food at *lunchtime* (*not Sun*).
✕🍺 **Rumwong** 16–18 London Road, Guildford (36092). Genuine Thai food in a friendly restaurant where, in the back room, the waitresses dance while you wait to eat. Sensible wine list. *L & D Reserve. (Closed Mon.)*
🍷✕ **Rowley's Wine Bar** 124 High Street, Guildford (63277). A wonderful selection of tasty food and tempting sweets in a fascinating beamed wine bar. *Open L & evenings (Closed Sun, & Mon evening).*
🍺 **Britannia** Millmead, Guildford. Overlooking the lock, this handsome red-brick pub has a very fine sign and an outdoor drinking area. Friary Meux real ale and *lunchtime* bar meals.
🍺 **Jolly Farmer** Shalford Road, Guildford. Upmarket riverside pub with its own jetty where customers may moor, and a terrace. Ind Coope real ale, and bar meals (*L & D*).
🍺 **Ship** Worplesdon Road, Guildford. Up the old Pilgrims' Way. Ind Coope real ale, *lunchtime* food and garden.
🍺 **Sea Horse** The Street, Shalford. Gale's real ale in a bright and friendly little pub. *Lunchtime* food and garden.
🍺 **Queen Victoria** Shalford, near the station. A nice homely local, serving Ind Coope real ale and snacks.
🍺 **Parrot** East of Broadford Bridge. A plain Watney's pub by the green. Pleasant walled garden, children's room and bar food.

Guildford

154 Godalming

Those who left the Thames to journey to Godalming will be sad their voyage is almost over. The River Wey provides one of the few local refuges from the stress of Surrey. The The gardens of very smart residences line the Farncombe bank as the river approaches Catteshall Lock, the highest on the river. There are good moorings at Lammas Lands on the towpath side above here, and it is only a short walk to Town Bridge, the usual head of navigation and the end of the National Trust section.

NAVIGATIONAL NOTES

Boats over 40ft in length must turn where the cut leaves the river either above or below Catteshall Lock. Small, shallow draught craft may be able to pass under Town Bridge to reach Boarden Bridge. Note there is a weir just above the railway bridge.

NOTES FOR WALKERS

The approach to Godalming is not unpleasant, and the towpath is in good shape. Above Town Bridge there is a tidy path through riverside gardens with a scattering of seats where you can rest your feet. The town lies to the south, beyond a vast car park.

Godalming

Surrey. EC Wed. All shops and services. By tradition a cloth-making town, Godalming has developed in a haphazard way over the years and so has no real centre. The head of navigation near the heavy stone bridge is to the north east of the town. A walk round the town gives the inevitable feeling that Godalming has always lived in the shadow of its more spectacular neighbour, Guildford,

and so has little contribution of its own to make. But in a small way its confusion of streets have something to offer. The early 19thC Market Hall with its open ground floor is pretty, and the church with its tall lead spire gives the town an interesting skyline. The spire is 13thC and is the best feature of the building.

BOATYARDS

Ⓑ **Farncombe Boat House** Catteshall Lock, Godalming (21306). Ⓡ Ⓢ Ⓦ Ⓓ Pump-out, gas, hire craft, day hire boats, long-term mooring, winter storage, narrowboat chandlery, books and maps, boat building, boat and engine sales and repairs, toilets. Ⓜ

BOAT TRIPS

Horse drawn trips in nb. *Iona* from Godalming Wharf. Details from Farnham 712414.

PUBS AND RESTAURANTS

There are several pubs along Meadrow (A3100), to the west of Catteshall Bridge.
🍺 **Railway Hotel** 1 Meadrow, Farncombe. North of Town Bridge. An un-named block of plain brick, wherein can be found Courage real ales and bar food.
🍺 **Three Lions** Meadrow. An old and friendly ale house serving Friary Meux real ale and bar food. Garden.
🍺 **King's Arms & Royal** High Street, Godalming. An old coaching inn, visited by Peter the Great in 1698 but now ruthlessly modernised. Ind Coope real ale, bar food and garden.
🍺 **Star** Church Street, Godalming. A homely town centre pub serving Courage real ale and bar food.

Near Godalming

A quiet mooring below Woodham Bottom Lock

BASINGSTOKE CANAL

Maximum dimensions:	Mileages
Length: 72'	*WOODHAM JUNCTION*
Beam: 13' 6"	*(River Wey) to:*
Headroom: 5' 10"	Woodham Top Lock 1½
	Goldsworth Bottom Lock 5¼
	Pirbright Bridge 8½
	Deepcut Top Lock 10½
	Mytchett 13
	Ash Lock 16
	Pondtail Bridges 20½
	Crookham Wharf 23½
	Barley Mow Bridge 27
	Odiham Wharf 29
	Limit of navigation 30¾
	Greywell Tunnel 31
	29 locks

Licences

Boat Licence Clerk, Basingstoke Canal Office, Ash Lock Cottage, Government Road, Aldershot GU11 2BS (Aldershot 313810).

An Act of Parliament for the building of this canal was passed in 1778, and the navigation opened to Basingstoke in 1794. Intended as an artery to and from London for mainly agricultural produce – timber, grain, fertilizers, chalk and malt – it was never a financial success. Built by the great canal contractor, John Pinkerton (who issued his own tokens or coins as payment to his navvies), it was originally estimated to cost £86,000. By 1796 £153,463 had been spent. Tonnages of goods carried averaged about 20,000 per annum, 10,700 tons below what was anticipated, and profit forecasts of £7,783 8s 4d proved wildly optimistic, the best figure achieved being £3,038 4s 2d in 1800–1.

The Napoleonic Wars, and the danger they brought to coastal shipping, benefited the Basingstoke Canal, which could transport goods bound for Portsmouth and Southampton in safety. But with the advent of peace, trade slumped – the canal managers commenting that 'some considerable injury must be sustained by the Canal'.

There was a minor boom in goods carried in 1839 to build the London & South Western Railway, but when this opened it was clear that the navigation had been instrumental in its own demise. Trade flourished for a while in 1854 with the building of the barracks at Aldershot, but this was short-lived. Plans for a revival by building a link canal from Basingstoke to the Kennet & Avon at Newbury came to nothing, and the company went into liquidation in 1866. A dissolution order followed in 1878.

Purchased by new owners in 1896, and re-named the Woking, Aldershot & Basingstoke Canal, a considerable amount of money was spent on improvements, to link with the new brickworks at Up Nately, but all to no avail, and by 1904 it was once again offered for sale. It was in 1910 that the last barge reached Basingstoke. The canal was owned by A. S. Harmsworth between 1923 and 1947 who did much to ensure its ultimate survival, despite the collapse of Greywell Tunnel in 1934. Munitions were transported on the canal during World War II, and the last commercial traffic, a load of timber to Spanton's Yard at Monument Bridge, came up the canal in 1949. In that same year it was auctioned and sold to the Inland Waterways Association. Now owned by the County Councils of Hampshire and Surrey, its restoration represents a magnificent achievement by both councils, the Surrey and Hampshire Canal Society and the IWA. Navigation from the Wey to Greywell Tunnel should be possible throughout by 1990.

KEY TO SYMBOLS USED IN CANAL SECTION

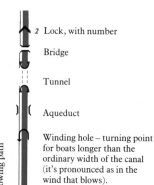

2 Lock, with number

Bridge

Tunnel

Aqueduct

Winding hole – turning point for boats longer than the ordinary width of the canal (it's pronounced as in the wind that blows).

Towing path

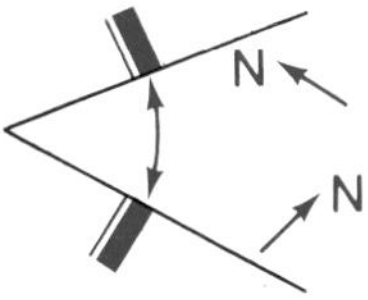

Where this occurs on a map it simply means that the actual route of the waterway would not fit neatly onto the page, so the cartographer has 'bent' the map, using two north points. The navigator on the water, or the walker on the bank, will find nothing amiss. Distances in this section should be measured along the thick blue line only, not including these gaps.

Other symbols used in this section are the same as those used on the River Thames and Wey sections.

Scale: 2 miles to 1 inch.

The final stages of restoration on the Basingstoke Canal

Woking

The Basingstoke Canal leaves the River Wey Navigation at Woodham Junction, near a large electricity sub-station and overshadowed by the M25 motorway. Its course is immediately lined with a fine mixture of mature trees, a feature which is to persist throughout most of its route to Greywell Tunnel. The Woodham flight of six locks (apart from Lock 1) was the last on the canal to be restored, and the re-establishment of through navigation has disturbed the peaceful, and almost secret, houseboat world which exists between Locks 1 and 3. These floating homes were established here around 1950, on narrowboat hulls brought from the Midlands.

Above Woodham Top Lock the waterway maintains its seclusion, with the large private gardens of an expensive residential area backing onto the canal. Horsell Common provides more open views before Woking is reached. The last commercial traffic on the canal brought timber to Monument Bridge in 1949. There is easy access to shops, banks and pubs from Lock 2 – walk south-west into West Byfleet; and to the south of Chobham Road Bridge.

NAVIGATIONAL NOTES

1. Navigation from the River Wey Navigation should open in the spring of 1990.
2. Facilities for boaters are at present fairly limited on the Basingstoke Canal. There is water available at St John's and Odiham, but no pump-out facilities. There are, however, many garages close to the route.

NOTE FOR WALKERS

The towpath is in excellent condition throughout the entire length of the navigation, and makes a very fine walk. British Rail stations are situated at regular intervals close to the canal (see maps), making it easy to plan short excursions on foot, without having to double back.

Woking
Surrey. EC Wed. MD Tue, Fri, Sat. All shops and services. Surrey's largest town, built around the railway, which came here in 1838. The original village, Old Woking, lies 2 miles to the south. Development carries on apace, making dormitory homes for the thousands of commuters who daily rush up and back to the city. It is, however, worth walking south from Monument Bridge, and taking the third turning on the right, Oriental Road, to see the Shah Jehan Mosque, built in 1889 and reminiscent of the Taj Mahal in India with its onion-shaped dome. Built by the enormously rich Begum Shah Jehan, ruler of Bhopal State in India, its design, by W. I. Chambers, is honest and dignified. A P & O captain was employed to take bearings to ensure an exact orientation towards Mecca. It is now the main centre for Muslims in England.

Woodham

Surrey. EC Wed. All shops and services. A typical commuter conurbation of dull, closely packed houses, only pretty in the more expensive areas, where large, spacious houses and gardens nestle among trees. Definitely at its best and most characterful by the canal.

Horsell

Surrey. Indistinguishable from Woking (see above), although if you look hard enough, you will find a few original cottages. St Mary's Church is unremarkable save for two interesting monuments – to Sir John Rose and his wife, on the west wall (1803), and to James Fenn and his wife, whom he faces across a jumble of books (1787).

PUBS

There are plenty of pubs in Woking and West Byfleet, although none are right by the canal.

🍺 **Claremont** Opposite West Byfleet Station, south of Lock 3. Friary Meux real ale, food and accommodation in a large, lively pub. Garden, games room.

Autumn on the Basingstoke Canal

Brookwood

The navigation passes through an area of extensive new development with busy roads, and tower blocks to the south. But it is heartening to see that few of these new buildings turn their backs to the canal – indeed they positively welcome its presence, with walk-ways and gardens linking with the water's edge. Gradually Woking is left behind as the canal rises through the five Goldsworth Locks to Kiln Bridge. Here there is easy access to shops, Indian, Chinese and Italian restaurants, and a launderette. The pub/wine bar by the bridge provides excellent moorings. The railway, which accompanies the canal to Frimley Green, comes very close at Knaphill, and is then replaced by the trees of Brookwood Lye. Houseboats moored here, by Hermitage Bridge, add a picturesque touch.
A collection of used cars are parked almost at the edge of Brookwood Bottom Lock, but the remaining two locks are pleasantly situated and once again the trees reappear. An old overgrown pill box still guards Pirbright Bridge. Beyond the bridge is the first of the Deepcut, or Frimley, flight of locks. The army now begins to make its presence felt, with distant pops and bangs from the rifle ranges.

Brookwood Cemetery A superbly landscaped expanse of heathland covering 2400 acres, to the south of Brookwood Station, where mature trees and eccentric mausoleums co-exist harmoniously. Founded by the London Necropolis Company in 1854, when the numbers of dead Londoners were becoming increasingly difficult to accommodate, it was once served by a railway – indeed one of the station buildings still survives. There is a military cemetery in the south-west corner – British and American soldiers are buried here, the latter in considerably more style, though whether they appreciate this is open to question.
Knaphill
Surrey. Basically a large Victorian village around the barracks and the gaunt Brookwood Mental Hospital, a mid-19thC asylum which was once entirely self-sufficient, generating its own electricity and running its own farm in the grounds. To the west is Bisley, famous for its annual rifle shooting competitions.
St John's
Surrey. PO, tel, stores, launderette. Swallowed up by Woking, the area around Kiln Bridge somehow, against all odds, manages to retain the feel of a village centre. Notice the well restored building topped by a clock tower, right by the bridge.

PUBS AND RESTAURANTS

🍺 **Station Hotel** Opposite Brookwood Station. A well preserved Victorian pub.
🍺 **Nag's Head** Knaphill, north of Brookwood Bridge. An attractive and welcoming pub offering Friary Meux real

ale, good food (*lunchtime Mon–Fri, lunchtime and evening Sat & Sun*) and a garden with children's play area.

Froggies 42–44 High Street, Knaphill. (Brookwood 80835). A restaurant/wine bar with a warm and cosy atmosphere, provided in part by a gas-log fire. Good value at lunchtime. *L & D (Closed Mon D)*.

Capstan's Wharf Kiln Bridge. (Woking 29282). A large rambling pub/wine bar with a canalside terrace and excellent moorings. Real ale is served along with food *lunchtime and evening* W.

Bridge Barn (Woking 63642). By Arthur's Bridge. A tastefully converted 16thC timbered barn now housing a Beefeater Steak House. Food *L & D*, morning coffee, real ale and canalside garden.

Star Wych Hill, Hookheath. (Woking 60526). South of Arthur's Bridge. Benskins, Friary Meux, Gales, Ind Coope and Tetley real ales in a pub/restaurant. Garden, children welcome, food *L & D*.

Houseboats by Hermitage Bridge

Deepcut

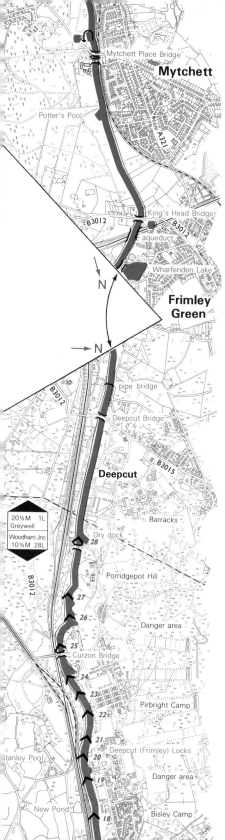

The Basingstoke Canal now climbs steadily up the Deepcut, or Frimley, flight of 14 locks, in a superb, tree-lined setting. Even the vast Pirbright Army Camp to the north hardly intrudes. Between many of the locks there are wide pools – check the depth of these carefully if you intend to stray off the direct course. Each of the locks has a footbridge, and a ladder in the chamber, but not all have an easy means of landing below the bottom gates, so it is a good idea for a member of the crew to walk ahead to open the gates when ascending.

Above the top lock is a dry dock, rebuilt in 1984. The building here was once a workshop and forge.

Having climbed 90 feet, the navigation now enters the dramatic Deepcut cutting, 1000yds long and up to 70ft deep. Lined with large, mature, deciduous trees, it is shady and remote.

Beyond Wharfenden Lake, now part of a country club, and the supposedly lead-lined aqueduct over the railway, the canal turns sharply south towards Mytchett, with wood and heathland rising to the east.

NAVIGATIONAL NOTE

Do not stray from the direct course of the canal without first checking the depth. Many of the wide pools are quite shallow.

Royal Army Ordnance Corps Museum
Deepcut. (Aldershot 24431). The general history of the RAOC. *Open 08.30–12.30 & 13.30–16.30 Mon–Fri. Free.*

PUBS

● **Potters** Above Mytchett Place Bridge. A large new pub with children's amusements, a public slipway in the garden and good off-line moorings. Food *lunchtime and evening*.
● **King's Head** By King's Head Bridge, Frimley Green. Courage real ale in a comfortable pub with a garden. Food *lunchtime and evening*.

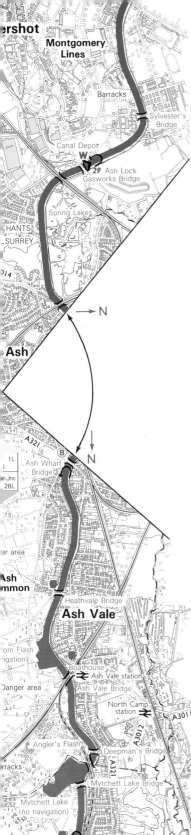

Ash

Mytchett Lake, owned by the army and renowned amongst anglers for the size of its pike, adjoins the canal, but is closed to navigation. The canal continues south, enclosed by the railway and thick woods on one side, and leafy gardens on the other. Just beyond the railway bridge at Ash Vale is the corrugated iron boathouse where 15 barges were built between 1918 and 1935. There is a pub here, by the station; a post office, off-licence and easy access to shops.

Greatbottom Flash is surrounded by trees, and signs indicate that this is a 'Danger Area', used by the army. The water is very clear, revealing just how shallow the canal is here.

Large houses with gardens landscaped to the water's edge face a busy road at Ash Vale before the navigation resumes its general westerly course, passing handy shops, a post office and Chinese take-away at Ash Wharf Bridge. It then crosses Spring Lakes on a 1000yd embankment, leaving Surrey and entering Hampshire. There are good moorings above Ash Lock, opposite the Canal Depot (slipway).

The reappearance of army property – barrack blocks behind high wire fences – announces the approach to Aldershot; the canal having climbed 195ft since leaving Woodham Junction.

Ash and Ash Vale

Surrey. EC Wed. PO, tel, stores. Villages now enclosed by the sprawl of Aldershot. St Peter's Church, Ash, is early medieval and retains a Norman window, a finely detailed south door, c1200, a 17thC wooden font and a Palladian memorial to John Harris, dated 1759.

Royal Army Medical Corps Museum

Keogh Barracks, Ash Vale. (Aldershot 24431). East of Mytchett Lake. The achievements of the RAMC in war and peace – the Duke of Wellington's hearing aids, Napoleon's dental instruments, and branding and flogging equipment used on soldiers. Fine medal collection. *Open 08.30–12.30 & 13.30–16.00 Mon–Fri. Free.*

BOATYARDS

Surrey & Hants Marine Services Ash Wharf Bridge. (Aldershot 319220). Chandlery, outboards and watersports equipment.

PUBS AND RESTAURANTS

✕🍴 **Ashram Tandoori** Ash Wharf Bridge. (Aldershot 313638). Typical Indian restaurant. *L & D.*

🍺 **Swan** At Heathvale Bridge. Warm welcoming Victorian-style pub with a large canalside garden offering children's amusements. Courage real ale, and food *lunchtime and evening.*

🍺 **Ash Vale** Opposite Ash Vale Station. Snug corner local serving Courage real ale and bar snacks. Garden and B & B. Occasional live music.

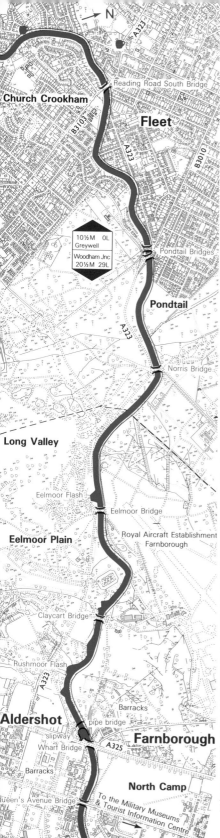

Fleet

Queen's Avenue Bridge is notable for its modestly ornate iron balustrades, bringing a little light relief from the army camps which now completely enclose the waterway. Do not be alarmed should you see soldiers wearing full combat gear – with helmets and gas marks, carrying rifles – trudging out of the woods, or above you 'guarding' the bridges. For the uninitiated the distant gunfire and clatter of helicopters can be a little unnerving. Beyond Eelmoor Bridge, the canal widens at Eelmoor Flash, a Site of Special Scientific Interest (SSSI) on account of its dragonfly population.

The canal continues its westward course through woods, which clear in places to reveal the runways and low buildings of the Royal Aircraft Establishment, Farnborough. Notwithstanding all this military presence, the course of the navigation is very rural and isolated, and approaches Fleet in a richly wooded cutting through Pyestock Hill. There is an excellent licensed supermarket at Pondtail Bridges, selling fresh meat and vegetables as well as the usual things – this marks the eastern extremity of Fleet. Houses and gardens back on to the canal and generally seem to appreciate it being there. A canoe slalom course is marked and there are some moored craft. Shops are close at hand to the north-west of Reading Road South Bridge.

NAVIGATIONAL NOTE

Wharf, Pondtail and Reading Road South bridges are all very low.

Fleet
Hants. EC Wed. All services. Useful for its shops and services, but little else of interest.
Tourist Information Centre Gurkha Square, Fleet. (Aldershot 811151).
Farnborough
Hants. EC Wed. MD Tue. All shops and services (but some distance north of the canal). A name synonymous with the famous biennial air show (see below), Farnborough is now just a northerly extension of Aldershot, the original village having been engulfed by light industry, housing and the military. Almost 2 miles north of Wharf Bridge is St Peter's Church, dating from around 1200, with a wooden porch and weatherboarded tower. A short walk further north of this is Farnborough Hill, the former home of the Empress Eugénie, wife of Napoleon III of France, from the time of her exile to England in 1881 until her death in 1920. The building is now a convent school. The Empress built an extravagantly French mausoleum for her husband, her son and herself in 1887, as well as an abbey, known as St Michael's, now occupied by English Benedictine monks.
Royal Aircraft Establishment
Farnborough. This aerodrome was set up in 1905 as His Majesty's Balloon Factory. The American showman, Samuel Cody, and a Red Indian friend, made the first powered

flight in Britain at Laffan's Plain, Farnborough, in 1908, when Cody was Chief Kiting Instructor at the Balloon School here. Cody died in an air crash in 1913. During the two World Wars extensive research into developing military aircraft was carried out at the airfield, and this still continues, although it has now broadened into the sphere of civil aviation. Much of the design and development work on Concorde was executed here. The world-famous Farnborough Air Show is held here biennially in *September*, and attracts over 200,000 visitors with its static exhibitions and dramatic flying displays. Considering the orientation of the main runway, you should get a good view from the canal.

Tourist Information Centre Farnborough Library, Pinehurst Avenue, Farnborough. (Aldershot 513838, ext 24).

Aldershot
Hants. EC Wed. MD Thur. All shops and services, cinema and theatre (but some distance south of the canal). In 1854 the army bought 10,000 acres of heathland surrounding the rural hamlet of Aldershot, bringing building materials on the Basingstoke Canal and descending upon the area in force. It has never been the same since. In spite of a great deal of redevelopment it is still, for the most part, an uninspiring place, the military being all pervasive. What is left of the original village, and it is not much, is to the south-east of the station. The spectacular biennial army display, held in *June*, attracts over 250,000 visitors.

Tourist Information Centre Aldershot Military Museum, Queen's Avenue, Aldershot (20968).

Aldershot Military Museum Queen's Avenue, Aldershot (314598). North of Queen's Avenue Bridge. Military history spanning 130 years, including a Victorian barrack room, photographs, models and personal mementoes. Some armoured vehicles and guns outside. *Open 10.00–17.00 daily Mar–Oct (to 16.30 Nov–Feb). Shop. Charge.*

Royal Army Dental Corps Museum Next door to the Military Museum (Aldershot 24431, ext 2782). The history of how soldiers have had their teeth attended to during various campaigns from 1660 to the Falklands in 1982. *Open 10.00–12.00 & 14.00–16.00 daily. Free.*

Queen Alexandra Royal Army Nursing Corps Museum Farnborough Road, Aldershot (24431). Nursing wounded soldiers from 1854 to the present. Florence Nightingale mementoes, and her Crimean carriage. *Open all year, by appointment. Free.*

Museum of Airborne Forces Browning Barracks, Aldershot (24431). Smaller exhibits include briefing models – outside there is a Dakota and various guns spanning Arnhem, Suez and the Falklands. *Open 09.00–12.30 & 14.00–16.30 (opens 10.00 weekends). Charge.*

Regimental Museum Royal Corps of Transport Aldershot (24431). History since 1800. *Open 09.00–12.00 & 14.00–16.30 Mon–Fri. Free.*

Gurkha Museum Church Crookham. (Fleet 3541). The history of the Gurkhas, including a collection of kukris, their traditional daggers. *Open 09.30–16.30 Mon–Fri (& Sat Jun–Oct). Free.*

PUBS

🍺 **Fox & Hounds** Crookham Road, Crookham. A friendly pub with a very large canalside garden and excellent moorings. Courage real ale, *lunchtime* food and family room. The Folk Club meets here *every Tue.*

🍺 **Oatsheaf** north-west of Reading Road, South Bridge. Friary Meux real ale and food *lunchtime and evening* in a large main-road pub. Garden. Fish & chip shop and Burmese take-away close-by.

Lock 20 on the Deepcut, or Frimley, Flight

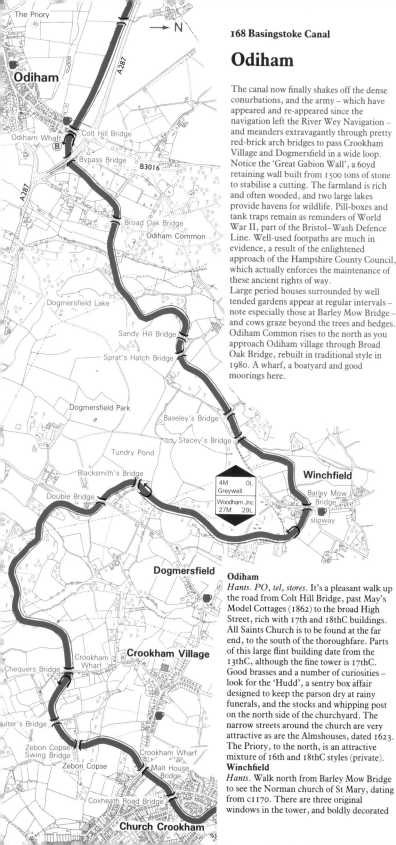

Odiham

The canal now finally shakes off the dense conurbations, and the army – which have appeared and re-appeared since the navigation left the River Wey Navigation – and meanders extravagantly through pretty red-brick arch bridges to pass Crookham Village and Dogmersfield in a wide loop. Notice the 'Great Gabion Wall', a 60yd retaining wall built from 1500 tons of stone to stabilise a cutting. The farmland is rich and often wooded, and two large lakes provide havens for wildlife. Pill-boxes and tank traps remain as reminders of World War II, part of the Bristol–Wash Defence Line. Well-used footpaths are much in evidence, a result of the enlightened approach of the Hampshire County Council, which actually enforces the maintenance of these ancient rights of way.

Large period houses surrounded by well tended gardens appear at regular intervals – note especially those at Barley Mow Bridge – and cows graze beyond the trees and hedges. Odiham Common rises to the north as you approach Odiham village through Broad Oak Bridge, rebuilt in traditional style in 1980. A wharf, a boatyard and good moorings here.

Odiham

Hants. PO, tel, stores. It's a pleasant walk up the road from Colt Hill Bridge, past May's Model Cottages (1862) to the broad High Street, rich with 17th and 18thC buildings. All Saints Church is to be found at the far end, to the south of the thoroughfare. Parts of this large flint building date from the 13thC, although the fine tower is 17thC. Good brasses and a number of curiosities – look for the 'Hudd', a sentry box affair designed to keep the parson dry at rainy funerals, and the stocks and whipping post on the north side of the churchyard. The narrow streets around the church are very attractive as are the Almshouses, dated 1623. The Priory, to the north, is an attractive mixture of 16th and 18thC styles (private).

Winchfield

Hants. Walk north from Barley Mow Bridge to see the Norman church of St Mary, dating from c1170. There are three original windows in the tower, and boldly decorated doorways. The pulpit (1634) is prettily decorated.

Dogmersfield

Hants. A well preserved village with pretty thatched and timbered houses. All Saints Church, built in 1843, stands separately to the south. Early English in style, it is of little interest apart from a brass (1590) and one or two monuments. Dogmersfield Park stands in its own grounds overlooking Tundry Pond, to the south of the canal. Built in 1728 on the site of an earlier building, where Arthur, the eldest son of Henry VII, and Catherine of Aragon first met, it is now a company training college. The new chapel contains fine carved tablets by Eric Gill, depicting the stations of the cross.

Crookham Village

Hants. PO, stores. Crookham Village and Dogmersfield have now merged, such is the extent of new development in these parts. Some pretty cottages, timber with red brick infill, but little of the cohesion which would give the village a focus.

BOATYARDS

Ⓑ **Galleon Marine** Colt Hill Bridge, Odiham (3691). Ⓦ Cruisers available for short-term breaks, rowing boats and punts (*Easter–Oct*), chandlery, boat storage, slipway.

TRIP BOAT

John Pinkerton This is a 56-seater boat operated by the S & HCS for public trips and private charter. Phone Aldershot 549037 for details. The **Mildred Stocks** is a 12-seater dayboat designed for the disabled. Details from Fleet 621501.

PUBS AND RESTAURANTS

🍴✕ **George Hotel** High Street, Odiham (2081). A handsome 16thC hotel with a Georgian façade. Inside are beams and an Elizabethan fireplace taken from Old Basing House. One of the upstairs bedrooms contains an early wall painting, and there is also a whipping post from the ministerial courts. Food *lunchtime and evening*, and real ale.

✕🍴 **Kings** 65 High Street, Odiham (2559). Smart Pekinese restaurant in a converted pub, not cheap, but good value. *L & D (closed Sun L)*.

🍴 **Water Witch** Colt Hill Bridge, Odiham. A comfortable and beamy pub decorated with canal artefacts and with a vast waterside garden. It replaced The Cricketers, closer to the bridge, when demand became such that the smaller building could not cope. Excellent food *lunchtime and evening*, and a choice of real ales including Ruddles and Websters. Children's play area, good moorings.

🍴 **Barley Mow** Barley Mow Bridge. Large country pub serving Courage real ale and *lunchtime* food. Garden.

🍴 **Queen's Head** Dogmersfield. A lovely sign announces the presence of this fine 17thC country pub, which has associations with Charles I. Courage real ale and food *lunchtime and evening*. Small garden.

🍴 **Black Horse** Crookham Village. A smart village local dispensing Courage real ale. The future of the **Chequers**, north of Chequers Bridge, is uncertain. Once an unpretentious pub, owned by the same family for over 200 years it is, at time of writing, closed.

The eastern portal of the collapsed Greywell Tunnel

Greywell

The course of the canal now becomes more open as it makes its approach to Greywell Tunnel. The few houses and gardens of North Warnborough are followed by a lift bridge, beyond which is the limit of navigation for cruisers, by Odiham Castle. It is then just a short walk to the eastern portal of the collapsed Greywell Tunnel (1230yds), passing the remains of Lock 30. This was built to raise the water level above here by 12ins, to give increased draft and aid navigation. A footpath leads over the tunnel portal to Greywell village, and the Fox & Goose pub. It is possible to follow paths over Greywell Hill to see what remains of the western entrance to the tunnel and a short isolated stretch of the canal passing the village of Up Nately. Greywell Tunnel is, of course, famous for its colony of bats.

NAVIGATIONAL NOTE

The limit of navigation is a few yards beyond Odiham Castle. Do not attempt to take your boat any further than this. Turn here.

Greywell

Hants. A village of charming red-brick houses around the pub and tunnel entrance. St Mary's Church is worth a visit. Parts of it date from c1200, and it has an interesting screen.

Odiham (King John's) Castle.

Dating from 1207, this picturesque pile of flint is all that remains of the only octagonal keep in England, a three-storied building used by King John as a stopping place between Windsor and Winchester. It was in June 1215 that the king rode from here to Runnymede to set his seal upon *Magna Carta* on the 15th of that month. Extorted from the king by the barons, *Magna Carta* set out the fundamental principles for the government of the realm – such as the right to a fair trial, and the preservation of ancient liberties. In the following year an invading French army besieged the castle for 15 days. The defending 'army' of 13 men gave such a good account of themselves that the French allowed them to surrender but retain their freedom. Later, the castle was given to the powerful wife of Simon de Montfort, who stayed here when her husband went to his final battle, and his death, at Evesham. The castle moat was cut through by the canal engineers.

North Warnborough

Hants. PO, tel, stores. A group of attractive houses, some thatched and dating from the 15thC. There is no church, the village being virtually an extension of Odiham.

PUBS

- **Fox & Goose** Greywell. Comfortable beamy pub with a log fire, serving Courage real ale and food. Small garden, family room.
- **Anchor** North Warnborough. A cheerful 18thC village pub offering Courage real ale and food *lunchtime and evening (not Sun)*.

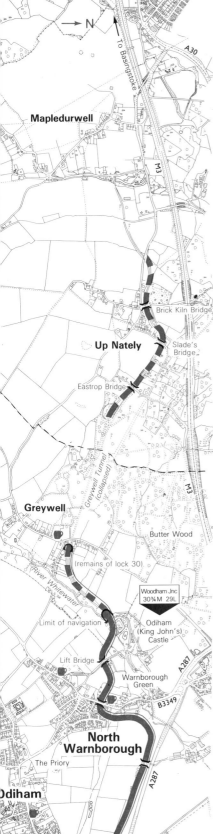

Plenty of traditional pub games, an open fire and a garden.

🍺 **Swan** At Swan Bridge. A dark, cosy local dating from the 16thC with a log fire, serving Courage real ale and food *lunchtime and evening*. Garden.

The steam dredger 'Perseverance'

INDEX

THAMES MILEAGES

Places (Bold type indicates locks – 45 in total)	Distances from Limehouse Basin	Distances from Inglesham
(Cricklade to Inglesham – 10½ miles)		
Inglesham – present limit of navigation for powered craft	146½	0
Lechlade	146	½
St John's Lock	145	1½
Buscot Lock	144	2½
Grafton Lock	140½	6
Radcot Lock	139	7½
Rushey Lock	136	10½
Shifford Lock	132	14½
Newbridge	129	17½
Northmoor Lock	127	19½
Bablock Hythe	125½	21
Pinkhill Lock	123	23½
Eynsham Lock	121½	25
King's Lock, and junction with Dukes Cut, Oxford Canal	119	27½
Godstow Lock	118	28½
Oxford, junction with Oxford Canal (Isis Lock)	116	30½
Osney Lock	115½	31
Folly Bridge, Oxford	114½	32
Iffley Lock	113	33½
Sandford Lock	111½	35
Abingdon Lock	107	39½
Culham Lock	104	42½
Clifton Lock	101½	45
Day's Lock	98½	48
Benson Lock	94½	52
Wallingford Bridge	93	53½
Cleeve Lock	88	58½
Goring Lock	87½	59
Whitchurch Lock	83½	63
Mapledurham Lock	81	65½
Caversham Lock, Reading	76½	70
Reading, junction with Kennet & Avon Canal	76	70½
Sonning Lock	74	72½
Shiplake Lock	71	75½
Marsh Lock	68½	78
Henley Bridge	67½	79
Hambleden Lock	65½	81
Hurley Lock	61½	85
Temple Lock	61	85½
Marlow Lock	59	87½
Cookham Lock	55	91½
Boulter's Lock	53	93½
Maidenhead Bridge	52	94½
Bray Lock	51	95½
Boveney Lock	47½	99
Windsor Bridge	46	100½
Romney Lock	45½	101
Old Windsor Lock	42½	104
Egham Lock (Bell Weir)	39½	107
Staines Bridge	38½	108
Penton Hook Lock	36½	110
Chertsey Lock	34½	112
Shepperton Lock, and junction with Wey Navigation	32½	114
Walton Bridge	30½	116
Sunbury Lock	29	117½
Molesey Lock, Hampton Court	26	120½
Kingston Bridge	23	123½
Teddington Lock	21	125½
Richmond Bridge	18½	128
Richmond Lock	18	128½
Brentford, junction with Grand Union Canal	16	130½
Hammersmith Bridge	11½	135
Putney Bridge	10	136½
Battersea Railway Bridge	8	138½
Chelsea Bridge	6½	140
Westminster Bridge	4½	142
London Bridge	2½	144
St Katharine's Dock	1½	145
Limehouse Basin, entrance to Regent's Canal and connection with River Lea	0	146½

All distances to nearest ½ mile